"A very welcome, timely, and important v

best thinkers currently working at the interface between empirical p ,
and Christian formation. It offers rich insights with practical application to the
nurture of flourishing Christian communities."

Joanna Collicutt, University of Oxford, author of *The Psychology of Christian
Character Formation*

"*Psychology and Spiritual Formation in Dialogue* is a fitting tribute to Dallas
Willard and a very helpful exchange of ideas for which I feel certain he would
be grateful. Dallas once said that the only way to divide the components of a
person is with the chapter titles of a book. I wonder if it could also be said that
the primary ways of dividing the disciplines of psychology and spiritual
formation are through the use of departmental headings, licensure boards, and
the timeline of focus. May this important work fan the flames of both Christian
spiritual theology and psychology and diminish the effect of nonhelpful barriers
and hidden assumptions."

Gary W. Moon, distinguished professor of psychology and spiritual formation,
Richmont Graduate University

"The brightest and best of Christian theologians, philosophers, and psychologists
are here amassed to grapple with how our understanding and enhancement of
the spiritual life of Christians can be aided by the insights of psychology. Many
striking insights are provided, resisting an overly strict adherence to
methodological naturalism that can create a barrier to a Christian understanding
of what it means to be fully human. Each chapter is worth a careful read for a
complete picture of the field. Biola's Center for Christian Thought (CCT), who
sponsored year-long weekly discussions on this topic, is to be commended for
such an achievement."

Peter C. Hill, Rosemead School of Psychology, Biola University, editor of the *Journal
of Psychology and Christianity*

"Pondering these essays on spiritual maturation was perturbing and gratifying.
It requires dialogue that disturbs our disciplinary comfort zones to realize
holistic Christian practice. The challenge of ministry in our age is to further an
understanding of how human persons are transformed, not merely morally and
spirituality, but toward genuine Christlikeness."

Stephen P. Greggo, professor of counseling, Trinity Evangelical Divinity School,
Deerfield, Illinois, author of *Assessment for Counseling in Christian Perspective*

"The dialogue between the discipline of psychology and the practice of spiritual formation is a timely and important discussion for our day, but it also remains one where too much misunderstanding remains. Very often folks from different disciplines fail to listen and learn from one another. Thankfully, this blended volume is another important step toward a healthier conversation that aims to push us toward more faithful reflections."

Kelly M. Kapic, professor of theological studies at Covenant College, author of *Embodied Hope*

"Psychology and spiritual formation are two of the most complex subjects on the planet, given the essential complexity and mystery of their subject matter. So it is no surprise that Christians today differ considerably regarding their relationship to one another. This book is distinguished by an especially fine set of essays in the first two parts of the book in which the Christian faith provides a guiding role in the relationship, followed by an excellent selection of contemporary conversation partners who offer various alternatives to the prior vision. Altogether one obtains here a lay of the land regarding the options practiced today by Christians. A remarkable contribution to the dialogue."

Eric L. Johnson, professor of Christian psychology, Houston Baptist University

PSYCHOLOGY AND SPIRITUAL FORMATION IN DIALOGUE

MORAL AND SPIRITUAL CHANGE IN CHRISTIAN PERSPECTIVE

EDITED BY
**THOMAS M. CRISP, STEVEN L. PORTER,
AND GREGG A. TEN ELSHOF**

An imprint of InterVarsity Press
Downers Grove, Illinois

InterVarsity Press
P.O. Box 1400, Downers Grove, IL 60515-1426
ivpress.com
email@ivpress.com

InterVarsity Press® is the book-publishing division of InterVarsity Christian Fellowship/USA®, a movement of students and faculty active on campus at hundreds of universities, colleges, and schools of nursing in the United States of America, and a member movement of the International Fellowship of Evangelical Students. For information about local and regional activities, visit intervarsity.org.

Scripture quotations, unless otherwise noted, are from The Holy Bible, English Standard Version, copyright © 2001 by Crossway Bibles, a division of Good News Publishers. Used by permission. All rights reserved.

While any stories in this book are true, some names and identifying information may have been changed to protect the privacy of individuals.

Cover design: David Fassett
Interior design: Daniel van Loon
Images: marble texture background: © NK08gerd / iStock / Getty Images Plus
      white marble texture: © undefined undefined / iStock / Getty Images Plus
      abstract blue watercolor: © kostins / iStock / Getty Images Plus
      abstract watercolor: © lutavia / iStock / Getty Images Plus
      blue water drop: © Deven Dadbhawala / Moment Collection / Getty Images

ISBN 978-0-8308-2864-7 (print)
ISBN 978-0-8308-7311-1 (digital)

Printed in the United States of America ∞

InterVarsity Press is committed to ecological stewardship and to the conservation of natural resources in all our operations. This book was printed using sustainably sourced paper.

Library of Congress Cataloging-in-Publication Data
A catalog record for this book is available from the Library of Congress.

P 25 24 23 22 21 20 19 18 17 16 15 14 13 12 11 10 9 8 7 6 5 4 3 2 1

Y 38 37 36 35 34 33 32 31 30 29 28 27 26 25 24 23 22 21 20 19

To Dallas Willard (1935–2013)

CONTENTS

INTRODUCTION

THOMAS M. CRISP, STEVEN L. PORTER,
AND GREGG A. TEN ELSHOF

There are various indicators of a renewed interest in the study of moral and spiritual change, especially among philosophers and theologians. For instance, within virtue ethics, discussion of how virtues are acquired has gone from almost absolute silence within the literature to a beehive of activity. In her edited book *Cultivating Virtue: Perspectives from Philosophy, Theology, and Psychology*, Nancy Snow observes, "The last thirty years have seen a resurgence of interest in virtue in Anglo-American philosophy. . . . Despite the rising interest in virtue, however, little attention has been paid to the question of how virtue is developed."[1] Snow's book aims to partly remedy that deficit in the literature with twelve new essays that address the cultivation of virtue. And within theology, attention to spiritual formation at a more popular level and sanctification at a more scholarly level has increased by leaps and bounds. For instance, Kelly M. Kapic introduces his edited book *Sanctification: Explorations in Theology and Practice* with this: "In recent decades debates about justification have dominated the attention of many

---

[1]Nancy E. Snow, ed., *Cultivating Virtue: Perspectives from Philosophy, Theology, and Psychology* (Oxford: Oxford University Press, 2015), 1.

Protestants. . . . [Now] there are indications that a new season, with new challenges, is at hand. Evangelicals in particular demonstrate strong signs of a growing need to revisit the topic of sanctification. Fresh concern about this vital theological locus is surfacing, which is wonderful since this is where the church so often lives and breathes."[2]

But while interest in the nature of spiritual formation has resurfaced afresh in philosophy and theology, psychologists have been engaged in this discussion all along. It is the modern dis-integration of psychology, philosophy, and theology—understood as distinct disciplines—that is partly to blame for this situation. Psychology, it could be thought, covers the domain of lived human experience, while modern philosophy and theology (perhaps particularly in their respective analytic and scholastic forms) are relegated to logical and conceptual analysis abstracted from the lived realities of human experience. The problem created by this fabricated separation is not simply that philosophy and theology are in need of the real-life observations of psychology, but psychology itself is starved of the epistemological and worldview considerations of philosophy and theology and driven instead by a naturalized, strict empiricism.[3] And so we end up with a situation in which psychological theory and research needs to interact with theological and philosophical resources as much as theological and philosophical conceptualizations are in need of data and reflections from psychology. This is particularly the case when it comes to the interrelationship of psychology and spiritual formation.

In what has been said thus far, we have been using the terms "psychology" and "spiritual formation" to refer to distinct bodies of research and theory grounded in different methodologies. Understood in this way, the two fields make putative claims to knowledge in need of

---

[2]Kelly M. Kapic, ed., *Sanctification: Explorations in Theology and Practice* (Downers Grove, IL: IVP Academic, 2014), 9.

[3]For a critique of this sort when it comes to the role of moral theory in clinical psychology, see Ronald B. Miller, *Facing Human Suffering: Psychology and Psychotherapy as Moral Engagement* (Washington, DC: American Psychological Association, 2004). See also Brent D. Slife, Kari A. O'Grady, and Russell D. Kosits, *The Hidden Worldviews of Psychology's Theory, Research, and Practice* (New York: Routledge, 2017).

integration. But we can also think of the two terms as pointing to the actual lived realities of human mental life and transformation in Christ. That is to say, with psychology we are concerned with the fundamental phenomena of lived, human existence as it is experienced, and with spiritual formation we are concerned with that lived, human existence as it is experienced in Christ Jesus. It is from the investigation of these phenomena that the discipline of psychology and the field of spiritual formation find their impetus.

But even in this way of thinking, there can remain an implicit division as if one can separate out the phenomenon of human mental life from the phenomenon of humans coming to have the mind of Christ. As Bruce Hindmarsh argues in chapter three of this book, there is an important theological case to be made that the end for which human persons were created shouldn't be separated out from an investigation of what is to develop as a human person. And so, to the degree that modern psychology has separated its examination of human development or mental life from the fullness of human life in Christ, these psychological accounts will be, at best, truncated.

And yet a treatment of the reality of transformation in Christ will itself be enervated if it does not take the psychological dimensions of that transformational process seriously. In the final chapter of this book, Justin Barrett contends that there is evidence from developmental theory indicating that there are particular seasons of human development that are especially conducive to spiritual formation. Of course, the Scriptures themselves point us to the significance of human psychology time and time again. It is "from within, out of the heart," Jesus says, that every manner of evil precedes (Mk 7:21-23). Jesus repeatedly directs his students to the "inside of the cup" (Mt 23:26), the "healthy tree" that bears good fruit (Mt 7:17), and the inner, psychological springs of sinful behavior (e.g., Mt 5:27-28). Moreover, it is interpersonal, loving union and communion with himself by faith that grounds the hope of salvation. "On that day many will say to me, 'Lord, Lord, did we not prophesy in your name, and cast out demons in your name, and do many mighty works in your name?' And then will I declare to them, 'I never knew you; depart from me, you workers of lawlessness'" (Mt 7:22-23). If we are ever tempted to return to a strictly behaviorist view of the person, a close reading of Jesus' theory of human personality should be enough to reign us back in.

It was thoughts and conversations such as these that fueled weekly discussions at Biola University's Center for Christian Thought (CCT) during our 2013–2014 year on the theme of "Psychology and Spiritual Formation." Over that year a group of sixteen CCT fellows and two pastors-in-residence gathered to discuss their own research on this topic as well as to hear from visiting scholars. This rich, interdisciplinary, year-long discussion culminated with an end-of-the-year conference drawing together the CCT fellows, pastors-in-residence, and many of the visiting scholars. Various papers from that conference were subsequently revised and are presented here in their final form.

Because of the interdisciplinary focus of Biola's CCT, these chapters are somewhat unique in that they were prepared for a multidisciplinary audience and were forged out of discussion between theologians, New Testament scholars, philosophers, educators, pastors, and psychologists around the CCT seminar table. Furthermore, the chapter authors are known as scholars who not only have expertise in their primary disciplines but also possess sincere regard for and extensive fluency in relevant disciplines outside their own. This makes for a volume that will speak across typical disciplinary divides on this important and timely topic.

OVERVIEW OF THE BOOK

The book is divided into three main parts. Part one treats issues regarding the relationship between psychology and theology. In the opening chapter, "Spiritual Theology: When Psychology and Theology in the Spirit Service Faith," John H. Coe reacquaints us with the ancient practice of spiritual theology. Spiritual theology, as Coe understands it, is a methodological approach to the study of Christian formation that recognizes the already existing unity of the teachings of Scripture with the dynamics of human experience. In doing spiritual theology, it is not merely that we bring empirical observation and reflection on human experience into conversation or dialogue with the deliverances of Scripture. Rather, Coe argues, the existential-experiential dimension is already contained within the biblical teachings on the nature, process, and directives of spiritual growth so that to fail to attend to the existential-experiential in biblical-systematics is to diminish what the Scriptures themselves have to offer. Thus spiritual theology is needed in biblical-systematic theology as well as in Christian psychology as it provides a fundamental episte-mological basis for a holistic integration of these two disciplines.

While Coe urges the retrieval of spiritual theology to undergird the relevance of psychology to spiritual formation, in "Is 'Spiritual Formation' More Cultural Than Theo-Anthropological? An Ongoing Dialogue," James M. Houston protests that professionalization within modern psy-chology undermines attempts to bring psychology profitably to bear on Christian formation. In particular, Houston contends that psychologists' professional identity can blind them to hidden assumptions of what it means to be human, to an ahistorical and restrictive scientific method-ology, and to the hubris that often accompanies disciplinary special-ization. Houston also directs our attention to a thin view of human depravity that is at work particularly in the North American context such that our views of spiritual formation are shallow when it comes to the need for "radical conversion" or *metanoia*. As remedy, Houston calls us "to critique the present status of the human sciences, as not being human enough" and to press forward with Karl Barth's notion of a "theo-anthropology . . . where the nature of God is indissolubly united with the nature of man."

In part two of the book, we consider theological insights for a psychology of spiritual formation. In chapter three, "'End of Faith as Its Beginning': A Christ-Centered Developmental Spirituality," Bruce Hind-marsh has us consider six theological propositions in order to reframe the conversation about human development and spiritual development.

Hindmarsh, akin to Houston and Coe, is concerned that to precede on the assumption that psychology and spiritual formation are two pre-existing subjects that only need to be brought into dialogue is a setup for failure. His central contention, then, is that "in order for developmental psychology to be deeply Christian at its foundations and for spiritual formation to be deeply human, there must be a vivid appreciation of the end for which humans were created." The idea here is that the final cause of human persons—namely, transformational, loving communion with God—is basic to human development, such that spiritual development cannot be merely one subtype of human development. Instead it is the essential core of human development such that every other aspect of human growth finds its place in light of persons-in-relation with God. This, Hindmarsh argues, rightly reorients developmental psychology and simultaneously humanizes spiritual formation.

In chapter four, "Living 'Before God': A Kierkegaardian View of Spirituality," C. Stephen Evans continues the exploration of a relational spirituality. Evans's chapter is a brilliant illustration of Coe's point in chapter one that the experiential-existential dimension is already present in Christian spirituality, rightly understood, such that to study spirituality is an inherently psychological task. Indeed, Kierkegaard's view of Christian living is a fruitful framework for the development of a Christian psychology.[4] Evans begins his chapter by distinguishing a sense in which all human persons are in relation to God whether they recognize that fact or not. "Generic human spirituality" is what Evans calls the sort of relatedness to God that the atheist, for instance, experiences despite his protests to the contrary. Evans shows that for Kierkegaard the atheist's claim that he does not believe in God is a volitional or characterological matter and not an epistemic matter. Evans writes, "If we do not believe, it is either because we do not want to believe (a kind of 'insubordination' that [Kierkegaard] sees as endemic to modernity) or else it is because we have lost the emotional and imaginative skills required to recognize God

---

[4]On this, see C. Stephen Evans, *Søren Kierkegaard's Christian Psychology: Insight for Counseling and Pastoral Care* (Grand Rapids: Zondervan, 1990).

at work in the world and our lives."[5] God is, in actual fact, relationally present to all persons in various ways (e.g., natural signs), including one's moral conscience. But once one acknowledges God's presence and moral claim, the spiritual life is a process of increasing degrees of awareness of God and striving to live life before him. Through Christ, the Spirit, and the church, Evans contends, the Christian has a unique awareness of God (i.e., Christian spirituality), which can be fostered or inhibited in various ways. Evans concludes his chapter with a Kierkegaardian treatment of several factors that inhibit spiritual life and several practices that foster spirituality (Scripture, prayer, worship, and Communion).

In chapter five, we reach our first author—Siang-Yang Tan—who is a psychologist. Tan is also a full-time pastor and approaches his psychology from a biblically engaged, pastoral perspective. Accordingly, in "Beyond Resilience, Posttraumatic Growth, and Self Care: A Biblical Perspective on Suffering and Christian Spiritual Formation," Tan takes up the topic of how a Christian perspective on suffering offers a corrective to the psychological literature on resilience, posttraumatic growth, and self-care. Tan argues that a Christian view of suffering sees a value in "sanctified suffering" that is more than the pursuit of "benefit-finding" typical of the psychological literature. Tan writes, "Concrete benefits and blessings may not be apparent or clear but God is doing his deeper work of grace in our hearts and lives through redemptive and sanctified suffering, and in so doing reveals his greatest glory in and through us." In particular, Tan argues, sanctified or redemptive suffering conduces to spiritual brokenness, humility, sharing in Christ's sufferings, and God's power perfected in our weakness. These outcomes, while good from a Christian perspective, are not always experienced as beneficial by the sufferer and are in tension with outcomes such as greater self-reliance and self-improvement that are reported in the posttraumatic growth literature. Moreover, Tan contends that suffering is ultimately for the glory of God, and yet the way in which suffering redounds to God's glory

---

[5]For a brief review of psychological research relevant to the "imaginative skills required to recognize God at work," see Justin Barrett's chapter in this volume.

may not be clear this side of heaven. Tan's contribution is an excellent example of how Christian theology reinterprets contemporary psychological research and theory for the sake of spiritual formation in Christ.

In chapter six, Ellen T. Charry invites us to join her in "Seeking the Tropological Import of Psalm 35." Psalm 35 is an imprecatory psalm—a psalm that invokes calamity on one's enemies—in which the psalmist, in this instance, requests God's vengeance on those who have done him harm. In conversation with evolutionary psychology and taking a figurative approach to this psalm, Charry finds in Psalm 35 a social critique of a lack of civility in Israel as well as a constructive way of dealing with the "dysfunction wrought by contempt when people honestly feel misunderstood and disrespected." The desire to be vindicated by God in such situations, contends Charry, is a constructive response because leaving vindication to God will restore the scorned to a place of confidence and wholeness. "The pastoral challenge of the scenario," writes Charry, "is that the wounded not emerge from the incident by becoming smug and that the scorners not emerge from it untouched." The imprecatory psalm provides a safe and empathic place for the complainant to express his hurt honestly and leave his grief and anger in the hands of God. The complainant, urges Charry, wants his oppressors to understand how he has been harmed and learn from their role in causing that harm. Charry's reading of Psalm 35 could be easily combined with similar themes of emotional honesty in psalms of lament, confession, and hope, which together offer a case for the role of the poetic in therapeutic healing. More significantly, Charry showcases the way in which biblical material often draws a profound psychological picture of the complex dynamics of instances of harm, abuse, and oppression at both individual and social levels.

Charry's chapter concludes part two of this edited collection. In part two, the chapter-authors endeavor to bring theological and biblical perspectives to bear on psychological themes. Part three turns the reader's gaze in the opposite direction, looking to psychology as an aid to understanding spiritual formation.

The first contribution is Earl D. Bland's "On Specks and Planks: Psychotherapy, Spiritual Formation, and Moral Judgment." Bland writes from the perspective of psychoanalytic, self psychology and brings depth psychological principles to bear on spiritual formation. For one, Bland argues that because spiritual formation is an embodied, lived process, it must include "deep and connective relational engagement" and that psychotherapy provides a unique relational context for that engagement. And yet Bland stresses that explicit usage of Christian language and interventions can blind the therapist and client to "unconscious enactments that operate to undermine lasting change." Bland proposes four ways in which therapeutic encounter, even if not explicitly Christian in presentation, can help accomplish Jesus' call to remove the plank from our own eye. First, psychotherapy helps identify and draw out into awareness defensive self-righteousness. Second, in the wake of trauma, psychotherapy can help relax inflexible certitude about one's faith. Third, psychotherapy provides a safe context in which the implicit understandings that lead to relational distancing and exclusion of others can be addressed. And, fourth, psychotherapy appears to be particularly helpful in treating persons who are unconsciously closed off to allowing their needs to be met or even admitting that they have needs.

In chapter eight, Robert A. Emmons addresses the "Queen of the Virtues and King of the Vices: Graced Gratitude and Disgraced Ingratitude." After summarizing some of the research showing the positive effects of gratitude on mental health, Emmons presents five possible explanations for this connection: gratitude increases spiritual awareness, gratitude promotes physical health, gratitude maximizes positive experiences, gratitude protects against negative experiences, and gratitude strengthens relationships. Emmons goes on to note the affinity of gratitude with humility in turning persons to beneficial realities beyond themselves on which they are dependent and of which they are undeserving (i.e., graced gratitude). But this turning from independent self to self-dependent-on-others does not come easily. Emmons puts forward two practices for the cultivation of virtuous gratitude: paying attention to blessings and remembering the benevolence of others. Both of these practices can be fostered through reflective gratitude exercises (e.g., gratitude journaling and letter writing) that turn our attention to the graced life in which we find ourselves.

With chapter nine, we come to a multi-authored chapter (Steven J. Sandage, David R. Paine, and Jonathan Morgan) titled "Relational Spirituality, Differentiation, and Mature Alterity." Sandage and his colleagues propose that alterity—relating to otherness—is an essential dimension of maturing Christian spirituality. They frame their discussion within a relational model of spirituality that emphasizes the significance of differentiated relationships between self, God (understood as a tri-unity of persons in relation), and others. Drawing off Emmanuel Levinas, Jessica Benjamin, Miroslav Volf, and Paul Ricoeur, Sandage et al. conclude that "benevolent alterity" involves differentiated relations between self and other with an orientation to what is good and just. Based on this conceptualization, the authors then turn to a discussion of empirical research on alterity by means of measuring intercultural competence and social justice commitment, both of which are associated with positive spiritual growth. Sandage, Paine, and Morgan conclude their chapter with several practical implications for spiritual formation centered around practices that aim to foster intercultural competence and social justice commitment.

Chapter ten continues the theme of drawing on psychological insights for deepened understanding of spiritual formation with Everett L. Worthington, Brandon J. Griffin, and Caroline R. Lavelock looking for resources in positive psychology in their "Cultivating the Fruit of the Spirit: Contributions of Positive Psychology to Spiritual Formation." The authors interact with Dallas Willard, James Wilhoit, Jeffrey Greenman, and George Kalantzis in order to arrive at an understanding of spiritual formation that emphasizes human participation with the Holy Spirit in community with others that brings about character formation for the benefit of the world. By positive psychology, Worthington and his colleagues intend the psychological science of the nature of eudaimonic virtue and virtue formation. On the basis of these definitions, Worthington, Griffin, and Lavelock turn to several hypotheses regarding eudaimonic virtue formation that are relevant to spiritual formation. Many of the hypotheses have to do with the social and contextual nature of virtue formation—for instance, the importance of being part of communities that value virtues and hold one accountable to act in accordance with virtue. The authors conclude that "much of spiritual formation is not through individual moral decisions but through arranging one's relationships with people, organizations, and things to maximize the number of times particular values reach momentary ascendancy in one's virtue hierarchy." The authors contend for a kind of automaticity when it comes to virtue formation that leads them to suggest the promotion of virtue through external "stimulus control procedures" as well as the voluntary practice of virtuous behavior.

Marie T. Hoffman takes up the significance of relational psychoanalysis and object-relations theory for Christian formation in her "Born to Relate: In Trauma, In Transformation, In Transcendence." Hoffman argues that spiritual formation is best understood and practiced from the perspective that humans are formed through relationship, disordered by relationship, and restored/transformed through relationship. In particular, object relations theory offers a helpful paradigm, suggests Hoffman, for understanding how one's early relational history can distort one's present experience of relational connection with both other human persons and the Divine persons. Hoffman contends that therapists can forge deep, loving relationships with their clients that free clients from their past patterns of relational dysfunction and in so doing, the therapist is in some imperfect way modeling the love and acceptance of Christ. Hoffman also challenges the critique that psychoanalysis only deals with the negative symptomology of psychopathology to the neglect of positive, life-enhancing development. Hoffman urges that therapeutic, relational healing not only involves relief from psychopathological symptoms but also helps bring about the formation of positive qualities and experiences.

Justin L. Barrett concludes this edited collection with "Give Up Childish Ways or Receive the Kingdom like a Child? Spiritual Formation from a Developmental Psychology Perspective." Echoing chapter three of this book in which Hindmarsh proposed that developmental theory stands to gain from a Christian view of human teleology, Barrett closes the loop, proposing that Christian formation stands to gain from sensitivity to one's developmental stage. Barrett observes that much of the spiritual formation literature assumes an adult or late adolescent population when there is reason to think that important opportunities exist for formation in young children and that the formative mechanisms involved would look quite different for children than adults (the same, he suspects, is true of older adults). Barrett proposes that childhood is a period of development that is particularly conducive to spiritual formation in part because research shows that children lose some psychological flexibility as they age. For instance, Barrett notes research from the cognitive science of religion that demonstrates that children have naturally occurring intuitions that favor theistic belief such that a belief in an invisible being with superpowers is easier to take on at a young age. Barrett goes on to discuss how faithfulness and kindness (which are called fruit of the Spirit) overlap with Jonathan Haidt's research on moral foundations drawing the conclusion that encouraging growth in particular moral foundations (e.g., authority/respect and in-group/loyalty) at a young age may enable children to more easily develop these fruit of the Spirit as they develop. These proposals by Barrett are meant to motivate further research and, accordingly, Barrett aptly concludes his chapter and the book with several questions to stimulate future research on spiritual formation from a developmental perspective.

ACKNOWLEDGMENTS

We conclude this introduction with a round of sincere thanks. First off, Evan Rosa and Laura Pelser are the backbone of Biola's Center for Christian Thought, and without their leadership and administration, the gatherings that brought about this collection of writings would not have come to be. In a similar vein, the leadership at Biola University have been indefatigable in their support of CCT. President Barry Corey and, at the time, Provost David Nystrom deserve particular thanks. Second, the insights and interactions of the CCT fellows for the 2013–2014 year served as the first (and sometimes second or third) audience for most of these papers. Those fellows were Betsy Barber, John Coe, Kaye Cook, Steve Evans, Todd Hall, Dave Horner, Eric Johnson, Chris Kaczor, Kelly Kapic, Jonathan Lunde, Alan Padgett, Greg Peters, Todd Pickett, Bill Struthers, Judy Ten Elshof, and Jim Wilhoit. Third, we are indebted to the Christian Association of Psychological Studies (CAPS)–IVP book committee for seeing merit in this edited volume as well as the good folks at IVP Academic. In particular, Pete Hill at CAPS and Jon Boyd at IVP have been a mainstay of support. Fourth, all of the fellowships, research, and events that came out of CCT's year on psychology and spiritual formation were made possible by a generous grant from the John Templeton Foundation. We particularly thank the program staff whom we interacted with most frequently: Michael Murray, John Churchill, and Alex Arnold. Of course, the views expressed in these pages are not meant to represent the views of the John Templeton Foundation.

Last, Dallas Willard was our dear friend and mentor and he had graciously accepted our invitation to join us as a senior visiting scholar over the course of the 2013-2014 academic year on the theme of psychology and spiritual formation. But that was not to be, and Dallas passed from this life to the next in May of 2013, a few months before we launched the theme year. And yet in many ways Dallas was with us at the Center throughout the course of that year. Dallas was referred to, quoted, or referenced at some point by just about every scholar who set foot in CCT during that year. Indeed, when you say the words "psychology and spiritual formation" it is hard not to think of Dallas Willard. Dallas's view of spiritual formation is a deeply psychological account of how it is that the Spirit of God reforms the innermost recesses of human persons: literally, our psyches (souls), and that includes, for Dallas, our thoughts, emo-tions, desires, intentions, and interpersonal relations—all mediated through an embodied existence in the world. Indeed, in many respects it was the writings and influence of Dallas that inspired the three of us to initiate this particular year of study. Dallas was fond of encouraging folks to think about what they would be doing five hundred years into their eternal future given that, as he put, we are unceasing spiritual beings with an eternal destiny in God's great universe. And so it is quite easy for us to imagine Dallas hard at work in the heavenly kingdom with which he was so intimately familiar while he lived on earth. In that spirit, Dallas, we offer this book for your perusal (if you have the interest and the time). Even though your fingerprints are all over these pages, we would have loved to have added your voice to the fertile discussions out of which these chapters bloomed.

PART ONE

THE

RELATIONSHIP

BETWEEN

PSYCHOLOGY

AND SPIRITUAL

FORMATION

SPIRITUAL THEOLOGY

WHEN PSYCHOLOGY AND THEOLOGY IN THE SPIRIT SERVICE FAITH

JOHN H. COE

A pastor once confided to me, "I know how to preach, teach and administrate a church. But when people tell me their spiritual problems, that they don't pray enough or that they struggle with anger or worry, and I quote to them the Bible that they should pray more, put off anger and not worry, they often respond 'I know that pastor—so what is wrong with me?' The truth is, I don't know what to say or do from there. I'm stuck." I don't think the problem is unique to this pastor. Those of us who preach would love to see transformation just by the speaking the Word: "Pray more; love God; put off anger!" And—poof—it is done. But that is a fantasy.[1]

---

[1]This chapter draws much from John Coe, "Spiritual Theology: A Theological-Experiential Methodology for Bridging the Sanctification Gap," *Journal of Spiritual Formation and Soul Care* 2, no. 1, (2009): 4-43. Permission to borrow material granted from *Journal of Spiritual Formation and Soul Care*. This recognition of the spiritual distance between what one believes to be true about the goals of Christian growth and an awareness of the reality of what is true in one's life has been called the "sanctification gap." For an insightful discussion of this "gap," see Richard Lovelace, "The Sanctification Gap," *Theology Today* 29, no. 4 (1973): 363-69. See also Steven L. Porter, "The Sanctification Gap Revisited" (paper and presentation, Evangelical Theological Society, Washington, DC, November, 2006).

There is a great need in the church for a robust methodology that takes seriously the study of spiritual growth. On the one hand, contemporary evangelical theological education has focused on doctrine and technical historical-textual studies but sometimes to the neglect of an in-depth understanding of sanctification.[2] Even when there exists an adequate doctrine of sanctification, what is still missing is how that truth of sanctification becomes a reality in the believer's life. On the other hand, Christian psychological training has focused on observation, reflection, and theorizing about psychological dynamics related to health, sin, and being sinned against. But it typically ignores the study of spiritual growth and the transforming ministry of the Holy Spirit in the believer's life and how the absence of the Holy Spirit affects the unbeliever's experience. Consequently, what is missing is an in-depth understanding of the process of growth in the Spirit. That is, there appears to be a gap in our theological and psychological training of pastors and Christian psychologists: In seminary the gap is between understanding the theological content of the faith and engaging thoughtfully in the praxis of spiritual formation, a gap that needs to be bridged by an understanding of the process of how we grow in Christ. In schools of Christian psychology, the gap is between the natural psychological processes of sin and growth and growth in the Spirit, a gap that needs to be bridged by an understanding of the dynamic processes of how the Spirit of God transforms the person.

---

[2]For example, William Shedd in his *Dogmatic Theology* spends over 50 pages on "Divine Decrees" and 6 pages on "Sanctification"; William G. T. Shedd, *Dogmatic Theology*, ed. Alan W. Gomes (Phillipsburg, NJ: P&R, 2003). Louis Berkhof in his *Systematic Theology* spends over 100 pages on the "Nature of Dogmatic Theology" and 17 pages on "Sanctification"; Louis Berkhof, *Systematic Theology*, rev. ed. (Grand Rapids: Eerdmans, 1996). Wayne Grudem in *Systematic Theology* spends over 100 pages on the "Doctrine of the Word" and 17 pages on "Sanctification"; Wayne Grudem, *Systematic Theology* (Grand Rapids: Zondervan, 1994). Millard Erickson in *Christian Theology* spends over 100 pages on "Revelation" and 18 pages on "Sanctification and the Christian Life"; Millard Erickson, *Christian Theology* (Grand Rapids: Baker Academic, 2013).

SPIRITUAL THEOLOGY AS A TASK FOR THEOLOGIAN, PSYCHOLOGIST, PASTOR, AND CHURCH

I want to reclaim for evangelical theological and psychological education and for the church a robust understanding of spiritual theology as pastoral-psychological-spiritual theology. Spiritual theology is the theological discipline that attempts to fill this gap of understanding the process of spiritual growth by integrating (1) the scriptural teaching on sanctification and growth with (2) observations, reflections, and experience (an empirical study) of the Spirit's work in the believer's spirit and experience, which is within the purview of both pastoral theology and a Christian doing psychology. Here is where theology and Christian psychology come together to understand the process of spiritual formation for the church. Thus it is unclear whether spiritual theology should be within the purview of theology or psychology, for it takes one versed in both to really do spiritual theology well. In that case, this study could just as well be called spiritual psychology or psychological spirituality or integrative spirituality than spiritual theology. However, I will use the term spiritual theology because it has a certain standing tradition in the history of theology, though the name is less important than the phenomena and methodology.[3] If schools of Christian psychology wish to give this a different name, that is fine. My experience teaching in a school of psychology is that what has been called "integration" has fallen short of this, being a study of the content of theology and psychology and less a focused understanding of the dynamic psychological-spiritual processes of growth in the Spirit based upon the work of Christ in salvation. And though the model developed here is an academic one, it would be a mistake to think it is for professionals only.[4] I will argue that theologians, pastors, and psychologists need to do spiritual theology if they are to understand all the dynamic process of growth in Christ. Nevertheless,

---

[3]For thoughtful Roman Catholic spiritual theologies, see Reginald Garrigou-Lagrange, *The Three Ages of the Interior Life* (Charleston: CreateSpace, 2013) and Jordan Aumann, *Spiritual Theology* (New York: T&T Clark, 1980).

[4]I am indebted to Jim Wilhoit for this type of concern in discussion at the Center for Christian Thought, 2014.

spiritual theology is implicitly the task for all believers who desire to integrate the truths of the word of God into the reality of how the Spirit works in our everyday lives.

THE DATA OF SPIRITUAL THEOLOGY: SCRIPTURE AND EMPIRICAL STUDY OF LIFE IN THE SPIRIT

On this model of spiritual theology, certainly Scripture is the central and most important datum for the content and understanding of the process of spiritual transformation—clearly a theological task. Nevertheless, this textual study needs to be combined with an empirical study and understanding of how these realities discussed in the Bible actually work in real life—a psychological-observational task. And both theologians and psychologists must stretch themselves to ask how the Spirit of God works in transformation in real life. I cannot overestimate the significance of this point—one that is sometimes difficult for the pastor, the theologian, and the psychologist to recognize. After all, how we put off anger in the Spirit and how we become filled with the Holy Spirit are very real questions for believers. And when I say there is a need for *empirical* study I do not mean the dogma of "empiricism" held by certain scientistic thinkers who restrict knowledge to what the senses provide. By *empirical*, I only mean the God-given use of observation, reason, experience, and reflection to understand certain dimensions of reality—namely, life in the Spirit. This is clearly the job of every Christian but also the specific task of the spiritual theologian.

This empirical element in spiritual theology will focus on two fundamental dimensions. First, because spiritual growth involves the work of the Holy Spirit in the believer's life—something that takes place in real life—it is insufficient to limit our study of the work of the Spirit to a textual study of the Scriptures if we are to have a full understanding of His work in sanctification. Rather, it is necessary to actually study the Spirit's work in the human experience (what we might call pneumadynamics). Second, because the Spirit does the work of transformation in the human person, we will also need to study the dynamic processes of the human spirit, sin, psychopathology, and response to the Spirit (psychodynamics). It turns out that these empirical tasks of observation and reflection are the work of spiritual theology and need to be done in both the schools of theology and psychology if pastors and Christian therapists are to have a robust understanding of the dynamics of spiritual growth. Of course, there may be different emphases and different goals to their work (on the one hand, for preaching and pastoral counseling, on the other, for doing therapy, etc.).[5] In that case, it seems even more clear how much theologians and psychologists need one another if they are to do spiritual theology in the most complete manner.

THE LACK OF SPIRITUAL THEOLOGY IN THEOLOGICAL AND PSYCHOLOGICAL TRAINING

In general, I think spiritual theology has been greatly ignored in theological and Christian psychological training as well as contemporary discussions of spirituality. The absence of this understanding of pneumadynmics and psychodynamics in our theological training has been largely due, I believe, to (a) the belief that this is the task of someone other than the theologian or psychologist, (b) the theologian/pastor's incorrect assumption that an adequate understanding of the process of spiritual growth can be gleaned from solely a textual study that involves little reflection on human experience, or (c) the psychologist's incorrect assumption that an adequate understanding of the process of spiritual growth can be gleaned from solely an empirical study of the dynamic processes of human growth (psychodynamics) apart from understanding dynamics of the Holy Spirit (pneumadynamics). But there is no good reason for this—theology and psychology must address the real questions of how growth takes place and how the Spirit works in transformation.

---

[5]For a more in-depth discussion of the nature of a robust Christian psychology whose methodology would legitimately study both psychodynamics and pneumadynamics, see John H. Coe and Todd Hall's chapter, "Transformational Psychology," in *Psychology and Christianity: Five Views*, ed. E. Johnson and S. Jones (Downers Grove, IL: InterVarsity Press, 2010). See also John H. Coe and Todd W. Hall, "Methodological Problems Confronting Contemporary Psychology as Science," in *Psychology in the Spirit* (Downers Grove, IL: IVP Academic, 2010), 121-31.

Perhaps a word about Christian psychology is relevant here. Christian psychology has done a marvelous job in seeking to understand human psychodynamics, as its secular counterpart has attempted. Unfortunately, however, it often ignores pneumadynamics altogether, given its tendency to mimic its secular counterpart's naturalistic and reductionistic methodology in doing science, which generally precludes the study of spiritual realities, particularly the experience of the ministry of the Holy Spirit. Even psychology of religion has fallen into this tendency.

The result of this hole or gap in our theological and Christian psychological training is an impoverished understanding of the process of growth in the Spirit. Overall, training in spiritual theology would greatly assist pastors, theologians, Christian psychologists, and believers in understanding the process of growth in the Spirit.

DEFINITION OF SPIRITUAL THEOLOGY AS A SPECIFIC FIRST-ORDER DISCIPLINE

Spiritual theology is the theological-empirical discipline, with its own unique data and methodology, that brings together (a) a study of the truths of Scripture—a historical-literary discipline—with (b) a study of the ministry of the Holy Spirit and spiritual growth in the experience of human beings—a broadly empirical discipline involving observation, reflection, and integration with other relevant disciplines. In that sense, it is at its core an integrative endeavor.

The purpose or goal of this spiritual theology is threefold:

1. To define the nature of this supernatural life in Christ (which is derived from the Bible and theology as the primary data)

2. To explain the process of growth by which persons move from the beginning of the spiritual life to its full perfection in the next life (which is derived from the data of the Bible, theology, and experience)

3. To formulate directives for spiritual growth and development (which are derived from the data of the Bible, theology, and experience)

Spiritual theology's task is to study all relevant data regarding growth. While the Bible is the central datum for this study, the peculiar and unique task in comparison to other kinds of academic disciplines (psychology, systematic theology, OT studies, NT studies)—that is, the task that is peculiar to this study in the universe of academic disciplines—is to integrate a theology of sanctification with a broadly empirical study of what is relevant to understanding spiritual growth in the real world. With God in heart and Scripture in hand, the unique task of spiritual theology is to go into the world of the church and the Spirit to study and understand all one can about the nature, process, and directives for spiritual growth.

This literary and empirical study of life in the Spirit would include dialogue and learning between theologians, Christian psychologists, philosophers, sociologists, anthropologists, etc. who are seeking to understand the person, human psychological-relational-cultural dynamics, and dynamics of the ministry of the indwelling Holy Spirit. This methodology blends particularly the work of the theologian and Christian psychologist in a robust sense. Thus it is unclear whether spiritual theology is most aptly in the purview of the Christian theologian or Christian psychologist—perhaps both can and should do this. Perhaps only both together can do this well. And though the work of spiritual theology can be captured by an academic discipline, it also has a general application in the life of any believer who attempts to understand how to obey and integrate truth into real Christian existence.

A PARTICULARLY EVANGELICAL-THEOLOGICAL CONCERN OVER SPIRITUAL THEOLOGY

Some may object that this view of spiritual theology contradicts the Reformation commitment to *sola Scriptura*—or at least to some people's interpretation of this doctrine, that the Scriptures alone contain all that we need for understanding the spiritual life or that all wisdom for living is contained in the Bible and, therefore, no wisdom for spiritual growth can be discovered outside the Bible. This has been the claim of the Biblical Counseling tradition for years.[6] According to some Biblical Counselors, all we need for spiritual growth is an understanding of the Bible and obedience to it. Spiritual theology, on the other hand, is interested in whether there is any extrabiblical wisdom that we can discover and that is helpful for understanding and participating in the process of spiritual growth.

JUSTIFICATION FOR DOING SPIRITUAL THEOLOGY

Because spiritual theology is controversial in certain circles of evangelicalism, there is a need to provide a justification for the need, even necessity for theologians and psychologists to do spiritual theology. The following are some of the more salient points.

First, spiritual theology is consistent with the Protestant view of *sola Scriptura*. The important use of *sola Scriptura* by the Reformers is a very subtle and complex matter that takes us beyond the scope of this chapter.[7] Suffice it to say that its original intent was not so much to employ *sola Scriptura* to mean that the Scripture alone provides all information or wisdom for spiritual growth. Rather, it was employed to affirm that Scripture alone and not some pope or council provides the constitutive tenets of the faith—that is, those central doctrines that constitute the faith and are essential for faith to which the believer must assent. It was also used with reference to providing a boundary condition on practice, so that no spiritual practice could be required of a believer that was not explicitly taught in the Scripture.[8] Of course, this does not preclude the possibility of finding wisdom outside the Bible that may assist in our

---

[6]For an understanding and response to the Biblical Counseling tradition and its insistence that there is no extrabiblical insight or wisdom for living, see John H. Coe and Todd Hall, "An Old Testament Model for a Transformational Science and Psychology," in *Psychology in the Spirit*, 132-65.

[7]For a more in-depth understanding of the nature and historical understanding of *sola Scriptura* and the epistemological implications, see Keith A. Mathison, *The Shape of Sola Scriptura* (Moscow, ID: Canon Press, 2001). See also Steven L. Porter, "Sanctification in a New Key: Relieving Evangelical Anxieties over Spiritual Formation," *Journal of Spiritual Formation and Soul Care* 1, no. 2 (2008): 129-48.

[8]I am indebted to my colleague historical theologian Alan Gomes for this reflection.

understanding of spiritual growth. However, some have stretched the meaning and commitment of *sola Scriptura* to disallow extrabiblical knowledge and wisdom.[9]

Second, the goal of all theology has something to do with spiritual theology insofar as all theology has a spiritual relevance. This is incontrovertible. The Christian faith teaches that the end of human existence, hence, all tasks, is a cluster of ends having to do with the love of God and neighbor and transformation into the image of Christ. There should be no controversy over whether pastors and theologians should do spiritual theology in the most general sense as bringing out the spiritual implications and application of theology, since the goal of all our teaching is the love of God and neighbor and the transformation of the listener into the image of Christ by the Spirit (Lk 10:27; Rom 8:29).

Third, spiritual theology is necessary if we are to apply Scripture to our lives. In some sense, all believers implicitly do spiritual theology in the sense that they seek to understand how the truths of Scripture apply to everyday life in the Spirit. One cannot seek to obey the command to "put off anger" or "be filled with the Holy Spirit" without asking themselves how to do this, what is the process by which one can obey this command in real life. Thus the church needs a meaningful theory-praxis of transformation (i.e., spiritual theology) that will be helpful to all believers, a practice of formation that is theoretically connected to theology and what is going on in human experience.

Fourth, spiritual theology is important if we are to understand how the ministry of the Holy Spirit actually works in our lives. Though the Bible is the sole or at least primary datum for expounding most doctrine (employing exegesis, biblical theology, and systematic theology), there is a need to employ observation and reflection on the Spirit's work in human affairs if we are to understand all that can be known about the

---

[9]For this approach to psychology and psychotherapy see J. E. Adams, *What About Nouthetic Counseling?* (Grand Rapids: Baker Books, 1976); M. Bobgan and D. Bobgan, *Psycho Heresy: The Psychological Seduction of Christianity* (Santa Barbara: East Gate, 1987); D. Hunt, *Beyond Seduction* (Eugene OR: Harvest House, 1987); and J. E. Adams, *The Christian Counselor's Manual* (Grand Rapids: Baker Books, 1973).

doctrines of sanctification and spiritual growth. This is because the loci of formation by the work of the Holy Spirit are the human soul and the church. That is, spiritual formation is an ongoing activity in the Holy Spirit-human spirit matrix in space and time (what I have termed *pneumatological realism*), which the Scriptures themselves affirm. If we are to understand all the work of the Holy Spirit, we will need to study his work in human lives and the church.

Fifth, the interpretation of passages having to do with the Holy Spirit requires some understanding of spiritual theology if we are to understand both the meaning and reference of those texts. To properly interpret or understand the meaning of the biblical texts having to do with the Spirit's work in transformation, we need to understand the referent of the texts that relate to human experience of the Spirit; that is, we need to understand what those texts refer to in our present experience of the Spirit in real space and time. In that sense, exegesis is not merely a literary investigation but depends upon empirical observation and reflection to understand the phenomena referred to in the text. To understand what Paul is saying about the ministry of the Holy Spirit in the person—that we are to be filled with the Holy Spirit (Eph 5:18), what is involved in walking and living by the Spirit (Gal 5:16, 25), having the fruit of the Spirit (Gal 5:22), putting to death the deeds of the body by the Spirit (Rom 8:13), being led by the Spirit (Rom 8:14), being filled with all the fullness of the Spirit in love (Eph 3:17-19)—we will need to open to empirical observation and reflection on our own and the church's present experience with the Spirit in order to understand something of the meaning and referent to which Paul is referring in these biblical texts.

Sixth, spiritual theology is helpful to understand how to live in dependence upon the Spirit. Because the whole of our spiritual life is a kind of dependence, response, and openness to the indwelling Spirit of God (Jn 14:16-17; Rom 8:15-16; Gal 5:16; Eph 3:16-19; 5:18), the Christian life is a form of doing spiritual theology insofar as it involves the common-sense practice of watching, sometimes waiting, and listening for the Spirit's work in space and time on the basis of the Scriptures.

Seventh, spiritual theology has a biblical justification in the integrative model of the Old Testament wisdom literature. The Old Testament wisdom literature in Proverbs insists there is an important extrabiblical source of wisdom for living, which God has provided and is discernable by observing and reflecting upon (a) the created world (Prov 6:6; 30:24-28; cf. natural sciences in 1 Kings 4:29-33) and especially (b) persons and their complex situations (Prov 24:30-34; 30:21-23). This serves as a kind of biblical model for doing spiritual theology.[10]

Eighth, spiritual theology services the church, theology, and psychology by bridging the theological content of the faith and the practice of the faith by providing a theory of the process of growth. The church needs a meaningful theory-praxis of transformation that will be helpful to all believers, a practice of formation that is theoretically connected to theology and what is going on in human experience. Thus a robust spiritual theology theoretically and experientially connects a purely biblical theology of sanctification with an understanding of the nature of growth in Christ—the developmental processes involved and the directives for growth, resulting in application and praxis.

Ninth, spiritual theology is necessary if psychology is to truly and most fully understand the human person as made for union with God by the indwelling Holy Spirit, who is the agent of true Christian transformation.[11] It is possible to do a naturalistic psychology that ignores those psychological capacities and dimensions that potentially interact with the Holy Spirit in both the unbeliever and believer. However, thinking that a naturalistic understanding is all psychology can offer is

---

[10]For an in-depth discussion of how the OT Wisdom Literature and OT Wise Man serve as biblical models for doing psychology in God, see Coe and Hall, *Psychology in the Spirit*.

[11]For a more thorough discussion of a Christian psychology or anthropology that requires a theological understanding of the person—insofar as the person is made for union with God and is only truly healthy when this is realized, see John H. Coe, "Beyond Relationality to Union," *Journal of Christianity and Psychology* 28, vol. 2 (2000): 162-64, as well as Coe and Hall, "The Person as Spirit: Beyond Relationality to Union," in *Psychology in the Spirit* (Downers Grove, IL: InterVarsity Press, 2010), 234-60.

to have a partial and even truncated understanding of the person. However, if we are to have a full-blown, Christianly robust psychology, then the Christian psychologist must be open to all empirical phenomena including what Scriptures say about the person as well as what we can empirically investigate and understand about the person. Unfortunately, Christian psychology has too quickly bought into integrating a naturalistic psychology with theology but has failed to do the firsthand, first-order discipline work of observing and reflecting on the full experience of the believer and the ministry of the Spirit in transformation or lack thereof in a person's life.

Last, spiritual theology is necessary for full, robust Christian theological and psychological training.[12] If spiritual theology is necessary for theology and psychology to reach its telos in understanding the person in God, then it is clear that this theological-empirical first-order discipline is within the purview of both theological and psychological training. This would be the natural nexus between the school of theology and school of psychology. This is where preaching, pastoral theology, theology, psychological theory, and therapy interface. If spiritual theology were taken seriously by both schools, integration would go to a whole new level in educational training, for both schools would take responsibility for this discipline and would necessarily need to interact. Up to now, theologian and psychologist have been satisfied with marginal interaction in their musings on integration. This could transform the schools.

EXAMPLES OF DOING SPIRITUAL THEOLOGY

I have argued that the primary task of spiritual theology—understood as a full-blown, academic, theological-empirical discipline—is to be intentional about discovering from the Scriptures and the experience of the Spirit working in the person: a kind of doing of psychology in the full-blown Christian sense. Its goals are to understand (1) the nature of

---

[12]See Coe and Hall, "Transformational Psychology in the Christian University and Seminary," in *Psychology in the Spirit*, 306-35.

growth, (2) the process of growth, and (3) directives for growth. There will be a dynamic interplay between doing theology, Christian psychology, and spiritual theology to understand Christian growth. The following are some brief examples.

Regarding the nature of growth. Although spiritual theology finds most of its content for the nature of growth from the Scriptures (as discussed above), even here observation and reflection assist the church in understanding the nature of growth in relationship to real life. One example of this is how spiritual theology can help make explicit the implication of the biblical truth of the double imputation of Christ's righteousness on the basis of our union "in Christ" for spiritual formation and the practice of spiritual disciplines (2 Cor 5:21). Because our sins have been imputed to Christ and his righteousness has been imputed to the believer, we are no longer guilty, under the condemnation of God, and we are no longer merely corrupt sinners in God's presence but are now clothed in Christ's alien righteousness (Rom 5:1, 8:1; Phil 3:8-11). This is the truth of justification taken from systematic theology.

One of the rich implications of our theology of justification for the Christian life is that all true growth is ultimately grounded "in Christ" so that God's work and not our own is what establishes our daily acceptance before Him. Spiritual theology, in turn, helps by observing and reflecting upon human experience in harmony with the Word of God in order to provide wisdom to believers regarding how to recognize when we are hiding from our feelings of neurotic or unhealthy guilt or when we are motivated to obey as a means of covering our shame—ways to find acceptance with God from our efforts rather than confessing our sin and finding acceptance in Christ.

Furthermore, observation and reflection on experience can provide wisdom to believers for determining the *nature* of the motivation in using spiritual disciplines, whether they are being employed in a healthy manner or are used "in the flesh" to deal with the believer's failure and guilt, whether they are employed as a way to merit acceptance or more love from God, or performed to obtain more love from others by being a good little boy or girl. Perhaps further reflection connects this unhealthy need to earn acceptance with God with one's early habituation in pleasing abusive parents to gain acceptance and love. Psychological observation and theory could be of great aid in this process. In this case, spiritual theology can provide insights into some of the early etiological impediments to trusting in Christ's imputed righteousness and not our own for finding acceptance with God.[13] The theological truth is that we are already fully loved, forgiven, and accepted "in Christ." Thus obedience and the spiritual disciplines are not to gain us acceptance but merely to open us more deeply to our need for Christ, to his sufficiency, to what Christ has already accomplished, to participating with the Spirit who is already willing and working his transforming work within us (Phil 2:12-13). The actual righteousness that results is always grounded in who we already are in Him. Thus the task of spiritual theology is, in part, to observe carefully what in fact believers are doing with spiritual disciplines and how they in fact respond to guilt and shame in order to address unhealthy and healthy motivations in obedience.[14]

Regarding the process of growth. Second, spiritual theology has been very helpful in exploring the developmental processes of growth. Whereas the Scriptures address this subject somewhat cursorily (e.g., 1 Cor 3:1-7; 1 Jn 2:12-14), theologians, pastors and spiritual writers of the church have given much attention to this. In particular, Bernard of Clairvaux of the twelfth century; St. John of the Cross and Teresa of Avila in the sixteenth century; theologians Gisbertus Voetius and Johannes Hoornbeeck's of the Dutch Second Reformation in the seventeenth century; and Reginald

---

[13]I want to thank Steve Porter, my colleague at the Institute for Spiritual Formation, for his thoughtful comments on this section. For further reflection on the "flesh," see Steven L. Porter, "The Gradual Nature of Sanctification: Σάρξ as Habituated Relational Resistance to the Spirit," *Themelios* 39, no. 3 (2014): 470-83.

[14]For more on this issue of unhealthy motivations in obedience, the temptation to use morality as a way to cover and hide from one's sin, and the deep connection of formation to justification, see John H. Coe, "Resisting the Temptation of Moral Formation: Opening to Spiritual Formation in the Cross and the Spirit," *Journal of Spiritual Formation and Soul Care* 1, no. 1 (2008): 54-78.

Garrigou-Lagrange of the twentieth century are types of spiritual theologians who have provided good examples of this.

Specifically, spiritual theology has been particularly helpful in providing thoughtful reflections on the developmental processes of growth related to consolation, desolation, and the "Dark Night of the Soul" phenomenon. Much has been written on this subject, but due to space, I will be brief.[15]

The ancient spiritual writers noticed both in themselves and in many of their committed disciples different seasons of experience of God. They observed that the convert or young believer (the "beginner") at some point often experienced a strong sense of the felt presence of God. On the other hand, they also noticed that the same believer at a later time, when more mature, often experienced a sense of spiritual dryness or the felt absence of God (an empirical observation). They came to call these times, respectively, *consolation* or the "felt presence" of God and *desolation* or the "felt absence" of God.

As they observed and reflected upon these phenomena in light of a theology of sanctification (the doing of spiritual theology), they developed a number of hypotheses about the felt presence of God.

First, at least at the beginning of the spiritual life, the felt presence of God (consolation) or felt absence of God (desolation) is not necessarily correlated to characterological maturity (a truth from observation and reflection). This phenomenon is contrary to what one might expect, namely, a pure correlation between maturity and experience of the presence of God. However, biblically we know that the Spirit is always present relationally in his people, which is a truth from Scripture (Col 1:27, "Christ in you"; 2 Pet 1:4, "partakers of the divine nature"). Thus, since God is always present, the felt presence or absence of Him (consolation

---

[15]For more on this developmental spirituality regarding the process of growth, see John H. Coe, "Musings on the Dark Night of the Soul: St. John of the Cross on a Developmental Spirituality," *Journal of Psychology and Theology* 28, no. 4 (2000): 293-307. See also St. John of the Cross, *Dark Night of the Soul,* trans. E. Allison Peers (New York: Image, 1959). For a thoughtful and historical account of various developmental approaches to spirituality, see Bruce Demarest, "Reflections on Developmental Spirituality: Journey Paradigms and Stages," *Journal of Spiritual Formation and Soul Care* 1, no. 2 (2008): 149-67.

and desolation)—at least at some times and perhaps in the beginning of
the spiritual life—are more gifts from God than the causal result of our
actions, more the result of differing ways the Spirit works in the soul at
different stages of our growth. Notice that this is a hypothesis from integrating both theological and empirical (psychological) reflections in
spiritual theology. In that case, it is hypothesized that consolation, for
the beginner, is often a filling of the Spirit ahead of one's character with
a purpose to encourage faith and reinforce the doing of spiritual disciplines.[16] Desolation, on the other hand, may be a sign of God withdrawing this beginner's consolation and the love of God as spiritual
pleasure in order to reveal one's true character to oneself and, hence,
discover a deeper love of God. This experience acts as a mirror to show
the reality of one's heart, one's true motivations. This is not a withdrawing
of the presence of the Spirit but rather is the Spirit drawing near in truth
apart from a feeling, to show the person the true state of some of the vice
elements of the character, of how the person is not truly filled with the
Spirit in those places of the heart but filled with oneself, and how God
can meet us ultimately in love in those dark places.[17]

Notice that in each of the cases above, the kernel of insight for this
developmental model was initiated from observation and reflection on
experience (consolation experience in the immature and desolation
experience of the more mature believer). This was then brought in dialogue with theological truth (that God is always with the believer, original
sin's effect on the heart, the need to put off the former vices of the heart)
and from there emerges a set of spiritual-theological-psychological

---

[16]As an aside, there is a "filling of the Holy Spirit" that is of consolation but in a deeper sense,
more congruent with character and maturity.

[17]For more on the coherency between this dark night of the soul phenomena and the content of
systematic theology, see John H. Coe, "Evangelical Boundaries in Spiritual Formation: An Evangelical Understanding of the Dark Night of the Soul," a paper presented to the Evangelical
Theological Society International Annual Meeting, Colorado Springs, November 2001, as well
as John H. Coe, "Opening to God When God Seems Far Away: Finding God in Dark Nights of
the Soul," a paper presented to the Evangelical Theological Society International Annual
Meeting, Providence, RI, November 2017. See also John H. Coe, "Musings on the Dark Night of
the Soul: Insights from John of the Cross on a Developmental Spirituality," *Journal of Psychology
and Theology* 28, no. 4 (2000): 293-307.

hypotheses regarding how to explain for this experience given what we know.

Regarding directives for growth. Throughout the history of the church, pastors, theologians, and mentors have developed practical directives regarding how to grow that are both consistent with and informed by Scripture while attempting to provide more specific details and particular wisdom from their experience for a people at a particular time. For instance, the Scriptures inform us to pray but do not give us any strict schedule or time allotment that is to be given to this other than a few suggestions about what saints such as Daniel or the psalmist, et al., did in particular circumstances. However, spiritual mentors throughout the centuries have instructed or suggested to their disciples different ways to pray, times to pray, and time allotments to pray. These spiritual-theological-psychological attempts to provide practical directives for growth can be good or bad depending upon the wisdom, particular relevance, and correct theological motivations and grounding provided. In general, spiritual theology can glean much throughout church history from the example of dedicated Christians who have given themselves to various forms of spiritual training for the sake of godliness, obedience, love, and transformation.

SUGGESTIONS FOR TRANSFORMING THEOLOGICAL AND PSYCHOLOGICAL TRAINING

I think it would be very wise and advantageous for the church were seminaries to develop departments of spiritual theology and hire or train spiritual theologians who seriously study both the Scriptures and the phenomena of the Spirit in human affairs. It would also be advantageous for Christian schools of psychology to teach spiritual theology also or even to see their training of Christian psychologists to include much of the work of spiritual theology. Both would discover a wealth of material in the history of the church that could greatly affect the training of pastors and psychotherapists in understanding and participating in spiritual growth. This includes such spiritual-theological-psychological writings from John Cassian's *Institutes* and Augustine's *Confessions* of the fourth and fifth centuries to Bernard of Clairvaux in the twelfth century to the Carmelites, Teresa of Avila, and John of the Cross in the sixteenth century to Puritans such as Richard Baxter and Jonathan Edwards to the great Dutch theologians Gisbertus Voetius and Johannes Hoornbeeck's *Spiritual Desertion* of the Second Reformation in the seventeenth century to Reginald Garrigou-Lagrange and Simon Chan of the twentieth century, to name just a few. Of course, these studies in spiritual theology would include exposure to all the areas of Christian psychology; philosophy; and observation and reflection on persons— the dynamics of sin and the Spirit for the sake of understanding spiritual growth. This would only compliment and not detract from an in-depth study of the Scriptures, the history of theology, and psychological theory relevant to spiritual growth.

Furthermore, whole courses could not only be taught in the history, theology, and psychology of spirituality but on existentially relevant topics in spiritual formation such as formation in the life of prayer; the heart's hindrances to growth; the ministry of the Spirit developmentally in the heart of the believer; the relationship of the spiritual disciplines and spiritual training to the work of Christ on the Cross and the Indwelling Spirit; the filling of the Spirit; how to put off the old man and put on the new; spiritual motivation in obedience; the role of neighbor love and missions in spiritual formation; the impact of childhood attachment on experience of God and prayer, etc. These courses would include not only theory but also praxis in applying what is learned for the sake of love and growth. These types of courses could greatly assist both students and faculty to address the sanctification gap theoretically and practically in their own lives as well and to make an informed bridge to the practical ministries of pastoral theology, Christian education, Christian psychotherapy, counseling, and missions for the edification of the saints.

Of course, a number of epistemological issues will arise regarding the justification of truth claims in spiritual theology. Time and energy will have to be spent in carefully developing a methodology and adjudicating procedures by which to scrutinize the study and findings of a spiritual theology insofar as they need to be informed, governed, and judged by a study of the word of God. Great care will need to be given in developing the criteria and guidelines for this study as it integrates within theological and psychological education.

Furthermore, all professors should be encouraged to do spiritual theology at least in the most general and minimal sense of application for the sake of the growth of the student and the church. This includes bringing out the formational relevance of what is taught as well as assisting students in experiential growth in prayer over the content of every course.[18]

The main hindrance to this process of bringing spiritual theology and formation into theological and psychological education will be, most likely, the professor. Our own experience or lack of experience of the Spirit and transformation—personal and corporate—will be the limiting horizon to our teaching. Furthermore, the absence or presence of spiritual theology in our education will be another limiting horizon for our teaching and life-application of the Bible and psychological insight, let alone our willingness and ability to do spiritual theology as a discipline. For Christian psychology, another main obstacle will be to overcome the naturalistic and reductionistic methodology that has precluded psychology from studying pneumadynamics and develop an approach to *scientia* (knowledge and study) that encompasses a robust study of life in the Spirit.

CONCLUSION

The evangelical church and its schools of theology and psychology—along with its pastors, professors, and leaders—needs to embrace a robust spiritual theology for the sake of providing a realistic and meaningful understanding of the process of spiritual growth in a full integrative

---

[18]For more on how to bring spirituality into the classroom, see John H. Coe, "Intentional Spiritual Formation in the Classroom: Making Space for the Spirit in the University," *Christian Education Journal* 4, no. 2 (2000): 85-110.

manner. This, in turn, finds its goal in the transformation of the believer into the image of Christ in the context of a community of saints. All agree that praxis is not to be separated from theory. However, I have argued here that much of Christian praxis is already theoretically disconnected from most of theology so that praxis appears often to dangle as an afterthought to our doctrine. And psychology is missing the fruit of spiritual theology much like a human body would miss the human spirit as its animating core. What is missing is a spiritual theology that both existentially and theoretically connects practice to theology, psychology to the Spirit. To be certain, I am not arguing that a person necessarily needs to be schooled in the spiritual theology to be holy and spiritually mature; however, the mature person will evince signs of implicit spiritual theology insofar as he or she seeks to understand and cooperate with the ministry of the Spirit as directed in Scripture and experienced in reality. The pastor, theologian, and Christian psychologist, however, have the responsibility to teach and train others in the spiritual life. To do this well carries with it both the obligation and opportunity to intentionally and explicitly do the work of spiritual theology for the sake of personal and corporate growth—whether it be through therapy, preaching, discipleship, or board meetings. God give us grace to embrace this task for the sake of growth in the kingdom of God.

IS "SPIRITUAL FORMATION" MORE CULTURAL THAN THEO-ANTHROPOLOGICAL?

AN ONGOING DIALOGUE

JAMES M. HOUSTON

In the current context, there are three ongoing challenges facing Christian scholars in psychology: (1) Christian blindness in having a professional identity that is not primarily—to use Pauline language—"in Christ," (2) cultural blindness in a shallow understanding of human depravity, and (3) the postmodern shift from social ethics, denominations, and ideologies towards the converted and the committed as a reshaping of personal identity for each Christian. As these have all been critically examined, they are simply a background—although essential—to our ongoing dialogue. I am simply reminding you of what these are, so that our identity given us as Christians—as being a person-in-Christ—can never be eclipsed by our own self-achieved "professional" identity.

CHRISTIAN BLINDNESS IN HAVING
A PROFESSIONAL IDENTITY

Hidden assumptions in psychological professionalism. We start by
looking at what is the Christian blindness in having a professional identity
as a psychologist. In focusing, of course, on psychology, we could say that
the same critiques could be applied to many more of our disciplines. But
let me share some of the hidden assumptions in psychological professionalism, for when we examine the interface between Christian formation and the disciplines of psychology, we face profound inconsistencies.
Max Weber, in seeking a place for religion, spoke of the "iron cage" of
rationalism, but I believe we are in a subtle trap in extending ourselves to
embrace the iron cage of professionalism.[1] Like the proverbial blind men
describing the elephant, each psychological discipline—whether it be
clinical, social, experimental, cognitive, or developmental psychology—is
biased toward some professional viewpoint. All assume we know what it
means to be human. If, then, one's personal identity is so restrained, all
one's perspectives of the human spirit become distorted and even blinded.
But to engage in critical thinking about the hidden assumptions of each
of these disciplines is to make one's own professional identity too vulnerable for sustained exposure.

An example of this is the irony that lies behind the history of Erik
Erikson's redirection from being a psychoanalyst to being a specialist in
identity studies. His new approach emerged when he started researching
on the *Young Man Luther* (1956). For in mid-life crisis, Erikson was discovering that his professional identity was coming under discredit. It was
not Luther's identity, rather probably Erikson's own discredited identity,
that motivated him in his study, for psychoanalysis began to be condemned under scientific scrutiny.[2] Ever since then, the fascination with
identity studies reflects, among other things, the precariousness of

[1]Max Weber, *The Protestant Ethic and the Spirit of Capitalism* (Kettering, OH: Angelico Press, 2014),
103.
[2]Steven Weiland, "Becoming a Biographer: Erikson, Luther, and the Problem of Professional
Identity," in *Contesting the Subject*, ed. William H. Epstein (West Lafayette, IN: Purdue University
Press, 1991), 193-215.

having only a professional identity. Indeed, the sociologist Zygmunt Bauman has even likened identity studies to being on a battlefield, "only coming to life when there is a battle going on."[3]

In the discipline of psychotherapy, C. Marshall Lowe observed in 1976 that with the crisis of conventional morality, psychotherapists had become the new moral authorities or "secular priests."[4] Then a series of writers began to recognize that the profession was accorded primacy within the mythic cult of self-fulfillment, with each individual the center of his or her own universe. It was what Philip Cushman called "the bounded, masterful self."[5] Further reactions have been toward virtue ethics or to being value-neutral, but such tend to be only moral chatter, vulnerable to cultural changes, and not grounded in basic human values.

Or take the dilemma of social psychology, which assumes the human being is social and yet deals with individuals, having individual properties. As Paul Ricoeur has observed of sociology, it has no reference to the neighbor as a moral category. "For one does not have a neighbor; I make myself someone's neighbor."[6] Indeed, "the world of the personal" remains indefinable. One of the founding fathers of sociology, Georg Simmel, was largely ignored because he was trying to give due diligence to individuality in a culture of bias toward sociality, which the more popular fathers of sociology—Comte, Durkheim, Weber—were all promoting. They were dealing with the rise of the urban, industrial expansion of the masses in new systematized forms of knowledge. In contrast, Simmel's nonconformity was seeking to cultivate morally educated individuals within society.[7] For he saw the uniqueness of the human being as being far more complex than what modern sociologists were

---

[3]Zygmunt Bauman, *Identity: Conversations with Benedetto Vecchi* (Malden, MA: Polity, 2004), 77.
[4]Quoted by Frank C. Richardson in *Critical Thinking About Psychology*, ed. Brent D. Slife, Jeffrey S. Reber, and Frank C. Richardson (Washington, DC: American Psychological Association, 2005), 18-19.
[5]Philip Cushman, *Constructing the Self, Constructing America* (New York: Addison-Wesley Publishing Company, 1995), 604.
[6]Paul Ricoeur, *History and Truth*, trans. Charles A. Kelbey (Evanston, IL: Northwestern University Press, 2007), 99.
[7]George Simmel, *On Individuality and Social Forms*, ed. Donald N. Levine (Chicago: The University of Chicago Press, 1971).

generalizing about, in the two notions of atomism: social and information atomism. The former is the idea that society is composed of self-contained individuals, each seeking their own purposes, while the latter is tied up with the general liberationist/individualist society so prevalent in the Western world.[8] Both types of agent fitted well into the Cartesian hyper-cognitive and instrumental self of both our modern and post-modern cultures.

Again, in cognitive psychology, the penchant for the scientific study of the human is as strong as in any other branch of psychology. Its focus is upon memory, perception, attention, learning, and their disorders. But its reliance on efficient causation and mechanism, enhanced greatly by the artificial intelligence gained in computer science and now also by neuroscience, exaggerates individualism. It presupposes what Charles Taylor calls "the punctured self"—a self viewed as free and rational to the extent it can fully distinguish itself from the natural and social worlds—and is able to treat these worlds instrumentally.[9]

Or finally, reflect upon the hidden assumptions of developmental psychology, what originally J. Piaget called "genetic epistemology." Trained as a biologist, Piaget argues that assimilation and adaptation are essential biological functions that are applicable to the development of human intelligence. Unstable and inflexible in the child, they become stabilized with adult development through four sets of childhood stages. As a liberal Protestant, he desired a reconciliation of religion with science, arguing God to be imminent, not transcendent, so that questions about God should not be sought biblically but simply empirically. Corresponding to Auguste Comte's three stages of man as the theological, the metaphysical, and the scientific/positivistic, Piaget posited three moral stages of the animistic or magical morality, the religious morality, and the morality of social reciprocity. When Nietzsche announced, "God is dead," in 1882, the theories of these psychologists were then coming to life!

---

[8]Robert C. Bishop, in Slife, Reber, and Richardson, *Critical Thinking,* 164.
[9]Charles Taylor, *Philosophical Arguments* (Cambridge, MA: Harvard University Press, 1995), 7.

However, today there is growing reaction to all these narrow views of personal reality, from many distinct perspectives. Such are (1) Heidegger's participatory philosophy of complex engagement with the world,[10] or (2) Clifford Geertz's "stratigraphic" cultural models of the self,[11] or (3) Charles Taylor's "moral space,"[12] or (4) Levinas and Paul Ricoeur's "self as the other."[13] Gaining more clarity about the self tends to leave developmental psychology fragmented and inchoate, as expressive of the cultural lack of moral cohesion.

Scientism as historical blindness of cultural changes. Further blindness occurs in being ahistorical about one's discipline. Doing one's profession is not the same thing as critiquing the history of each field, that is, as seeing its own subculture arising within a specific temporal context. This is more than knowing that Wundt created the first laboratory in 1879 in Leipzig for experimental psychology, or that Freud first developed interest in the interpretation of dreams at the end of the nineteenth century for the later elaboration of psychoanalysis, or that William James first began to explore varieties of human consciousness about the same time. Each has had a historical contextual development in creating new sub-cultures, each having their own social concerns, ideas whose time had come to be explored. Something new had appeared, which challenged exploration of a new territory in need of being known in the ongoing history of ideas.

Historically, psychology is as old as philosophy, both arising from the Western classical tradition. But the new prominence given to psychology as a "science," as an independent series of disciplines in the latter nineteenth century, gave psychology the opportunity to seek a similar emancipation from philosophy. Now the mirage appeared that

---

[10]M. Heidegger, *Being and Time,* trans. J. Macquarrie and E. Robinson (New York: Harper & Row, 1962).

[11]Clifford Geertz, *The Interpretation of Cultures* (New York: Basic Books, 1973).

[12]C. Taylor, "The Moral Topography of the Self," in *Hermeneutics and Psychological Theory,* ed. S. B. Messer, L. A. Sass, and R. L. Woolfolk (New Brunswick, NJ: Rutgers University Press), 290-320.

[13]Paul Ricoeur, *The Self as the Other,* trans. Kathleen Blamey (Chicago: The Chicago University Press, 1992).

in being ahistorical, psychology could become also a new series of sciences.[14] The assumption was then added that method uncovers truth, which then deepened the pursuit of empirical knowledge as the scientific method to follow. Yet even in science, verification is less capable of application the more complex the system becomes. So now many scholars within psychology readily grant that human beings are less subject to falsification, a corollary of verification, than simpler physical systems. Mathematical models also can only go so far in interpreting human behavior.

Without critical appreciation of cultural history, one remains blinded by one's specialization, especially when it concerns the deep mysteries of being human. Again, without psychology becoming a moral science, it will always tend to see only the canons of normativity, never of good and evil.[15] In general, the whole profession of psychology is too embedded in the mores of Western individualism and therefore cannot be a critical voice against contemporary culture. So Reinhold Niebuhr adds to his brother's voice, American/Western Christianity is implicitly about selfhood—not personhood.[16] Yet the mystery of being a person reflects upon the mystery of the Trinity, of the God-Man.

The blindness of hubris. A third source of professional blindness is taking one's research assumptions for granted, never seeking plausible alternatives because of the desire to quickly succeed in a narrow field. Like the pursuit of success itself, it entails a restrictive quest that generates its own seeds of failure by being too narrowly and too hastily focused. Recent scientific studies have demonstrated that articles in *Nature* or other specialized journals now report more frequent claims than in the past, so that the number of discoveries that are then found to be false has intensified because of impatient self-ambitions to claim fame. Such self-deception prevails in the vanity of desiring new

---

[14]See Daniel N. Robinson, *An Intellectual History of Psychology,* 3rd ed. (Madison: The University of Wisconsin Press, 1995).

[15]Svend Brinkmann, *Psychology as a Moral Science: Perspectives on Normativity* (New York: Springer, 2011).

[16]Reinhold Niebuhr, *The Self and the Dramas of History* (London: Faber & Faber, 1954).

discoveries to express one's own cleverness rather than in the generosity of teamwork; it becomes a form of professional narcissism. In a powerful chapter, "Self-Deception and the Structure of the Social Sciences," Robert Trivers explores how self-deception is so ingrained in our human condition that "the greater the social content of a discipline, especially in the sphere of 'the human,' the greater will be biases due to self-deception and the greater the retardation of the field compared with less social disciplines."[17]

Actually, many of the contemporary forms of psychology are expressive of nineteenth century theories whose problems and methods are now questionable. This is well surveyed by Daniel Robinson in his book *An Intellectual History of Psychology*. The claim that psychology is a science is a nineteenth century idea, which cuts it off from the longevity of psychology as a twin discipline with philosophy, both traceable back to Greek culture. Rather, the two great axial dimensions of human mental intelligence and emotional consciousness are such that philosophy and psychology should never be separated. Likewise, to link psychology morally with Judaism and Christianity, a much more fruitful dialogue, would prevent such folly as to eliminate the category of the soul from the history of humanity. Likewise, if secular psychologists assume human consciousness can only be understood as a-religious, then they are also assuming such human studies are also ahistorical. Some schools of philosophy have tried such imperialism, notably logical positivism, but they have failed by being too reductionist of the human condition, which must always include the ethical.

Indeed, hidden assumptions tend to be most hid from reductionist thinkers. As Brent D. Slife and his colleagues ask in their book *Critical Thinking About Psychology: Hidden Assumptions and Plausible Alternatives*, psychologists are taught to be critical analysts of myths and popular assumptions, yet how much do they critique their own "scientific

---

[17]Robert Trivers, *The Folly of Fools: The Logic of Deceit and Self-Deception in Human Life* (New York: Basic Books, 2011), 303-4.

assumptions"?[18] Covering six major psychological sub-disciplines, the authors critique assumptions peculiar to each field, such as the dualism of mind and body, the truth of efficient causation, and the discrete unit known as the individual. Such tacit assumptions are all to be questioned. For value-neutral assumptions may suit well the academic postures of the disciplines, but they also distort the mystery and fullness of the human condition.

Trivers has a section on "the psychology of self-deception" as a form of psychic immunology that we all inherit in our social behavior. The hallmark of self-deception is the denial of self-deception. Trivers even explores the possibility that neurophysiology may open up how the human brain is itself self-deceiving, within its distinct functions.[19] Certainly, Freud was himself self-deceived in claiming psychoanalysis to have the status of a science. Religiosity too can be hugely self-deceptive, but the vigorous denials of secularism and materialism can also be self-deceptive. Indeed, whatever quest for self-possessiveness is exercised in egotism, ambitious power, and pride, will all contain their own seeds of deception. It is the deepening of humility and consciousness, the sharing with good friends, and the meditative life in reverence, that will all help to make us less vulnerable to self-deception.[20] This leads me to the further cultural blindness of overseeing our American heritage of sedimented individualism without a background in European cultural history.

CULTURAL BLINDNESS IN SHALLOW UNDERSTANDING OF HUMAN DEPRAVITY

The contrasted socio-political environment of Western Europe. The intensifying individualism on North America, on an "empty" continent, non-invaded by the two great wars of the twentieth century, is contrasted by the history of Western Europe. Culturally, things were very different

---

[18]Slife, Reber, and Richardson, *Critical Thinking*.
[19]Slife, Reber, and Richardson, *Critical Thinking*, 53-54.
[20]Slife, Reber, and Richardson, *Critical Thinking*, 329-33.

in Western Europe, where the Enlightenment Prussian culture was destroyed after World War I. Then a variety of thinkers, notably Jewish and Germans, in societies like the Patmos Club, tried to re-imagine eschatologically, like John of Patmos, what a new German society could become. Its members were as diverse as Karl Barth, Martin Buber, Georg Simmel, Max Scheler, Dietrich von Rosenstock-Huessy, and Dietrich von Hildebrand. Some of their mentors like Edmund Husserl and Max Weber were sympathetic. Austrians like the economist Ludwig von Mises were also highlighting the role of the human agent acting not only from necessities but from ideals. As a consequence, European thinkers in the human sciences were much more influential in conceiving of the human being much less individualistically, as an agent of social change and of moral reconstruction.

Now in "the malaise of modernity," as Charles Taylor has been describing disenchantment with the Enlightenment, we are rereading these European thinkers with fresh appreciation. They are helping us to expose and to question American individualism, as American culture seems incapable of doing for itself.

For example, American pastoral theology tends to be more therapeutic than theological. The more we contrast the continuous, uninterrupted individualistic heritage of North American culture with the huge European cultural discontinuities of the last century, with two major wars, the more we will realize that the ongoing heritage of "the Monarchical/ Hobbesian Self," "the Possessive/Lockean Self," and "the Romantic/ Rousseauian Self" have never been seriously challenged in American culture. Yes, Freud made modifications, as did Dewey and William James, but only to re-shape and deepen its sedimentation of individualism. After the 1960s, some sociologists began to be alarmed by the increasing narcissism the therapeutic culture was promoting.[21] The fundamental good in the nature of man that Enlightenment theorists like Adam Smith believed has given way to profound despair that economics merely intensifies

---

[21]Notable examples were Philip Rieff, *The Therapeutic Revolution* (New York: HarperCollins, 1966) and Nicholas Lasch, *The Culture of Narcissism* (New York: W. W. Norton, 1978).

self-interest. Even the Cartesian identity has given way to "I spend therefore I am," as Philip Roscoe has recently reminded us.[22] The traditional bonds of social obligations are being stripped away to expose unmitigated selfishness.[23] Now also the strong bias toward the cognitive self is further reinforced by the technological revolution.

Meanwhile, the unreflective liberal theological assumptions of the Niebuhr brothers, those of "Christ and culture," have been accepted into pastoral theology as a nominal assumption, rarely challenged theologically.[24] Instead it was a psychiatrist, Karl Menninger, who asked *Whatever Became of Sin?*[25] He asked this as our culture began to shift away from awareness of guilt and personal responsibility. "Sin" is a pivotal theo-anthropological category, expressive of human alienation from God. But evil is by its very nature unaware of its evil. As Karl Barth recognized it, human nature is unaware of its sinfulness. "The access to the knowledge that he is a sinner is lacking in man because he is a sinner."[26] We can only know sin in the reality of Jesus Christ: to quote Barth again, "Only when we know Jesus Christ do we really know that man is a man of sin, and what sin is, and what it means for man."[27] For the emotional healing of the emotions or the cognitive corrections of the mind do not cover the whole personal realm of the human being as a moral agent. Rather it was from Germany that Bonhoeffer wrote on *The Cost of Discipleship*. Likewise, it was courageously in Berlin in 1933 that Dietrich von Hildebrand publicly lectured on "Transformation in Christ." It was Karl Barth's friend Thurneysen who wrote a serious pastoral theology. It was Barth himself who used the radical term "theo-anthropology" for the union between God and Man, as the *imago Dei*. In contrast, American pastoral theology has been more psychology than serious theology.[28] So

---

[22]Philip Roscoe, *I Spend Therefore I AM* (Toronto: Random House, 2014).

[23]Roscoe, *I Spend*, 6.

[24]It was challenged by Kenneth Hamilton, but his was a lone voice. Kenneth Hamilton, *The Doctrine of Humanity in the Theology of Reinhold Niebuhr* (Ontario: WLU Press, 2013).

[25]Karl Menninger, *Whatever Became of Sin?* (New York: Hawthorn, 1973).

[26]Karl Barth, *Church Dogmatics*, IV/1, 360.

[27]Karl Barth, *Church Dogmatics*, IV/1, 389.

[28]For instance, Albert C. Outler, *Psychotherapy and the Christian Message* (New York: Harper, 1954).

I submit we need to review our use of spiritual formation, for historically its origin is shallow—exercising confession, perhaps even reformation of a way of life, but not radical conversion.

"Spiritual Formation" as based on "Priestly Formation." Spiritual formation is part of the curriculum adopted by the ATS (Association of Theological Schools) for students in training for church ministries. Its predecessor was the various responses to the Second Vatican Council's teaching on the priesthood.[29] The United States National Conference of Catholic Bishops intensified their efforts to redefine norms of priestly formation after the sex scandals brought against various dioceses. In the American Protestant context, a strong cultural emphasis on "leadership" conjoins with the National Conference of Catholic Bishops, which emphasizes that priests are the assistants of the bishops and requires "priestly formation" as a life, according to the Evangelical Counsels.[30] With Catholics the bias can be either sacramental or pastoral priestly ministry, whereas with Protestant seminaries the bias can be homiletical, or pastoral, or often just administrative.[31] Spiritual formation for the priesthood of all believers is left in suspension, dependent upon the nature of the Christian college. All of these ministries suggest that spiritual formation reflects a cultural crisis or series of crises on the credibility of the Christian communication of faith today. For Catholics, it is the sexual scandal of some priestly abuse.[32] For evangelical Christian colleges, it is the unreflective embrace of Richard Niebuhr's "Christ and Culture," where "'belief in Jesus Christ,' so manifold the interpretation of his essential nature, that the question must arise whether the Christ of Christianity is indeed one Lord."[33] Consequent on this unexamined

---

[29]Charles M. Murphy, *Models of Priestly Formation* (New York: Crossroads Publishing, 2012), 41-57.

[30]National Conference of Catholic Bishops, *Norms for Priestly Formation* (Washington, DC: United States Catholic Conference, 1993), 178-91.

[31]Paul J. Philibert, *Stewards of God's Mysteries: Priestly Spirituality in a Changing Church* (Collegeville, MN: Liturgical Press, 2004), 21-29.

[32]David L. Toups, S.T.D., *Reclaiming Our Priestly Character* (Omaha, NE: The Institute for Priestly Formation, I.P.F. Publications, 2008), 133-208.

[33]H. Richard Niebuhr, *Christ and Culture* (New York: Harper & Row, Harper Torchbooks, 1951), 11-12.

marriage of Niebuhrian "Christianity and culture" with social sciences in our Christian colleges is the uncritical embrace of deistic/atheistic premises for the creation of human sciences in the nineteenth century. If deism is not expressive of the living God, how then can Enlightenment human sciences ever be "human" enough? Is this not the basic cause for even the secular disenchantment or "malaise of Modernity," to use Charles Taylor's phrase?[34] It is no wonder that to educate our students and faculty in our Christian colleges "to be conformed to the image" of Christ makes spiritual formation our greatest challenge imaginable (Rom 8:29).

Actually, it was originally Ignatius of Loyola's reform vision, adopted by the Counter Reformation, that to reform the church there must be a reform of the priesthood. But with equality today, priestly identity is raising questions. Is the indelible mark of "priesthood," a unique category only given to the Roman Catholic priestly identity, with sacramental powers not given to the ordinary catholic members? Are there two priestly identities, one liturgical and the other pastoral? Clearly in a Protestant context, where the priesthood of all believers is upheld, such spiritual formation cannot be theologically the same process as the catholic/liturgical identity.

Instead, should not spiritual formation mark the identity of every true Christian? Confusion also arises from the mix of personal and social ethics that give shape to a Christian identity. This issue goes to the heart of the contrasted leadership of the papacy now being evidenced between Pope Benedict XVI and his successor, Pope Francis.

I have read widely the recent Catholic literature on priestly formation, much of it devotionally inspiring, yet it remains institutional and social, rather than indicative of the quest for a differing personal identity that should mark all Christians. Likewise, exposure to spiritual formation or the opportunity to make it an educational specialty is not limited to those privileged with seminary training. There is clearer awareness today

---

[34]Charles Taylor, *The Malaise of Modernity* (Concord, ON: Anansi, 1991).

that spiritual (including priestly) formation is ongoing, but how this is sustained is not investigated in the literature.[35] Nor is priestly formation being treated theo-anthropologically but more usually with reference to psychologists such as Erikson, who, perceptive as they may be, are not interpreting "identity" biblically.[36] The relapse into unbelief and atheism of Christian leaders is evidenced by such ventures as TCP (The Clergy Project), which has been set up to shelter religious leaders who have lost their faith and are adjusting to a new way of life as atheists.[37] Pope John Paul II, in *Pastores Dabo Vobis*, recognized there was indeed a crisis of priestly identity.[38]

For the ordinary lay Christian, this too is raising a host of questions. Can nominal church membership express adequately the challenge of conversion? Can theological education get to the heart of Christian identity? Can programs in spiritual formation eradicate our cultural individualism? In our colleges, is spiritual formation an elective course, or is it at the core of the college's mission? Should all courses have some focus on this educational process?

THE POSTMODERN SHIFT TO A PERSONAL IDENTITY: CONVERTED AND COMMITTED

Beginning in the twelfth century, one of the chief vectors of change has been individuation. Devotional movements began to fructify with the increasingly greater sense of personal commitment. Now we see an acceleration of individuation intensifying in the present millennial age, with much more laicisation and the increasing decline of institutional religion. At the same time there is more de-coupling of belief and practice, or of believing but not belonging. Barriers are breaking down between belief groups, while secularization has intensified and atheism greatly extended. Yet the retreat of nominal religion

---

[35]National Conference of Catholic Bishops, *Norms for Priestly Formation*, 2:333.
[36]Philibert, *Stewards of God's Mysteries*, 49-51.
[37]John Lombard, "Bingo, I Was an Atheist," *National Post* March 17, 2014, 13A.
[38]Toups, *Reclaiming Our Priestly Character*, 79.

is also being resisted by the deepening of personal faith, and more than ever believers need a strong individual Christian identity and an anchored commitment of life.

The extremities to which narcissism is going in our culture today—as in the excesses of Michel de Foucault's aesthetic self and the broadening call to utilize technologies of the self for radical freedom—have great appeal to our youth in the tech revolution. Christians are being called to become radical in response, but a weak sense of sin and a low profile about conversion make their witness effete (i.e., weak, powerless). So we have to ask, is even our term *conversion* adequate to express the criteria in the New Testament for *metanoia*? Today, theologians who are grappling most seriously with such questions are also having to critique our culture. David Ford, Regius Professor of Divinity at Cambridge, does so in his book *Self and Salvation: Being Transformed*.[39] Mark McIntosh, in his *Mystical Theology*, seeks to do so by integrating spirituality with theology.[40] The corpus of Hugel von Balthasar, focused on sacrifice and contemplation, is deeply challenging. But the voices I find most challenging are those Christian philosophers like Charles Taylor and Paul Ricouer or the literary critic René Girard, who delve into the issues of self-identity, which require transformation. Here Charles Taylor is weaker, for he is more optimistic about the goodness of the self, and significantly he makes no confession of an experience of conversion, though his transitions from Marxist Catholicism to a more conventional Catholic orthodoxy have been significant. But both Ricoeur and Girard had definite conversion experiences.

In his essay "Conversion in Literature and Christianity" (1999), Girard points out that the problem with the Latin word *conversio* is that it only means a turning around in a circle, as one does with a translation.[41] But Christian conversion is linear, open-ended, and irreversible, so *conversion*

---

[39]David F. Ford, *Self and Salvation: Being Transformed* (Cambridge: Cambridge University Press, 1999).
[40]Mark A. McIntosh, *Mystical Theology: The Integrity of Spirituality and Theology* (Oxford: Blackwell Publishers, 1998).
[41]René Girard, *Mimesis and Theory* (Stanford: Stanford University Press, 2008), 263-73.

is too weak a word. But the Greek-speaking early churches used the word *metanoia* as a type of penance, reflecting *metanoeō*, or a change of mind, involving a radical transformation. This can have no reversal, no "re" that suggests the possibility to recant, reform, even repent, when one is under pressure. Metanoia produces martyrs, unafraid of death, like the Donatists of North Africa. It is metanoia that produces great literary classics like those of Cervantes, Dante, Dostoevsky, and Proust, who had a profound turn around in their personal lives and could then depict the hell of their own society and become profoundly turned away from the darkness.

What gives Girard such force is that he takes up one aspect of sin, the dark force of envy, and builds up a remarkable, universal, all-encompassing interpretation of human culture around this primordial role of mimesis. As a cultural anthropologist as well as literary critic, he sees envy carrying out its complex logic in all aspects of the human condition. We could react and ask, "And what about all the other six or seven cardinal sins recognized by the Desert Fathers?" Perhaps we should encourage our brightest students to explore the ramifications of pride, of the other evil ecosystems that breed in their own dark places of the human psyche. It was their own conversions that allowed these great novelists to each become a literary genius. Likewise, in our teaching we need to recover the immense communicative need of restoring conversion to become the greatest challenge to our cultural confusion today.

The historic moment, the turning point, the change of mind—this sets every Christian on a pilgrimage from which he or she cannot go back. Pivotal to our conversion is the resurrection, which turned fearful and bewildered disciples into men and women who were each given a new identity. Then was created the notion of an "individual," each one accountable for his or her life, but in complete equality, where "there is neither Jew nor Greek, there is neither slave nor free, there is no male and female," for all are now one "in Christ Jesus" (Gal 3:28). To *individuate* is then to liberate with equality, while to *personalize* is to give moral space to be the self for the other, as indeed in love of God and love of neighbor. It is then your mandate as Christian psychologists to critique the present status of the human sciences as not being human enough. Without this our human future, as human persons, lies in jeopardy.

RECOVERING THEO-ANTHROPOLOGY FOR "SPIRITUAL FORMATION"

With the shattering of European culture(s) after World War II, European theologians were challenged to interpret Christian faith in more radical ways. Notable is Barth, who defied the pressures of the Nazi Führer culture in the German state church as early as June 24, 1933, when regional ecclesial führers were being appointed: reform of the church "ought to issue from obedience to the Word of God, or else it is no reform of the Church."[42] In his *Church Dogmatics*, Barth went on to develop the new theme of "theo-anthropology," where the nature of God is indissolubly united with the nature of man. Eberhard Jungel then proceeded further that theology has to become the narrative of God's love story for humanity.[43]

Another radical call was made by the Catholic convert, Dietrich von Hildebrand, who began public lectures in Berlin, also in 1933, that Christians need "transformation in Christ." But since his book was translated in America in 1948, there has been very little interest in his stirring call for such *metanoia* of church members, Catholic or Protestant.[44] "True surrender of self" is his closing theme, as the key to such "transformation." This we can sing about in our church services, but is it too radical for what we describe as "spiritual formation"?

A further European approach has been to reconsider the nature of theology as pastoral. The Dutch theologian Jacob Firet, in his work *Dynamics in Pastoring*, helpfully defines three modes of practical

---

[42]Karl Barth, *Theological Existence Today! A Plea for Theological Freedom*, trans. R. Birch Hoyle (London: Houghton & Stoughton, 1933), 19.
[43]Eberhard Jungel, *God as the Mystery of the World*, trans. Darrell L. Guder (Eugene, OR: Wipf & Stock, 2009), 219-23.
[44]Dietrich von Hildebrand, *Transformation in Christ* (Manchester, NH: Sophia Institute Press, 1948), 481-500.

theology—that is, implementing theological teaching.[45] First is the mode of Kerygma, the act of the proclamation of a new state of being Christian, healing and transformative in its biblical teaching. God enters into our world with his salvation. Second is the mode of Didache, or catechetical instruction of Christian doctrine. For now God points to a new way of being and living. Third is the mode of Paraklesis, of being persuasive to entreat, encourage, nurture, comfort, console, liberate, that the whole process of spiritual formation would be furthered. All three modes should be integrative of the whole process of doing theology. Thus a pastor who claims only to be a preacher and is not also a shepherd is an oxymoron.

It is therefore the failure to integrate theology and spirituality, and to interpret all theology as being pastoral in intent, that splinters off our specialties, such as "spiritual disciplines," and "spiritual direction," "spiritual formation." It has been timely for Ellen Charry to illustrate historically from the teachings of the Fathers the pastoral function of Christian doctrine.[46]

SPIRITUAL FORMATION CAN ONLY BEGIN WITH *METANOIA*

The only way we can prevent our ministry of spiritual formation from continuing to be merely a cultural feature of our times is by the vital "agogic break," when we allow the Holy Spirit to break into our mindset with the experience of *metanoia*. The Greek *agōgos* was a guide who led one to make a change in one's life. Such a moment of dramatic change is illustrated by Job, who concludes the series of dialogues he had been engaged in: "I have uttered what I did not understand . . . I had heard of thee by the hearing of the ear, but now my eyes see thee; therefore I despise myself, and repent in dust and ashes" (Job 42:3, 5-6). Job has had a change of paradigm, a *metanoia*, a process affecting one's whole existence.

---

[45]Jacob Firet, *Dynamics in Pastoring* (Grand Rapids: Eerdmans, 1986).
[46]Ellen T. Charry, *By the Renewing of Your Minds: The Pastoral Function of Christian Doctrine* (New York: Oxford University Press, 1997).

Recently great classical fiction is being re-appreciated as illustrative of *metanoia*, such as Dante's pilgrimage from *The Inferno* or Bunyan's *Pilgrim's Progress*. Even the medieval pilgrimage to Jerusalem was geographically limited, whereas only fiction is boundless, if the power of the Holy Spirit is not realizable. But the symbol of pilgrimage remains powerful, as the Exodus of Israel reminds us.

However, living as a Christian pilgrim can be a historical reality, as the epistle to the Hebrews cites in chapter eleven. Biblical *metanoia* alone can be a personal reality. Then our motives for Christian scholarship itself will be subject to transformation, all perhaps becoming increasingly interdisciplinary, as well as more personally lived out in embodiment.

Beginning as a mild liberal scholar at Tübingen, Joseph Ratzinger's writings have been described significantly as "mapping a Theological journey." Then as Pope Benedict XVI, he came to realize, "metanoia is not just any Christian attitude but the fundamental Christian act per se . . . that of transformation, conversion, renewal and change. To be a Christian, one must change not just in some particular area but without reservation even to the innermost depths of one's being."[47] As the apostle Peter himself admonishes us all, "In your hearts set apart Christ as Lord" (1 Pet 3:15).

---

[47]Joseph Ratzinger, *The Ratzinger Reader*, ed. Lieven Boeve and Gerard Mannion (London: T&T Clark, 2010), 57.

PART TWO

THEOLOGICAL

INSIGHTS

FOR A

PSYCHOLOGY

OF SPIRITUAL

FORMATION

"END OF FAITH AS ITS BEGINNING"

A CHRIST-CENTERED DEVELOPMENTAL SPIRITUALITY

BRUCE HINDMARSH

The APA's *Encyclopedia of Psychology* closes its article on the history of developmental psychology with this sentence: "There is increased awareness that values matter in development, and that science cannot provide those values."[1] It is precisely here where I think the conversation may be joined by those who bring a theological perspective to bear on the development of human persons as spiritual creatures. There is a danger, though, if we begin with "spiritual formation" and "developmental psychology" as two isomorphic categories, two pre-existing subjects that must somehow be brought into dialogue, since this will likely not probe deeply enough.

---

[1] John D. Hogan, "Developmental Psychology: History of the Field," in *Encyclopedia of Psychology* (Washington, DC: American Psychological Association, 2000), 3:13. Cf. Balswick, King, and Reimer, who write, "Defining good or optimal development has not been a traditional task of the psychological sciences. Psychology has not focused on teleological issues." Jack O. Balswick, Pamela Ebstyne King, and Kevin Reimer, *The Reciprocating Self: Human Development in Theological Perspective* (Downers Grove, IL: InterVarsity Press, 2005), 28.

This isomorphism was there from the beginning. Developmental psychology has its roots in the observational psychology that followed the trajectories established in the eighteenth century by John Locke and Jean-Jacques Rousseau at precisely the moment in Western thought when efforts were made to separate religion and ethics. As moral philosophers were looking to ground ethics in human nature as such, apart from divine revelation, there was great faith on the part of European elites in the possibilities of education to take the young from a point of innocence in a state of nature, like blank slates, and form them toward civilized ideals. In the case of Rousseau, his mature subject Émile is led to embrace natural religion rather than revealed religion.[2] The split is complete. So we must recognize the macro-context that set the parameters of the discussion both of the emergent psychology and of the pastoralia in the modern period. The trajectories were separate: developmental psychology would be concerned with intra-mundane goods and the enclosed psyche, and the spiritual life would be priva-tized and compartmentalized as something other than public philosophy or universal science. Indeed, Robert and Beverley Cairns go even further in their history of developmental psychology: "The goal of many of them [the early developmentalists] was to formulate a developmental science, which, in its highest application, would supplement—or supplant—religion."[3]

Prior to the ascendancy of mechanical philosophy and empirical science in early modern Europe, there was not the same isomorphism. In Johann Arndt's exceedingly popular treatise, *True Christianity* (1606), the first three books trace the progress of what we would rec-ognize as the spiritual life. However, the fourth book demonstrates how far we are from Arndt's world, since in this section he expounds the way in which the very life of God in the human soul was also the vital

---

[2]Jean-Jacques Rousseau, *Émile, or, On Education* (1st English ed., 1763).
[3]Robert B. Cairns and Beverley D. Cairns, "The Making of Developmental Psychology," in *Theoreti-cal Models of Human Development*, ed. Richard M. Lerner, vol. 1 of *Handbook of Child Psychology*, ed. William Damon and Richard M. Lerner (Hoboken, NJ: John Wiley & Sons, 2006), 123.

force of the material world—the same divine Spirit animating both the human and the non-human creation. In this pre-Cartesian, pre-Newtonian world, there was as yet no split between observational science and spirituality, between "the starry heavens above me and the moral law within me."[4]

In the following century Charles Wesley wrote a splendid poem celebrating the Holy Spirit in similar terms to Arndt as Spirit who was the "Author of every work Divine, Who doth through both creations shine, The God of nature and of grace." The same Spirit whom he invokes in another hymn, "Come, and in me delight to rest," is here the "Universal Soul, The plastic power that fills the whole, And governs earth, air, sea, and sky."[5] And Jonathan Edwards made this a matter of first philosophy that connected "affections that are truly spiritual" with a comprehensive metaphysic and natural philosophy of divine presence and relationality.[6] But all these figures—Arndt, Wesley, Edwards—were fighting a rearguard action, and increasingly public science and private piety were separated as alien approaches to an understanding of human nature.[7] So the fact that we are thinking in this book about two separate fields (spiritual formation and psychology) and that these fields are largely reified prior to our conversation—this problem has its roots in this macro-context of seventeenth and eighteenth-century Western thought. It was not always so, and it takes some imagination to see it otherwise.

In this chapter, I would therefore like to argue a set of six theological propositions that I think are necessary at our point in history to reframe the conversation about human development and spiritual development. My central contention is that in order for developmental psychology to be deeply Christian at its foundations and for spiritual

---

[4]The allusion is to Immanuel Kant's famous conclusion to his *Critique of Practical Reason*.

[5]John and Charles Wesley, *Hymns of Petition and Thanksgiving for the Promise of the Father* (Bristol: Felix Farley, 1746), 31-32.

[6]Michael J. McClymond and Gerald R. McDermott, *The Theology of Jonathan Edwards* (Oxford: Oxford University Press, 2011), 60-76, cf. 93-115.

[7]W. R. Ward, *Early Evangelicalism* (Cambridge: Cambridge University Press, 2006).

formation to be deeply human, there must be a vivid appreciation of the end for which humans were created. From this perspective of final causes, developmental psychology is spiritualized and spiritual formation is humanized.

THE HUMAN PERSON AS SPIRITUAL

First, then, spiritual development ought to be seen as basic to human development, not as simply one more layer in a contextual or systemic developmental psychology or a bolt-on addition to an evolutionary framework of adaptation or an aspect of humanistic ego transcendence.

On the contrary, the human person is spiritual all the way down and all the way up. For the apostle Paul, the unbeliever and the believer alike are ensouled: *psychikos anthrōpos* (1 Cor 2:14-15). This fundamental reality cannot be ignored at any point in the lifespan. Scripture uses several words and metaphors to communicate the interior mystery and depth dimension of anthropology: the soul (or in Greek, *psyche*), the spirit, the heart, even the kidneys and the loins of a person. I don't think we can or ought to avoid some kind of substance ontology of the soul, as we speak about these things, even if human nature is still always composite and contingent. We live because the very breath of God has been breathed into us (Gen 2). And we are created in and by the very word of God (Jn 1). So Eugene Peterson writes, "Most of what makes us human is God. When we say 'soul' we are calling attention to the God-origins, God-intentions, God-operations that make us what we are." And then he continues, pointing to the very different anthropology at work in much of modern psychology: "In our current culture, 'soul' has given way to 'self' as the term of choice to designate who and what we are. Self is the soul minus God. Self is what is left of the soul with all the transcendence and intimacy squeezed out, the self with little or no reference to God (transcendence) or others (intimacy)."[8]

---

[8]Eugene Peterson, *Christ Plays in Ten Thousand Places: A Conversation in Spiritual Theology* (Grand Rapids: Eerdmans, 2005), 37.

Like the word *soul*, "the image of God" is a key phrase in any theological anthropology.[9] The image of God in human persons has been understood variously and sometimes in a hyper-rational way, but it certainly signifies that at our core we are persons-in-relation, and especially that we stand in relation to God as divine person, even as we stand in relation to human others and the non-human creation. There is here also therefore a relational ontology of the soul, wherein we remain as creatures always fundamentally open and porous to God. Hans Urs von Balthasar describes this beautifully: "Man was created to be a hearer of the word [of God], and it is in responding to the word that he attains his true dignity. His innermost constitution has been designed for dialogue. . . . Man is the creature with a mystery in his heart that is bigger than himself." And so when God comes to a human being, he does not need to build a temple: "the room itself does not need to be built: it is already there and always has been, at the very center of man."[10] Again he writes, the human "creature is a perpetual question addressed to God. . . . [God] is the answer to the question which I am."[11] How dangerous therefore for pastoral ministry and clinical practice today if we work with a shrunken anthropology, viewing the people around us merely as enclosed selves rather than as creatures made in God's image and intended for his likeness, able to commune with the God of the universe, meant to share his eternal glory.

The postmodern context has opened the human sciences more to the importance of spirituality, though as one of my colleagues has written, the will-to-self-definition of high modernism has hardly been abandoned.[12] Still, even the very secular DSM has for a number of years now had a V Code for flagging problems as having a spiritual or

---

[9]The early and medieval doctrine of the image of God is outlined in Lars Thunberg, "The Human Person as Image of God: I. Eastern Christianity," and Bernard McGinn, "The Human Person as Image of God: II. Western Christianity," in *Christian Spirituality: Origins to the Twelfth Century*, ed. Bernard McGinn, John Meyendorff, and Jean Leclercq (New York: Crossroad, 1989), 291-330.

[10]Hans Urs von Balthasar, *Prayer*, trans. Graham Harrison (San Francisco: Ignatius, 1986), 22-23.

[11]Balthasar, *Prayer*, 156.

[12]Craig Gay, *Way of the (Modern) World* (Grand Rapids: Eerdmans, 1998), 224.

religious dimension.[13] And so in this context of a more heightened awareness of spirituality, there have been many efforts by Christians to study and write about human development from the point of view of a more robust theological anthropology, doing this from first principles now rather than smuggling it in as contraband.[14] May their tribe increase.

BEYOND THE BIRTH-TO-DEATH LIFESPAN

Second, a theological anthropology will begin the account of human development earlier and end it later than is typical for developmental psychology, since the human person has pre-natal origins and a post-mortem destiny.

Not only are human beings spiritual top to bottom, they are also so from beginning to end. One of the ways the psalmist speaks of this is to describe us as under the loving gaze of God from before ever we came to be: "My frame was not hidden from you when I was made in the secret place, when I was woven together in the depths of the earth. Your eyes saw my unformed body; all the days ordained for me were written in your book before one of them came to be" (Ps 139:15-16 BCP Psalter). No matter how far back we stretch our imaginations to the roots of our being, God has been there first, looking upon us with love. The first of the ten meditations in Francis de Sales's *Introduction to the Devout Life* (1619), designed to take the spiritual directee from a merely conventional faith to an entire consecration of her life to God, is a meditation on our creation. It seems to me to be where a Christian developmental psychology might begin. Says Francis,

---

[13]Allan M. Josephson and John R. Peteet, eds., *Handbook of Spirituality and Worldview in Clinical Practice* (Washington, DC: American Psychiatric Publishing, 2004), 38.

[14]For example, James E. Loder of Princeton Seminary in *The Logic of the Spirit: Human Development in Theological Perspective* (San Francisco: Jossey-Bass, 1998). See also the Fuller Seminary psychologists Balswick, King, and Reimer in *Reciprocating Self*, who have sought seriously to address developmental issues across the lifespan by focusing at every stage on the human person as a "reciprocal self," the term they use for identifying the human person as always standing in relationship to God and to others even as they develop from infancy to old age. And see K. V. Cook and K. C. Leonard, "A Relationally Integrated Systems Model for Faith and Learning in Developmental Psychology," *Journal of Psychology and Theology* 42 (2014): 150-63.

Consider that a certain number of years ago you were not yet in the world and that your present being was truly nothing. My soul, where were you at that time? The world had already existed for a long time, but of us there was as yet nothing. God has drawn you out of that nothingness to make you what you are and he has done so solely out of his own goodness and without need of you. Consider the nature God has given you. It is the highest in this visible world; it is capable of eternal life and of being perfectly united to his Divine Majesty.[15]

This is where both human formation and spiritual formation coincide in their deepest beginning, in the freedom of God to create beings to be blessed with his blessedness.

So also the terminus of human development taps out not in idealism with some vague Kantian ideal of universal disinterested virtue or in the senescence of old age merely but with a continued post-mortem existence in the presence of God. The long *ars moriendi* tradition of the medieval and early modern church was predicated on death as itself one last developmental task, one for which to prepare and one that would introduce a qualitatively new existence. In the prophetic words of Job: "I know that my redeemer lives, and that in the end he will stand on the earth. And after my skin has been destroyed, yet in my flesh I will see God; I myself will see him with my own eyes—I, and not another" (Job 19:25-27 NIV).[16] The Puritan Richard Baxter set himself to meditate with all his powers on this post-mortem developmental stage in his book, *The Saints' Everlasting Rest* (1650), in which he kept before himself and the reader the connection between this life and the life to come beyond death. One of his favorite of many ways to describe our eternal rest in God was to refer to the believer's glorified post-mortem existence as our "fruition" in God.[17] Note that this

---

[15]Francis de Sales, *Introduction to the Devout Life*, trans. John K. Ryan (New York: Image Books, 2003), 41.

[16]All Scripture quotations in this chapter follow the NIV unless otherwise noted.

[17]"The Rest here in question is the most happy estate of a Christian, having obtained the end of his course: or it is the perfect, endless fruition of God by the perfected saints, according to the measure of their capacity." Richard Baxter, *The Saints' Everlasting Rest*, ed. John T. Wilkinson (London: Epworth Press, 1962), 29.

is a developmental metaphor: fruition. Acorn to oak tree. We will
return to this concern below, but here I would simply like to underline
that a developmental psychology that takes Christian anthropology
seriously will at least conceptually begin earlier and end later than the
standard textbooks: it will look back to our pre-natal origins and
forward to our post-mortem destiny. This is, finally, a deeply christo-
logical reality, since Christ is in the book of Hebrews the author and
finisher of our faith, just as in the book of Revelation he is the Alpha
and Omega, the First and the Last, and therefore the beginning and
end of any series we can imagine.[18]

THE HUMAN PERSON'S DESIRES

Third, it is basic to a Christian anthropology to recognize the developing
human person as a desiring creature, fundamentally constituted by his
or her loves.

In considering human persons there is something more basic than
the evolutionary model of an organism adapting to its environment
primarily in terms of the drive to survive and to reproduce: the inner
compulsion to love. There is something more too than the Piagetian
conception of the developing mind, with the child as a little scientist,
or of humans as simply striving to make meaning. The focus upon the
rational part of the personality in the classical developmentalists, including in many ways James Fowler on faith development, present a
view of the human person that is partial by being hyper-cognitive.
While other models of human development are more relationally focused, and certainly psychoanalytic models strongly emphasize desire,
I think we can reflect more theologically on the drive of the human
creature for its Creator across the lifespan. The human psyche was, for
Augustine, in the image of God "insofar as it is capable of him (*capax*

---

[18]One of the original stanzas of Charles Wesley's hymn, "Love Divine, All Loves Excelling," made
this sentiment a prayer in the lines: "Take away our *power* of sinning, / Alpha and Omega be,
/ End of faith as its beginning, / Set our hearts at liberty." Charles Wesley, *Hymns for Those That
Seek and Those That Have Redemption in the Blood of Jesus Christ* (London: William Strahan,
1747), 11.

Dei) and can participate in him."[19] This capacity within the finite creature for union with the infinite God constitutes the human person as insatiable. For Gregory of Nyssa, this was a never-ending desire, a thirst of the creature for the Creator that is only further intensified even when it is slaked.[20] There is always more of God to know and to desire. Charles Wesley wrote in the same spirit when he exclaimed in one of his poems,

> Eager for thee I ask and pant;
> So strong the principle divine,
> Carries me out with sweet constraint,
> Till all my hallow'd soul is thine;
> Plunged in the Godhead's deepest sea,
> And lost in thine immensity.[21]

Similarly, Thomas Traherne wrote, "You must want like a God that you may be satisfied like God. Were you not made in his image?"[22]

Is there not then a longing of the human spirit, a restlessness that drives deeper even than the parent-child bond, or the libido, or the fear of death? As Henry Scougal wrote, "What is a little skin-deep Beauty . . . to satisfy a Passion which was made for God?" Or, again,

> What an infinite Pleasure must it needs be, thus as it were to lose ourselves in him; and being swallowed up in the overcoming Sense of his Goodness, to offer ourselves a living Sacrifice, always ascending unto him in Flames of Love? Never doth a Soul know what solid Joy is, till it give itself up unto the Author of its being, and feel itself become a hallowed and devoted Thing.[23]

The human creature has transcendent desires for what J. R. R. Tolkien recognized in fairy stories as a "joy beyond the walls of the world, poignant

---

[19]Augustine, *The Trinity*, trans. Edmund Hill (New York: New City Press, 1991), 379.

[20]Gregory of Nyssa, *From Glory to Glory*, comp. Jean Daniélou, ed. and trans. Herbert Musurillo (Crestwood, NY: St. Vladimir's Seminary Press, 2001), 142-48.

[21]John and Charles Wesley, *Hymns and Sacred Poems* (London: William Strahan, 1739), 184.

[22]Thomas Traherne, *Centuries* (London: Faith Press, 1960), 21. And, again, Traherne offers praise to God "for giving me desire, / an eager thirst, a burning ardent fire," "[a] restless longing heavenly avarice, / That never could be satisfied." *Thomas Traherne: Selected Poems and Prose*, ed. Alan Bradford (London: Penguin, 1991), 68.

[23]Henry Scougal, *The Life of God in the Soul of Man* (London: 1677), 18, 21.

as grief."[24] The desire is for something beyond the walls of this world. While not all persons may be able to express this, or acknowledge it, with the acuity of Augustine in his *Confessions* or C. S. Lewis in his autobiography, *Surprised by Joy*, there is surely a similar story to be told of spiritual exile, spiritual homesickness, and spiritual desire for all human beings. Augustine's treatise *On Christian Doctrine* provided a framework for Christian discipleship based entirely on the premise that human beings are constituted essentially by their loves and concerned therefore with the developmental task of the just reordering of those loves. In the biblical tradition disordered human loves are idolatrous—a violation of the first command—and are inevitably enslaving. We become the *homo in se incurvatus*, curved in upon ourselves rather than open to God and to others. Jonathan Edwards and later Thomas Chalmers wrote of the expulsive power of a new affection, a new attachment that was the work of the Spirit in the heart of the converted believer.[25] This new affection is capable of increase as one develops spiritually. Bernard of Clairvaux's developmental scheme built on Augustine and was conceived as four stages in the transformation of our loves, from a natural self-love, to a grateful love that responds to divine self-giving, to a disinterested love that loves and worships God for his own sake as lovely, to an ecstatic bond of love that displaces the ego and is ultimately eschatological.[26] Spiritual formation and human development coincide in a theological anthropology that understands human growth as essentially a matter of the redirection and intensification of love.

THE TELOS OF THE HUMAN PERSON

Fourth, basic to Christian anthropology is an appreciation of the goal of human formation as glorification in the presence of God.

---

[24]J. R. R. Tolkien, "On Fairy-Stories," in *Essays Presented to Charles Williams*, ed. C. S. Lewis (Grand Rapids: Eerdmans, 1966), 81.

[25]Jonathan Edwards, *A Treatise Concerning the Religious Affections* (Boston: S. Kneeland and T. Green, 1746); Thomas Chalmers, *The Expulsive Power of a New Affection* (Edinburgh: Thomas Constable, 1855).

[26]*Bernard of Clairvaux: Selected Works*, trans. G. R. Evans (New York: Paulist Press, 1987), 192-96.

This is to return us to the question of final causes and the ultimate end for which God created human persons. A recent book on developmental psychology states flatly, "Psychology does not have the epistemological tools to address issues of teleology."[27] Yet few questions are more important in spiritual theology.

In the fourth century, John Cassian began his *Conferences* by asking, "What is the goal of the spiritual life?" He states his answer in different ways, saying the ultimate goal is the kingdom of God (echoing the Synoptics), that it is eternal life (echoing the Fourth Gospel), and that it is to reach the high point of love, but more than anything else he comes back to the words of Christ—"Blessed are the pure in heart, for they will see God" (Mt 5:8).[28] The instrumental—or, if you like, developmental—goal is the purification of the heart, and the terminal or ultimate goal is to see the very face of God. Human persons are created to this end, to be beatified in the presence of their Creator. We were made for glory. The remaining 911 pages of Cassian's book follow from this clear and distinct grasp of the telos of human development.

In our own more secular age, final causes are occluded in the modern preoccupation with instrumental causes and intra-mundane goods. Modern society assumes the goods of economic prosperity and intimacy in relationships—what Charles Taylor nicely calls the goods of "production and reproduction"—but beyond this level of material and companionate human flourishing, we have very little to say.[29] And likewise the model of an organism adapting to its environment yields at best a functionalism, but not a teleology, nothing beyond the language of "well adjusted" on the one hand or "dysfunctional" on the other.

How wonderful then to contemplate that we are truly made for glory. *Glory* is the biblical word for beauty, God's own beauty.[30] And in this

---

[27]Balswick, King, and Reimer, *Reciprocating Self*, 28-29.

[28]John Cassian, *The Conferences*, trans. Boniface Ramsay (New York: Paulist Press, 1997), 49.

[29]Charles Taylor, *Sources of the Self* (Cambridge: Cambridge University Press, 1989), 211.

[30]This is densely considered in Hans Urs von Balthasar, *Glory of the Lord: A Theological Aesthetics*, vol. 1, *Seeing the Form* (Edinburgh: T&T Clark, 1982).

is the perfection of our nature. In the second century, Irenaeus fa-mously wrote, "For the glory of God is a living man; and the life of man consists in beholding God."[31] And the psalmist writes similarly of our recovery by grace, "Turn us again, O God; show the light of thy countenance, and we shall be whole" (Psalm 80:7, 14, 19 BCP Psalter). The perfection of our nature is to see the face of God. This is a devel-opmental goal worth celebrating.

With this end in view, Irenaeus gives the first and clearest outline of human development in Christian theology:

> Now it was necessary that man should in the first instance be created; and having been created, should receive growth; and having received growth, should be strengthened; and having been strengthened, should abound; and having abounded, should recover [from the disease of sin]; and having recovered, should be glorified; and being glorified, should see his Lord.[32]

Christian experience is thus developmental because it is teleological. Beginning and ends are linked, first causes and final causes, through the anthropology of "image" and "likeness": created in Christ's image and intended for his likeness.

The key vocabulary in the New Testament that links the final glorifi-cation of human persons with their development is *metamorphóomai*, to be transfigured or transformed. The transfiguration of Christ is a turning point in all three Synoptic Gospels and is linked to Peter's confession and the call to discipleship (Mk 8:31—9:13 and par.).[33] Anthropologically, the event looks back to the Adamic glory of the original human person and

---

[31]Irenaeus, *Against Heresies*, in *Ante-Nicene Fathers*, ed. Phillip Schaff, vol. 1, *The Apostolic Fathers, Justin Martyr, Irenaeus*, ed. Alexander Roberts and James Donaldson (Peabody, MA: Hendrick-son, 1994), 490.

[32]Irenaeus, *Against Heresies*, in *Ante-Nicene Fathers*, 1:522. Clement of Alexandria draws on the same precedent in St. Paul to describe "the training and nurture up from the state of childhood, that is, the course of life which from elementary instruction grows by faith; and in the case of those enrolled in the number of men, prepares beforehand the soul, endued with virtue, for the reception of gnostic knowledge." Clement of Alexandria, *Stromata*, in *Ante-Nicene Fathers*, vol. 2, *Fathers of the Second Century*, ed. Alexander Roberts, James Donaldson, and Arthur Cleveland Coxe (Peabody, MA: Hendrickson, 1994), 480.

[33]See further Eugene H. Peterson, "Saint Mark: The Basic Text for Christian Spirituality," *Crux* 29 (1993): 2-9.

to the final glory of the human person in Christ as the new Adam. The transfiguration is thus anamnestic and adumbrative of the human person, even while setting apart Christ as the one upon whom the Shekinah glory uniquely rests. *Metamorphóomai* is also the word used by Paul for the transformation of believers who contemplate the Lord's glory with unveiled face: they are transfigured or transformed by the Spirit into his image from one degree of glory to another (2 Cor 3:18). Here the ideas of *metamorphóomai* as developmental transformation of one's nature and *metamorphóomai* as transfiguration in glory are fused.

The Christian is intended to become no less than a divinized human person, transfigured by the presence of God, living in union with Christ and filled with the Spirit of God. The pure in heart shall, finally, see God. And "we know that when Christ appears, we shall be like him, for we shall see him as he is. All who have this hope in him purify themselves, just as he is pure" (1 Jn 3:2-3). The vision of God is that for which all men and women were created, and it is the proper end of their nature. Development in these terms is a matter of beatification.

Henry Scougal recognized the implications of this high theological anthropology for human relations. Even when we see a weak and rugged human being, unlovely to us, he says, we should consider that this one is "capable of all that Wisdom and Goodness, wherewith the best of Saints have ever been adorned, and which may one Day come to be raised unto such Heights of Perfection as shall render a fit Companion for the holy Angels."[34]

A theological anthropology ought therefore to lead to a kind of hushed reverence that bows before the holy mystery of another human person.

---

[34]Scougal, *Life of God*, 45. C. S. Lewis wrote about this similarly in his famous sermon, "The Weight of Glory," but he also spoke of the stark alternative, in that the very human nature capable of glory may also choose its own damnation. Human development is therefore a matter of grave moral seriousness. He ended his reflections on human glorification with a reminder of this solemnity: "It is a serious thing to live in a society of possible gods and goddesses, to remember that the dullest most uninteresting person you talk to may one day be a creature which, if you say it now, you would be strongly tempted to worship, or else a horror and a corruption such as you now meet, if at all, only in a nightmare. All day long we are, in some degree, helping each other to one or the other of these destinations." C. S. Lewis, *The Weight of Glory and Other Addresses* (New York: Macmillan, 1975), 18-19.

Negative theology, like the dark center of an Orthodox icon of the transfiguration, acknowledges that in all our language about God, however true, we do not exhaust or circumscribe God. By analogy, may we not say something similar about human persons, made in God's image? As Balthasar writes, "The highest instance of the *analogia entis* is the *analogia personalitatis*."[35] If this is true, then we must be on guard against all modern anthropologies, implicit or explicit, that would reduce the human person to fit the heuristic tools of the observational human sciences. A properly "negative" theological anthropology will always stand in awe of another human person as made in God's image, and limit for this sake the claims made to explain human nature and behavior. On the basis of the analogia personalitatis, one will remember, always, the partial and heuristic nature of any empirical research into human nature. For positive psychologists, for example, to operationalize a theological virtue, determine its salience in a population, and then design corresponding interventions, there is a necessary series of reductions of quality to quantity as the view of the human person is constrained to fit the tools. Theological anthropology invites some modesty here about the extent of our findings and chastens our claims to understanding. On this theological view of psychology and spiritual formation, science is always taken up into wisdom, and knowledge into love.

HUMAN AND SPIRITUAL DEVELOPMENT
AS ANALOGOUS

Fifth, the growth of a Christian in his or her discipleship is analogous but not coincident with the stages of human development from infancy to old age.

The analogy between spiritual growth and the biopsychosocial development of the human person was there in Irenaeus, but it perhaps most clearly developed in Aquinas and his later interpreter, Reginald Garrigou-Lagrange in his opus, *The Three Ages of the Interior Life* (1938).

---

[35]Balthasar, *Prayer*, 23.

Drawing on the precedent in Aquinas and fusing this with the teaching of John of the Cross, Garrigou-Lagrange saw a correlation between the three stages of childhood, adolescence, and adulthood, and those of the spiritual beginner, proficient, and perfect, following the classical threefold path of purgation, illumination, and union. There are three corresponding conversions. Beginners are preoccupied with repentance as a first conversion. Like the disciples were called to leave everything in childlike obedience to follow Christ, so it is with beginners. But there follows in due time the need for a second conversion, which is like the crisis of adolescence, in which the disciple must continue faithful in the absence of sensible consolation. This middle conversion has its parallel in the experience of Simon Peter during the dark night of the passion during which he denied Christ, repented, and was re-established. But as the adolescent transitions to the freedom and responsibility of adult commitments, so in the spiritual life one is called to a third conversion of the spirit, to an utter transparency to grace in the absence of all spiritual consolation. This is like the period between the Ascension and Pentecost, when the disciples continued through a kind of desolation, enduring the physical absence of Christ, until a fiery Pentecostal grace consumed them entirely.[36] As another writer says, there is first the experience of baptismal grace, followed by a strengthening eucharistic grace, which is finally fulfilled in a charismatic grace.[37]

Other writers have also developed this analogy between spiritual growth and human development, but I think we are right still to see these two lines as distinct: the line from biological birth to death, and the line from spiritual conversion to spiritual maturity. These lines are analogous but not coincident. This is the meaning of Jesus' words to Nicodemus in John 3: "Flesh gives birth to flesh, but the Spirit gives birth to spirit. You should not be surprised at my saying, 'You must be born again'" (Jn 3:6-7).

---

[36]Réginald Garrigou-Lagrange, *The Three Ages of the Interior Life: Prelude of Eternal Life*, trans. M. Timothea Doyle, 2 vols. (Rockford, IL: Tan Books, 1989), 225-46.

[37]A monk of the Eastern Church, "The Essentials of Orthodox Spirituality," in *Exploring Christian Spirituality: An Ecumenical Reader*, ed. Kenneth J. Collins (Grand Rapids: Baker Books, 2000), 118-20. Conceptually, the eucharistic grace may be considered climactic.

The biological development of human life is constrained in a way that the spiritual life is not. Even higher levels of human experience, while still constrained, become ever more complex and undetermined, and the more so as we approach the intellectual, emotional, social, and other complex dimensions of the mystery of human life. As Michael Polanyi argued in his little book *The Study of Man* (1959), there is an increasingly rich and complex relation to the object of study as one rises from the hard sciences to the study of another human person, face to face in history.[38] This seems to be something appreciated as developmental psychology has moved beyond nature-nurture debates and maturationist-environmentalist polarities to emphasize more complex contextual and systems-oriented models of human development, and to reckon with the evidence of neuro-plasticity across the lifespan.[39] There is less danger now of reductionism but a new danger perhaps of the incoherence of micro-narratives and the loss of universals.

The basis for human freedom in theological terms derives from God's own freedom. God relates to his human creatures not out of necessity but in the freedom of a divine person, and his word is always therefore fresh and new. Balthasar makes the point that one of the reasons we need to be attentive to God's word is that he might say something today that he did not say yesterday. This is also the meaning of divine election: "It is possible for us to hear the word of God because God's world is open to us" as "a miracle of the Father's utterly free love. Every day it should astonish us anew. . . . A whole world of love-mysteries opens up to us" and all this is because of the "miracle of his merciful election."[40]

---

[38]Speaking of the contrast between the distinctness of human nature beyond the harmonies of the inanimate world or even the excellence of lower forms of life, Polanyi says, "This is the spiritual foundation of freedom. . . . And this is also the framework, therefore, within which man *writing* history confronts the men who *made history.*" Again, "This is to say that when we arrive at the contemplation of a human being as a responsible person . . . our knowledge of him has definitely lost the character of an observation and has become an encounter instead." Michael Polanyi, *The Study of Man* (Chicago: University of Chicago Press, 1959), 86, 94-95.

[39]See further Philip David Zelazo, "Developmental Psychology: A New Synthesis," in *The Oxford Handbook of Developmental Psychology*, vol. 2, *Self and Other*, ed. Philip David Zelazo (Oxford: Oxford Handbooks Online, 2013), doi.org/10.1093/oxfordhb/9780199958474.013.0001.

[40]Balthasar, *Prayer*, 38-39.

What corresponds to this in the human creature is an answering freedom. The response to blessing is *parrhesia*, a boldness to approach God in the freedom and dignity of human persons (2 Cor 3:12; cf. Heb 4:16).[41] This is very different than a linear, locked-in, one-size-fits-all escalator of spiritual development or a natural mysticism of ascent by the naturalization of the soul. The purgation-illumination-union scheme that early Christians took up from Platonism had to be adapted in precisely this more personal direction, as we find in Bonaventure's treatise on the *Enkindling of Love*. Although there is a shape to the Christian life and a sense of beginning, middle, and end, there is a uniqueness to every human itinerary and to the free response of each human person to God's own freedom. There is a wonderful moment when the character John in C. S. Lewis's allegory *The Pilgrim's Regress* looks back on his circuitous journey north and south, and round the earth from east to west, and across the chasm of conversion. His Guide reassures him about the Divine Landlord's providence, "You may be sure the Landlord has brought you the shortest way: though I confess it would look an odd journey on a map."[42] In the nature of things, there is something about spiritual formation that will always "look an odd journey on a map."

SPIRITUAL AND HUMAN FLOURISHING

Sixth, the progress of a Christian toward maturity involves the sort of deepening experience of relationships with others, with creation, with oneself, and with God that constitutes the flourishing of human persons generally.

Becoming more deeply Christian means becoming more deeply human. The spirituality of the early church, East and West, and of the Middle Ages was always in danger of isolating or losing the individual, subsuming him or her into larger patterns of the ascent to God along the lines of the *exitus-reditus* scheme of emanation and return. It is not the

---

[41]Balthasar, *Prayer*, 45-46.
[42]C. S. Lewis, *The Pilgrim's Regress* (London: Geoffrey Bles, 1933), 173.

case that the soul is somehow naturally divine and naturally returns to its source, or that it simply participates in the cosmic procession from and return of all things to God. Our ascent to God is not the return of the soul to an original unitive state but communion with a person. Christ himself is the beginning, middle, and end, and our ascent takes place only in personal communion with him. Julie Canlis argues that John Calvin reformed the doctrine of ascent in precisely this direction: "Calvin has relocated 'participation' from between impersonals (the soul in the divine nature) to personals (the human being in Christ, by the Spirit)."[43] Recovery of the dynamic of spiritual formation as a matter of personal communion with Christ by the Spirit returns us to our humanity, resisting the gnosticizing tendency to see spirituality as a matter of an isolated individual (the alone to the alone) or of a spiritualism that abandons our humanness.

The rise of evangelical religion in the eighteenth century certainly signaled a reaffirmation of the uniqueness of personal spiritual experience, and the greatest testimony to this is the enormous deposit of personalia—letters and testimonies and diaries—left behind in manuscript, a mountain of archival material from ordinary Christians speaking to their personal experience of God's grace. In John Coe's chapter in this book (chapter one), calling us to close empirical observation of the spiritual life, he echoes what so many of the early evangelicals did. Indeed, they pioneered in this sort of close attention to spiritual experience. In many ways, John Wesley's voluminous journal—over a million words—was like the notebook of a social scientist. It was a series of very precise observations on the spiritual life of those he encountered, and sometimes of himself, over six decades.

His contemporary, the evangelical pastor John Newton, likewise had an especially keen sense for the way God's grace operated across a variety of circumstances in the life of the believer, including the life stages of the believer. He corresponded with hundreds of women and men about their

---

[43]Julie Canlis, *Calvin's Ladder: A Spiritual Theology of Ascent and Ascension* (Grand Rapids: Eerdmans, 2010), 50.

particular experience and helped them to see this in light of the common work of grace to bring believers to maturity. For one of his directees he outlined three stages of spiritual formation from desire though conflict to contemplation, and he denominated these stages as simply A, B, and C. Of the work of God's grace in the mature Christian, C, he writes:

> C may be rich or poor, learned or illiterate, of a lively natural spirit, or a more slow and phlegmatic constitution. He may have a comparably smooth, or a remarkably thorny path in life; he may be a minister or a layman: these circumstances will give some tincture and difference in appearance to the work; but the work itself is the same.[44]

Here Newton writes with the sensitivity of contextual and systemic models of human development. He appreciates that God sees the whole of our lives: "Our great and merciful High-priest knows the whole; he considers our frame . . . makes allowances, pities, bears, accepts, and approves, with unerring judgment." Newton discerned the beauty of God's work of spiritual formation, refracted by the particular experience of men and women, as if by a prism, into the varied colors of grace. The mature believer has become transfigured as "the object and residence of divine love, the charge of angels, and ripening for everlasting glory."[45]

The disciplined observation and attention of psychologists to human development across the lifespan can only enrich this perception of God's work in human persons. What is God doing in this person's life here and now, at this time? Love always notices details in the beloved. And so, as in the Franciscan tradition from which science first arose, love closely attends to particulars, and this humanizes spirituality, especially where there is a danger of flight: flight to abstraction, flight to isolation, or flight to discarnate ascent. No, if I am to attend to God's work in this particular person, here and now, love would call me to pay attention to conditions of their life at this biological, cognitive, and psychosocial stage, in this culture at this moment in history. And this means considering all the

---

[44]John Newton, "Spiritual Letters on Growth in Grace," in *The Life and Spirituality of John Newton*, ed. Bruce Hindmarsh (Vancouver: Regent College Publishing, 1998), 110.
[45]Newton, "Spiritual Letters," 111.

insights of developmental psychology. Sensitivity to the need for secure attachment in infancy and childhood, attention to the issues of identity formation in adolescence, awareness of the importance of forging memories in old age, and so on—all of these are paths of love, and they serve to humanize the work of spiritual formation.

CONCLUSION

Indeed, a robust theological anthropology will, in the end, see a union between human development and spiritual development. We may conclude therefore with the joyful exhortation of John Paul II in this respect:

> Human formation, when it is carried out in the context of an anthropology which is open to the full truth regarding the human person, leads to and finds its completion in spiritual formation. Every human being, as God's creature who has been redeemed by Christ's blood, is called to be reborn "of water and the Spirit" and to become a "son in the Son." In this wonderful plan of God is to be found the basis of the essentially religious dimension of the human person. . . . The human individual is open to transcendence, to the absolute; he has a heart which is restless until it rests in the Lord.[46]

---

[46]Pope John Paul II, *Pastores Dabo Vobis* (Vatican: Libreria Editrice Vaticana, 1992), w2.vatican.va/content/john-paul-ii/en/apost_exhortations/documents/hf_jp-ii_exh_25031992_pastores-dabo-vobis.html, 45.

LIVING "BEFORE GOD"

A KIERKEGAARDIAN VIEW OF SPIRITUALITY

C. STEPHEN EVANS

I wish in this chapter to present a Kierkegaardian view of what it means to be "spiritual" or to exist as "spirit." (Kierkegaard does not distinguish between these ways of putting the matter.) The thesis is simple: spirituality is fundamentally relational. To exist as spirit is to exist "before God," aware that life is lived in God's presence. However, this relational spirituality comes in two forms. There is a generic human spirituality that may be found in many religions and even in the lives of those who call themselves "spiritual but not religious." This generic human spirituality must be distinguished from Christian spirituality, where a person relates to God through Jesus of Nazareth and through the Spirit who is present within the Christian, both as an individual and in the community. I shall begin with a discussion of generic human spirituality.

KIERKEGAARD ON THE NATURAL KNOWLEDGE OF GOD

If spirituality is fundamentally a quality of a life lived in relation to God, then a generic human form of spirituality will depend on the possibility of a generic human relation to God. Such a relation may seem problematic.

Much of philosophy of religion in the West has wrestled with the problem of whether God exists and has treated this question as a profoundly difficult one to answer. If a person cannot even know that God exists, how can that person have a relation to God?

Kierkegaard believes that there is something fundamentally wrong with this whole picture. He believes that a natural knowledge of God is not hard to obtain. God is in some ways present to all or virtually all humans. If there are difficulties, the difficulties do not lie in the evidence for God's reality but in ourselves. If we do not know that there is a God, it is either because we do not want to know God, or else it is because we have lost the ability to recognize God's presence in the world or see God at work in our lives. If the former is true, we need a change of heart; we need to want to know God. If the latter is true, then what we need is not new evidence, but rather the ability to see and rightly interpret the evidence that is right before us. If this view is right and God is present to all humans, this means that there is a sense in which all human beings have the ability to live their lives "before God." This is Kierkegaard's view, and it underlies his understanding of humans as spiritual beings.

The view that a knowledge of God is commonly present in humans seems implicit in the Christian biblical writings as a whole and sometimes is explicit. The biblical writers do not argue for God's existence or see any need to offer such arguments. The individual who "says in his heart" that "there is no God" is characterized as a "fool" (Ps 14:1 NIV).[1] Paul claims that "what may be known about God" is plain even to those who have not received any special revelation from God. God has made his reality plain to them since God's "eternal power and divine nature" can be "clearly seen" in the created order (Rom 1:20). God's moral law has also been revealed to all humans, since the "requirements of the law are written on their hearts, their consciences also bearing witness" (Rom 2:15).

---

[1] All Scripture quotations in this chapter are given in the NIV unless otherwise noted.

That Kierkegaard endorses the view that God's reality should be obvious to all can be seen from an obscure footnote in Kierkegaard's *Philosophical Fragments*, in which Johannes Climacus, the pseudonymous author, describes a man who wants to prove the existence of God as "a superb subject for crazy comedy."[2] In Kierkegaard's *Papirer* we find a much a longer version of this footnote that was deleted from the final manuscript of the book.[3] In the long version, Kierkegaard (and at this stage of the game the book is attributed to Kierkegaard himself rather than the pseudonym) explains why the situation is comical by imagining "a man deluded into thinking that he could prove that God exists—and then have an atheist accept it by virtue of the other's proof." This is comic because both the man producing the proof and the atheist are "fantastic" figures, that is, figures that cannot exist in real life: "Just as no one has ever proved it [God's existence], so there has never been an atheist, even though there certainly have been many who have been unwilling to allow what they know [that God exists] to have control of their minds."

Did Kierkegaard really think that there has never been an atheist? Since the long version of this footnote was deleted, one might think that Kierkegaard thought better of this extravagant claim before publishing the book. However, a more plausible explanation of the deletion is this: Kierkegaard made the change to the book at the last minute, when he decided to attribute the book to the humorist Johannes Climacus, removing his own name as author and inserting it as editor. Since Climacus as a pseudonymous character does not claim to be a Christian, it is plausible to think that the footnote accurately expressed Kierkegaard's own viewpoint, but he recognized that it did not fit with the views of the

---

[2]The rest of this paragraph and the next one contains a revised version of material taken from C. Stephen Evans, "Kierkegaard, Natural Theology, and the Existence of God," in *Kierkegaard and Christian Faith,* ed. C. Stephen Evans and Paul Martens (Waco: Baylor University Press, 2016), 25-38. The footnote occurs in the Hong translation of Søren Kierkegaard, *Philosophical Fragments,* ed. and trans. Edna H. Hong and Howard V. Hong (Princeton, NJ: Princeton University Press, 1985), 43.
[3]The full version of the footnote can be found in the "Supplement" in the Hong version of Kierkegaard, *Philosophical Fragments,* 191-92.

enigmatic Climacus, who does not tell us explicitly (in *Fragments*) what his own religious commitments are.

In any case this quotation aptly captures the attitude Kierkegaard takes toward God's existence in his authorship as a whole. It is true that Kierkegaard claims that faith involves a "leap" and that faith is something that the human understanding often finds unreasonable, even "absurd." However, those claims are made about Christian faith, centered as it is on the "Absolute Paradox" that Jesus of Nazareth was both fully human and fully divine. The kind of *Socratic faith* that merely involves belief in God requires no leap and does not seem unreasonable to humans.

We can see this attitude clearly in *Concluding Unscientific Postscript*, also attributed to Johannes Climacus.[4] Climacus surely speaks for Kierkegaard when he criticizes the idea of proving God's existence: "To prove the existence of one who is present (*er til*) is the most shameless affront, since it is an attempt to make him ridiculous; . . . For how could it occur to anyone to prove that he exists, unless one had permitted oneself to ignore him, and then makes matters worse by proving his existence right before his nose."[5] God is (or ought to be) present to a human being, and if a person feels the need to argue for God's existence, that is a reliable sign that the person is ignoring the ways God is present to that individual—or has lost or never acquired the skill whereby one recognizes God. Climacus goes on to compare God to a king and says that if a person who was in the "majestic presence" of a king tried to prove the king's existence, he would in effect be making a fool of the king. No, one indicates an awareness of the king by an appropriate expression of submission. Similarly, one "proves" God's existence by worship.

Recognizing that this is Kierkegaard's view helps us understand Kierkegaard's lack of interest and even disdain for natural theological

---

[4]The rest of this paragraph is also taken from Evans, "Kierkegaard on Natural Theology."

[5]Søren Kierkegaard, *Concluding Unscientific Postscript*, ed. and trans. Edna H. Hong and Howard V. Hong (Princeton, NJ: Princeton University Press, 1992), 1:545. The above translation is my own, taken directly from Kierkegaard's *Samlede Værker*, 1st ed. (Copenhagen: Gyldendals, 1901-1907), 7:475.

arguments for God's existence. He is uninterested in such arguments because they are unnecessary to gain knowledge of God's reality. He disdains such arguments because they presuppose a wrong picture of our epistemic situation, and this contributes to a misleading picture of the causes of the decline of religious belief among intellectuals. A concern with arguments makes it seem that the problem with religious belief lies with the evidence. However, Kierkegaard thinks that this is a mistake that gives the unbeliever way too much credit. In effect, skeptics wants us to think that if there were sufficient evidence they would believe, but, since there is not enough evidence, they cannot believe. Kierkegaard thinks that the real problem lies in ourselves. If we do not believe, it is either because we do not want to believe (a kind of "insubordination" that he sees as endemic to modernity) or else it is because we have lost the emotional and imaginative skills required to recognize God at work in the world and our lives.

GOD'S PRESENCE THROUGH CONSCIENCE

How is God present to humans? Since my initial focus is on generic human spirituality, I want to focus on how God might be known to humans through general revelation, through the created order rather than through specific historical events. I personally believe that God can be known in many ways, through "natural signs" that he has planted in the natural order to point to himself.[6] Some of these are found in the natural world, as Paul says in Romans 1. However, an important natural sign for God is conscience, which Paul also mentions in Romans 2. In conscience God is present as the one with authority who demands of us that we become a certain kind of person; God is the Lord, and if he is not known as the one who must be obeyed, he is not really known at all.[7]

---

[6]See C. Stephen Evans, *Natural Signs and Knowledge of God: A New Look at Theistic Arguments* (Oxford: Oxford University Press, 2010), 26-46, for a fuller explanation of this concept.
[7]Some parts of this paragraph and the next two are also taken from Evans, "Kierkegaard on Natural Theology."

Kierkegaard's *Climacus* makes this point by arguing that one place where God is not clearly present to humans is in world history. We do not see God in history because "as it [world history] is seen by humans, God does not play the role of Lord; as one does not see the ethical in it, therefore God is not seen either."[8] We see God when we see the world through ethical lenses. To understand history correctly, however, we must not look through such lenses, for world historical importance does not correlate with moral character. Evil people such as Hitler and Stalin have left their impact on world history quite as strongly as the Mother Teresas of this world. To see God, you must not look at history but within yourself, and every person who does this sees God, because "every existing individual has a possibility-relationship with God."[9] Kierkegaard does not deny that God is providentially guiding human history; he just thinks that we humans cannot see the plan, at least we cannot in our earthly lifetime.

For Kierkegaard, anyone who has a moral conscience has an awareness of God's requirements, for to have a conscience is simply to have a "relationship in which you as a single individual relate yourself to yourself before God."[10] Similarly, in *Sickness unto Death*, Kierkegaard's pseudonym Anti-Climacus explains that God's judgment, unlike the judgment of a human judge or authority, cannot be evaded by humans mutinying as a group or crowd because God judges humans as single individuals.[11] Kierkegaard actually says that God's judgment in eternity will be easy (he says "a child could pass judgment in eternity") because

[8]Kierkegaard, *Concluding Unscientific Postscript*, 156. Again, I cite the Hong edition but use my own translation.
[9]Kierkegaard, *Concluding Unscientific Postscript*, 156.
[10]Søren Kierkegaard, *Upbuilding Discourses in Various Spirits*, ed. and trans. Edna H. Hong and Howard V. Hong (Princeton, NJ: Princeton University Press, 1993), 129.
[11]Søren Kierkegaard, *Sickness unto Death*, ed. and trans. Edna H. Hong and Howard V. Hong (Princeton, NJ: Princeton University Press, 1980), 123-24. Strictly speaking, the author is not Kierkegaard, but the pseudonymous persona Kierkegaard has created, Anti-Climacus. However, this is a Christian pseudonym, and Kierkegaard uses it only because he does not think he himself measures up to the strict Christian ideals that Anti-Climacus lays out. To avoid confusing readers, in this chapter I shall simply refer to Kierkegaard as the author of *Sickness unto Death*.

human persons through conscience make a "report" about their guilt each time they sin. Thus Anti-Climacus simply identifies a God-relationship with conscience.[12]

Support for this view is also found in *Works of Love*, where Kierkegaard claims that God is the source of our ethical duties. God has a justifiable claim on our obedience because he is the one who created us out of nothing and has destined us for a life of love and happiness in relation to himself and others. Just as human lovers acquire obligations to each other through their history of interactions, so God has a claim on us due to our history with God: "But that eternal love-history has begun much earlier; it began with your beginning, when you came into existence out of nothing, and just as surely as you do not become nothing, it does not end at the grave."[13] Because of this debt to God, we must obey God: "But you shall love God in unconditional obedience, even if what he requires of you might seem to you to be to your own harm, indeed, harmful to his cause; for God's wisdom is beyond all comparison with yours. . . . All you have to do is obey in love."[14]

SPIRITUALITY AS RELATIONAL

Increasingly, individuals in contemporary American society describe themselves as "spiritual but not religious." Is this possible? From Kierkegaard's perspective, the answer is clearly yes. For him to be spiritual is simply to exist "as spirit." The definition he gives of spirit is very similar to the definition of conscience, which is, as we have just seen, the mode in which God is present to all humans. A human being is spirit because a human being "relates itself to itself" and does so by "relating itself to another."[15]

What does this mean? I think it means that humans are doubly re-lational creatures. On the one hand, to be a human being is to "relate

[12]Søren Kierkegaard, *Sickness unto Death*, 123-24.
[13]Søren Kierkegaard, *Works of Love*, ed. and trans. Edna H. Hong and Howard V. Hong (Princeton, NJ: Princeton University Press, 1995), 149-50.
[14]Kierkegaard, *Works of Love*, 20.
[15]Kierkegaard, *Sickness unto Death*, 13-14.

yourself to yourself." To be a self is to be self-conscious, and self-consciousness involves a distinction between the self as an object of awareness (the self I am conscious of) and the self that is the subject of awareness (the self that is conscious of itself). This ability to "step back" from ourselves creates yet another duality within the self. This is the distinction between the self that I am aware that I am, and the self that I am aware of myself as wanting to be. This gap is present because part of what it means to be a self is to project an ideal for oneself, a true self by which the actual self can be measured. I am conscious of myself as having certain qualities acquired through my past, but I also define myself by the qualities I see myself as striving to realize in my projected future.

However, Kierkegaard thinks that this intra-psychic process in which a person "relates himself to himself" also involves a relation to something outside the self. We are not autonomous, isolated individuals. The "ideal self" we are striving to become is not fashioned out of nothing but is made possible by the social processes that form the self. We always relate to ourselves by virtue of a relation to an "other" that is not the self.

Who is this "other"? One might think the other is necessarily God. Ontologically, this is true. God is the one who creates the human self and is its ground. However, psychologically humans often ground their ideal self in something other than God. Kierkegaard calls the ideal self the "criterion" (*Maalestok*, literally "measuring stick," or that by which the self measures itself). A crucial passage from *Sickness unto Death* makes this quite clear:

> A cattleman who (if this were possible) is a self directly before his cattle is a very low self, and, similarly, a master who is a self directly before his slaves is actually no self—for in both cases a criterion is lacking. The child who previously has had only his parents as a criterion becomes a self as an adult by getting the state as a criterion, but what an infinite accent falls on the self by having God as a criterion.[16]

---

[16]Kierkegaard, *Sickness unto Death*, 79.

If my ideal self is derived from my relation to the cattle I am taking care of, there is a sense in which I fail to be a self at all. The bar is set too low in such a case, because "being smarter than a cow" does not really describe a recognizably human life. The slave owner whose identity is grounded in owning slaves also fails to be a self, because the status he gains at the expense of the slaves depends on their being regarded as property. Because his slaves are property, the recognition of him they afford is a forced recognition, unable to give the slave owner a genuine human self.

Kierkegaard implies that a child begins to be a self by deriving an ideal self, a "criterion" of selfhood, from the child's parents. It is only when the child becomes an adult and is part of society that the child gains some distance on this childhood ideal. However, even in this case the criterion of self is not invented by the self out of nothing. Rather, the child who is becoming an adult is absorbing broader socially informed ideals, which Anti-Climacus says, following here the views of Hegel and his followers, are embedded in the laws of the state. We might say the child learns "cultural scripts" from the broader society about what it means to be a self, and these may differ from those learned from the parents.

The state is not the ideal "other" in which to ground my identity, however. For Kierkegaard it is possible for the self to exist "before God." "And what infinite reality the self gains by being conscious of existing before God, by becoming a human self whose criterion is God."[17] Of course Kierkegaard's thought here is not that the self aspires to be or become God. Rather, the self aspires to become the self that God desires that individual to become. It is God's recognition that counts. "At every person's birth there comes into existence an eternal purpose for that person, for that person in particular. Faithfulness to oneself with respect to this is the highest thing a person can do, as that most profound poet said, 'Worse than self-love is self-contempt.'"[18]

---

[17]Kierkegaard, *Sickness unto Death*, 79.
[18]Kierkegaard, *Upbuilding Discourses*, 93. The "profound poet" is Shakespeare, a reference to *King Henry the Fifth*.

We can here see the origins of Kierkegaard's "individualism" and his critique of social conformism, which defines the task of the self as simply becoming like "the others." However, it should be clear that the authentic individual self Kierkegaard affirms is thoroughly relational. It is formed by a relation to God, which by no means nullifies the human social relationships that largely define the self. Rather, the God-relation makes it possible to transcend the power of those social influences. When I hear God's call and respond, I am no longer defined purely by my parents or my friends or my society, important as those continue to be.

In a sense, "spirit" is an ontological category. Every human being is created by God as an embodied spirit. The structure of spirit is given in creation. But an essential part of that structure is that spirit must be self-determining. God, who is pure spirit, is completely determined by his own nature; no outside influence can change who he is. Humans cannot be spirits in this sense since they are not God. However, they have been given the dignity of playing a role in their own development. In order that humans can exist as finite, creaturely spirits, God does not create humans as fully determinate products but endows them with possibilities to be actualized. Thus for humans, we are spirits, but our task as spirits is to "become what we are." For this reason, although every human is in one sense spirit, we can also speak of spirituality as a task and therefore of degrees of spirituality, depending on how much of the task has been actualized.

As creaturely spirits, human persons are partly defined by things we have no control over. We are born male or female, to a particular set of parents, in a particular culture, and at a particular time. However, since we are self-conscious creatures, we are not simply passive products of these factors. Still, the ideal selves we strive to be are heavily shaped by them. Kierkegaard believes that a God relationship offers the possibility of partial transcendence of our finitude. When God addresses me and I answer God's call, I am not completely determined by my parents or society. To be spirit is to be autonomous or self-determining. Only God is truly spirit in this sense. However, when we are rightly related to God, that relation allows us a kind of relative autonomy or independence, in that we can partially transcend the factors that make us who we are. Serving God is thus liberating; it frees up individuals to be the true selves God intends them to be.

When we think of spirit in ontological terms, it is a status God has given to all humans. All of us are created by God and all of us are addressed by God, and thus we have the opportunity to live our lives *coram Deo*, before God. However, when we think of spirit as a task, then we can understand spirituality as something that comes in degrees. The degree of spirituality a person possesses is a direct function of the degree to which the person is aware of God's presence and is striving to live before God. In this "degree" sense of spirituality, a more intense awareness of God leads to a more spiritual life, as does a more adequate conception of the God who is present. Spirituality in this sense is "the practice of the presence of God," as Brother Lawrence so memorably expressed the idea in the book published under that title.

This relational understanding of spirituality also makes possible the distinction I have made between generic human spirituality and Christian spirituality. Generic human spirituality, though possible outside of Christianity, as the figure of Socrates demonstrates to Kierkegaard, is not actually present in all humans except as a capacity or potentiality. Kierkegaard himself speaks of a kind of paganism that lacks an understanding of God; "paganism is 'to be without God in the world.'"[19] Such paganism is possible both in cultures that have not heard the gospel as well as in Christendom, where people may be familiar with the Christian message verbally but have totally lost the ability to hear with understanding. In fact, the "spiritless" person in paganism is actually in a better position than the spiritless person in Christendom, since a pagan who lacks this spirituality may still be a person who longs for it and is looking for it. The "pagan" person in

---

[19]Kierkegaard, *Sickness unto Death*, 81. The allusion is to Ephesians 2:12.

Christendom, however, is running away from the spiritual life, not seeking it.

Such generic human spirituality should be distinguished from the kind of spirituality that is possible when God is present to the individual through the Christian revelation. When God addresses someone through the Scriptures and through the Christ that the Scriptures testify to, the person's relation to God changes dramatically. When God is present to someone through the Christian sacraments and the Spirit that unites Christians to Christ and Christ's body, the church, spirituality takes new forms. All forms of spirituality involve a life that is lived before God, but the life, death, and resurrection of Christ make possible not only a qualitatively different understanding of God and what it means to live in God's presence but also new resources to enable such a life.

SPIRITUALLY ENABLING QUALITIES
AND SPIRITUAL FRUITS

To say that spirituality is fundamentally relational in character does not of course mean that there are no distinctive qualities in people with greater degrees of spirituality. For both generic and Christian spirituality there are qualities that are spiritually enabling, qualities that lead to greater awareness and/or understanding of God, and also qualities that are best seen as products or fruits of spirituality. Spirituality is also enabled by removing factors that function as barriers to spirituality. Kierkegaard has a special interest in removing such barriers. He does not believe one ordinary human can directly instill spirituality in another; only God can establish the relation with himself that is required. However, a human can help by removing barriers that might block a person from hearing God's address. In the remainder of this chapter I will speak briefly about the qualities that foster spirituality and those that hinder, both for generic and Christian spirituality. In general it is correct to say that factors that enable or hinder generic human spirituality will function in a similar way for Christian spirituality. This is to be expected since Christian spirituality is a species of spirituality and thus will share some characteristics with other forms of spirituality. There are, however, also distinctive factors that foster or inhibit Christian spirituality.

ENABLING QUALITIES OF GENERIC HUMAN SPIRITUALITY

In the beginning of this chapter, I mentioned Kierkegaard's conviction that the decline of faith in modern Europe among intellectuals is not due to increased scientific knowledge or lack of evidence, but rather in impoverished capacities on the part of those intellectuals. The problem is not that our brains are too big, but that our imaginations are puny and shrunken and that our emotional capacities are impoverished. Kierkegaard uses the terms *inwardness* and *subjectivity* more or less interchangeably to refer to those areas of human life that need to be strengthened if we are to regain our ability to live spiritual lives.

Rekindling subjectivity. The contrast with subjectivity is objectivity. For Kierkegaard, *objectivity* is a kind of intellectual stance or attitude in which the subject ignores the implications of a question for the self who is doing the thinking. This kind of thinking has its place and in that place it has value. For example, in mathematical thinking or when one is studying the results of an experiment, it is proper to avoid or minimize subjective bias, so as to make it possible to see things as they really are. Some of the greatest modern Western philosophers have claimed that this intellectual stance is the proper one to take when one is doing philosophy as well. Spinoza taught that the philosopher should strive to see the world "*sub specie æternitatis*" (under the aspect of eternity).[20] In effect, the philosopher ought to see the world from God's point of view. Hegel, who was deeply influenced by Spinoza, similarly claimed that "philosophy must keep up its guard

---

[20]Baruch Spinoza, *Ethics*, in *A Spinoza Reader: The Ethics and Other Works*, trans. and ed. Edwin Curley (Princeton, NJ: Princeton University Press, 1994), 85-265.

against the desire to be edifying." The aim of the philosopher is "Absolute Knowledge."[21]

Kierkegaard thinks that this attitude has profoundly shaped modern Western thought in deleterious ways. It can be seen in the "scientism" that regards natural science as the proper means of answering all significant questions. Scientism says that science can tell us whether humans have free will or whether there are objective moral obligations. It can also be seen in the assumption that our human problems stem primarily from lack of objective knowledge. If our business corporations are showing a lack of ethical integrity, we can solve the problem by teaching ethical theory at business schools. If pornography is ruining people's lives, or if teenagers are having children before they are mature enough to be parents, the answer must lie in sex education. We can solve our problems without taking moral stands, or stands of any kind, except the stand of the detached knower who has forgotten that he himself is an existing human being. All human problems can be solved by objective knowledge.

We may believe that in taking this "objective" viewpoint we are more likely to arrive at truth, but Kierkegaard thinks that just the opposite is the case when one is dealing with moral and religious truths. The truth is that we are not God and we cannot see the world from God's point of view. There is no such thing as the "view from nowhere."[22] When we attempt to take such a stance, we cut ourselves off from the insights that are possible for an engaged human being who must choose and, in choosing, define the self. Here is an example: Kierkegaard says that one can't really understand sin unless one understands sin as something serious and terrible. To think about sin without recognizing that sin leads to destruction is like thinking about what path to take on a foggy mountain and ignoring the possibility that a path may lead one toward

[21]Georg W. F. Hegel, *Phenomenology of Spirit*, trans. and ed. Terry Pinkard (Cambridge: Cambridge University Press, 2018).

[22]Thomas Nagel's memorable phrase to describe the objective, scientific standpoint. See his book *The View from Nowhere* (Oxford: Oxford University Press, 1986).

a cliff. Any honest thinking about sin that involves real understanding of sin must then engage the emotions.

The alternative to this objective point of view is not to become unthinking or mindless but to think hard about our human problems in a way that takes seriously our situation. For example, if I want to think about death and what it means to die, it is essential for me to face seriously the fact that I am going to die. This does not mean simply registering a fact, such as "all humans are mortal," but thinking about what my impending death means for the whole of my life and its significance. This is not an excuse for wish fulfillment; the subjective thinker in Kierkegaard's sense cares deeply about truth. But it means that the subject will be engaged with a kind of thinking that is imbued with passion. To think about sin or death without passion is for Kierkegaard tantamount to thoughtlessness.

One strategy Kierkegaard employs to help rekindle subjectivity among his readers is what he calls "indirect communication." If Kierkegaard merely gives a scientifically accurate diagnosis of the problem, he may exacerbate the problem, even if the diagnosis he gives is correct. People who think that a full and rich human life requires only objective knowledge may not be helped by giving them more objective knowledge, even by giving them the objective knowledge that there is more to life than objective knowledge. Rather, Kierkegaard strives to engage and even seduce his readers through humor and through parables. He does not simply tell us that it is bad to live for momentary pleasure but gives us a concrete literary portrait of a seducer in *Either/Or I*, a portrait that is both beguiling and horrifying. This kind of imaginative portrayal of truth has a better chance of engaging the emotions of readers than a more straightforward philosophical treatise.

I believe that C. S. Lewis was trying to do something similar when he added such imaginative works as the novel *Till We Have Faces*, the Narnia books, *The Screwtape Letters*, and *The Great Divorce* to his Christian writings such as *Mere Christianity*, *The Problem of Pain*, and *Miracles*. In this way Lewis himself hoped to help remedy the problem he diagnosed in *The Abolition of Man* as endemic to modern society, which has created "men without chests" who cannot grasp moral truths because they have lost the emotions which make it possible to grasp such truths.[23]

Becoming individuals. Another barrier to spiritual life that Kierkegaard saw as pervasive in modern, Western society was a tendency to think in terms of collective abstractions that prevent an individual from thinking responsibly as an individual. There are several forms this malady can take.

One form consists in assuming that my religious and moral status is simply a function of the group to which I belong. This is the main error of "Christendom," which equates being a Christian with being a member of an allegedly Christian society. According to this way of thinking, Denmark is a Christian country, so if I am a Dane, and I don't happen to be Jewish, then I must be a Christian. The antidote is a recognition that Christian existence, while always situated within a particular human culture, can never be identified with any such culture. The Christian's highest allegiance can never be to the nation-state, and one can never equate cultural socialization with Christian formation.

Another form consists in believing that my human task is essentially a function of the historical age to which I happen to belong. Of course, Christian existence must have a particular historical location in time, just as it must have a particular cultural location, and this will certainly make a difference to the form a particular expression of the Christian life must take. However, Kierkegaard believes the essential human tasks are not altered by the historical era in which one happens to live. Every human has the task of becoming the self God intends that person to be, and though that self is always individual and particular, there are universal qualities that will be included in every individual vocation. Every person has the task of learning to love God whole-heartedly and of loving the neighbor as oneself. Every person has the task of becoming compassionate and forgiving, honest and transparent before God. To think that because one lives in a modern or postmodern

---

[23]C. S. Lewis, "Men Without Chests," in *The Abolition of Man* (New York: HarperOne, 2001), 1-26.

world, one somehow has a different calling is an illusion. Even if it were true that the modern or postmodern worlds have somehow advanced over previous eras, this makes no difference to the task of the self. Someone who thinks that the advance of history makes human life easier is as foolish as a novice dancer who thinks that modern ballet has advanced so far that he or she does not have to waste time learning traditional moves and steps but can move right into the most advanced forms of dancing.[24]

The final form I shall briefly mention is one that Kierkegaard is well-known for criticizing: a kind of social conformism that thinks the answers to life's questions are given by what "the others" or "most people" think.[25] Kierkegaard compares this kind of social conformist to a child at a fancy party who has not yet learned proper table manners and must look around to see what fork or spoon others are using before eating.[26] The antidote is to have the courage to become yourself before God. Kierkegaard says that a person who is listening to God's call in this way has a quality termed *Primitivitet*. The Hongs translate this as "primitiveness" or "primitivity," but it might better be rendered as *authenticity*.[27]

In the Kierkegaardian sense, becoming an individual is not a matter of seeking some unique non-conformist lifestyle, as was done by the beatniks in the fifties or the hippies in the late sixties. The point is not to be different from other people but to be yourself. That self is something that must be formed; it is not a ready-made object already present as when our contemporaries speak of "finding yourself." Taking responsibility for becoming a self in this sense is the beginning of the ethical life, for it amounts to taking my choices seriously as acts I am accountable for and thereby, the discovery of the self as something distinct from a social product. And, as I have already noted, for Kierkegaard, the

---

[24]This illustration is Kierkegaard's. See Søren Kierkegaard, *Fear and Trembling*, trans. and ed. Howard V. and Edna H. Hong (Princeton, NJ: Princeton University Press, 1983), 46.

[25]Kierkegaard, *Sickness unto Death*, 33-34.

[26]See Kierkegaard, *Concluding Unscientific Postscript*, 244.

[27]Kierkegaard, *Sickness unto Death*, 33.

authentic ethical life is the beginning of spiritual life. The voice of conscience is the voice of God, even if that voice is often heard in a confused and distorted fashion. Beginning to live as spirit is then to recognize oneself as accountable to a moral power higher than oneself and distinct from society.

CHRISTIAN SPIRITUALITY

Christian spirituality, if Kierkegaard's relational account is correct, will consist in recognizing God's presence in specifically Christian ways and thereby developing a new relation to God. Although all humans live before God, some are unaware of this, and Kierkegaard calls them spiritless. Of those who are aware of God, there are degrees of awareness and clarity. The Christian also lives before God but things are now radically different. The Christian does not merely hear God speak through conscience or nature but hears God speak through the history of Israel—culminating in the life, death, and resurrection of Christ—and the founding of Christ's church. God is also heard through the Scriptures, the divinely inspired and authoritative revelation God offers us. Hearing God speak through these forms or (to change the metaphor) seeing God as present through those forms makes possible an awareness of God that is both clearer and more intense than is possible through generic human spirituality.

If one asks how this kind of spirituality is to be nourished, in one sense Kierkegaard's answers are quite traditional: through reading Scripture and meditating on it, through prayer, and through participation in public worship, in particular the sacrament of Communion. Although these are standard Christian answers, Kierkegaard has something important to say about each of them.

Reading Scripture. That Kierkegaard was himself an ardent and devoted reader of Scripture can easily be seen from reading his works, which contain multiple scriptural quotations and allusions on virtually every page, not only in the signed religious writings but usually in the pseudonymous writings as well. However, Kierkegaard's best-known and most important views on how Scripture should be read can be found in one of his "Discourses," titled "What Is Required in Order to Look at Oneself with True Blessing in the Mirror of the Word?"[28] This sermon-like essay is a meditation on James 1:22-27, focusing especially on verses 22-25.

Kierkegaard begins with James's admonition to be a doer of the Word and not merely a hearer of God's Word. Naturally, however, one cannot be a doer of the Word if one has not heard it or read it, and that becomes Kierkegaard's theme: How can we read or hear the Scriptures so that we can become doers of the Word and thereby obtain true blessing? James himself compares the Scripture to a mirror and says that a person who merely listens and does not obey is like a man who looks in a mirror but then immediately forgets what he looks like. Kierkegaard thus proceeds to consider the Word of God as kind of mirror and asks what this means for us as readers. Specifically, what are the practices whereby we can become people who hear God's Word?

The first point he makes is that we are not to focus on the mirror of Scripture itself but on "seeing oneself in the mirror."[29] One way we can go wrong is by making God's Word simply an object of scholarship to be studied rather than reading it to hear God speak to us. When reading God's Word, it is easy to get lost in the intricacies of scholarship and forget the purpose of reading the Bible:

> As for ways of reading, there are thirty thousand different ways. And then this crowd of scholars and opinions, and learned opinions and unlearned opinions about how the particular passage is to be understood. . . . Is it not true that all this seems to be rather complicated! God's Word is the mirror—in reading it or hearing it, I am supposed to see myself in the mirror—but look, this business of the mirror is so confusing that I very likely never come to see myself reflected—at least not if I go at it this way.[30]

Kierkegaard even expresses some suspicion that some of this scholarly machinery is "human craftiness," providing an excuse for our failure to

---

[28]This is part one of Søren Kierkegaard, *For Self-Examination,* trans. Howard V. Hong and Edna H. Hong (Princeton, NJ: Princeton University Press, 1990), 13-51.

[29]Kierkegaard, *Self-Examination,* 25.

[30]Kierkegaard, *Self-Examination,* 26.

obey God, since by approaching Scripture in a scholarly way we never become clear on what God actually requires of us.

We must be careful here not to make the mistake of thinking that Kierkegaard is here disparaging honest biblical scholarship. He makes this clear by an extended analogy. Imagine that you are in love but that the person you love speaks a foreign language you do not understand. You receive a letter from your lover, one that you long to read. However, in order to understand what your lover wrote, you must laboriously translate the letter, and this requires working to understand the grammar and vocabulary of the foreign language, perhaps even enlisting the help of experts in that language. However, all of this labor is not the same thing as reading the letter; it is preliminary work, and if the letter is never read as a letter from one's beloved, then in a sense it is pointless and wasted labor. So Kierkegaard does recognize the importance and value of good translators and those who can help us understand obscure passages. However, this kind of scholarly labor is a precursor to actually reading God's Word. If we never get to the point of reading the Scriptures to hear God speak to us, then we have forgotten what drew us to the Bible in the first place. So the first practice Kierkegaard recommends is the practice of reading Scripture so as to understand God's ideals so we have a clear understanding of ourselves in light of those ideals.

It is true of course, and Kierkegaard recognizes this, that there is much in the Bible that is obscure and hard to understand. Kierkegaard says that this fact gives us no excuse for not reading God's Word:

> When you are reading God's Word, it is not the obscure passages that bind you but what you understand, and with that you are to comply at once. If you understand only one single passage in all of Holy Scripture, well, then you must do that first of all, but you do not first have to sit down and ponder the obscure passages. God's Word is given in order that you shall act according to it, not that you shall practice interpreting obscure passages.[31]

---

[31]Kierkegaard, *Self-Examination*, 29.

If the one who received a letter from a lover did not understand parts of the letter, this would not excuse the lover from immediately complying with some desire that the lover clearly expressed in another part of the letter. When we read God's Word we should strive to read like that lover reads the letter.

The second practice Kierkegaard recommends is that when we read God's Word, we should be alone.[32] He does not of course mean that God's Word should never be read as part of corporate worship or even that there is no place for a group reading and discussion. He does mean that we must somehow open ourselves up to hear God's address as it is directed to us as individuals. If we always read Scripture as part of a Bible study or class, then we will be tempted anew to treat the Scriptures as if they were simply an object of scholarship. When we read alone and are honest, we will recognize much that we can understand easily; the hard part is obeying. It is just for this reason most of us want to avoid being alone with God's Word. We do not want to obey, and also do not want to admit that we fall short of God's standard.

The third practice Kierkegaard recommends is that we constantly remind ourselves that the Scriptures are talking about us. "Remember to say to yourself incessantly: It is I to whom it is speaking; it is I about whom it is speaking."[33] While Christendom would like us to believe that such a practice is vanity and narcissism, Kierkegaard says it is actually essential to "earnestness" or "soberness" before God. Kierkegaard draws on the story of David and Bathsheba and the confrontation between David and Nathan the prophet to make this point. David, of course, lusting after Bathsheba, has managed to get her husband killed and has taken her for his wife. Nathan tells David a story about a rich man with many sheep who steals one from a poor neighbor who has one little lamb who is a pet, and the rich man feeds the lamb to a guest. David is wrathful and expresses the view that the rich man deserves death. Nathan responds, "You are the man."

---

[32]Kierkegaard, *Self-Examination*, 30.
[33]Kierkegaard, *Self-Examination*, 35.

As Kierkegaard notes, David already knew that it was morally wrong for him to have another man killed so he could marry his wife. He did not need to know an objective moral principle. What he needed was to apply that principle to himself: "this was the transition to the subjective."[34] No matter how much knowledge we have of what the Scripture teaches, we will not hear God's Word until we say to ourselves what Nathan said to David, "You are the man (or the woman)."

Kierkegaard illustrates this practice by giving a reading of the story of the Good Samaritan. When we read of the priest or the Levite who passed by the wounded traveler, we should recognize that we are people who pass by those who are hurt and wounded in our world. When we read of the Samaritan who stopped to help, we must read the story as describing the self we ought to become. What Christ said to the Pharisee who agreed that the Samaritan had acted as a neighbor must be applied to ourselves: "Go and do likewise."

The next practice Kierkegaard recommends is a kind of immediate commitment to remembering (and obeying) what God says. If we are not to be like the person who looks in a mirror and then forgets what he looks like, then we must remember what God has said to us and about us. However, the best way to ensure that this is the case is to promptly remind yourself to remember. Grand resolutions are of little help: "Ah, my friend, it is far better that you never forget to remember promptly than that you promptly say, I will never forget it."[35]

Finally, Kierkegaard recommends the practice of silence if we are to hear God's Word. If we are always chattering about what God has said, and perhaps talking about how to obey, we will never really hear God speak. In discussing this, Kierkegaard claims—in a way that will seem sexist to contemporary readers—that this is something that women, who have been told to keep silent in the churches, have learned well. However, it is clear that he thinks this is a lesson that men need to learn as well. The woman of his society is not being "put

---

[34]Kierkegaard, *Self-Examination*, 38.
[35]Kierkegaard, *Self-Examination*, 44.

in her place," but put forward as a model that men ought to strive to follow.

Prayer. There is less to say about Kierkegaard's view of prayer than his view of Scripture reading. We know that Kierkegaard prayed on a daily basis, but of course we do not have access to the contents of his private prayers. We do know how important and vital he considered prayer: "The Church Fathers were right in observing that to pray is to breathe. Here we see the stupidity of talking about a why, for why do I breathe? Because otherwise I would die—and so it is with praying."[36]

Although we do not know the content of Kierkegaard's private prayers, Kierkegaard wrote out many prayers, which are used at the beginning of virtually all of his edifying or upbuilding writings. A large number of these published prayers have been collected and published separately by Perry Lefevre; they repay close reading and can helpfully be prayed by one seeking to grow spiritually.[37] Lefevre organizes the book by classifying the prayers by the persons of the Trinity primarily invoked, thus displaying the Trinitarian character of Kierkegaard's prayer life.[38] There is also a helpful section of prayers Kierkegaard composed for special occasions such as confession, weddings, and funerals. Lefevre also includes a thoughtful treatment of Kierkegaard as a man of prayer.

Kierkegaard's prayers largely consist of worshipful adoration of God and a recounting of what God does for us and offers to us. He thereby helps us avoid a common fault in prayer life, in which prayer is reduced simply to a series of requests for divine aid. In prayer we do not simply ask God for things, but we focus our hearts and minds on who God is and what God has done.

---

[36]Søren Kierkegaard, *Søren Kierkegaard's Journals and Papers*, ed. and trans. Howard V. Hong and Edna H. Hong (Bloomington: Indiana University Press, 1975), 3:568, entry # 3432.

[37]Søren Kierkegaard, *The Prayers of Kierkegaard*, cd. Perry Lefevre (Chicago: University of Chicago Press, 1996). There is also a remarkable choral musical setting of some of Kierkegaard's prayers composed by Samuel Barber.

[38]For a wonderful example of Trinitarian prayer, see the prayer at the beginning of *Works of Love*, which invokes each member of the Trinity and the roles of the Divine Persons in creating and fostering love.

Kierkegaard does recognize the importance of intercessory prayer as well and certainly affirms that we should bring our needs before God as frail humans. However, Kierkegaard's requests of God are mainly for spiritual gifts: that we will learn what God wishes us to learn and acquire the qualities God wants to instill in us. When we ask God for finite goods, such as healing of illness or suffering, our requests should always be accompanied by a desire that God's will be done, not just our own wills, because he does not think we can ever be sure of what is really for our good.

We can see this clearly if we look at Kierkegaard's treatment of the book of James, Kierkegaard's favorite book of the Bible (which is quite unusual for a Lutheran). Kierkegaard returns again and again to James 1:17: "Every good and perfect gift is from above, coming down from the Father of lights, with whom there is no variation, neither shadow that is cast by turning" (ASV).[39] Kierkegaard's exegesis of this text stresses the fact that what makes a gift "good and perfect" is not determined by the content of the gift but by the fact that it comes from God. When received with gratitude from God's hand, every "gift" is a good and perfect, even the gift of suffering. In fact, when we pray in Jesus' name, what we are really doing is affirming that we want the will of Jesus to be done. When I pray in this way, "I dare put the name of Jesus to my prayer, that is, picture him, his holy will, together with what I am praying about."[40] This practice is also the antidote to the problems with prayer James identifies later: "When you ask you do not receive, because you ask with wrong motives, that you may spend what you get on your pleasures" (Jas 4:3).

Public worship and Communion. Because of Kierkegaard's attack on the state church at the end of his life, it may be odd to picture Kierkegaard as someone who sees participation in public worship as one of the ways we encounter God. However, we should remember that for almost all of

---

[39]Kierkegaard says this was "the first text I ever used," and he returned to it frequently, including a final discourse published at the very end of his life, during the attack on the state church. See "The Unchangeableness of God." This is included in Søren Kierkegaard, *The Moment and Late Writings*, trans. and ed. Howard V. Hong and Edna H. Hong (Princeton, NJ: Princeton University Press, 1998).

[40]Kierkegaard, *Journals and Papers*, 3:371, entry #3441.

his life, Kierkegaard was a faithful church attender. He was particularly fond of the Communion services the Danish Church held on Fridays in those days.

Kierkegaard gives us a clear picture of the purpose of participation in public worship. All too frequently, even in Kierkegaard's day and certainly in our own, those who go to church see the service as a kind of performance, which they are entitled to judge. Understood in this way, Christian worship becomes a kind of aesthetic experience, and the worshiper confuses himself with an art critic.[41] When the worshiper sees the service as a performance, with those attending constituting the audience, then the quality of the pastor's sermon, the choir's singing, or even the quality of the voice of the liturgist become the primary focus of attention, and much of the attention is directed to the artistic quality of the service.

Kierkegaard says that the true worshiper sees things entirely differently. Those attending the service are not the audience but rather the performers who are there to perform the act of worshiping God. The audience is God himself, and God does not judge the worship on aesthetic grounds. The pastor, organist, choir director, and liturgist are seen as "prompters" for the worshipers, much as in the theater the actors sometimes need prompters to help them remember their lines and do their parts correctly. When we see ourselves as active in worship, and God as the primary audience for our activity, our view of worship will change fundamentally.

Kierkegaard not only regularly attended Friday Communion services but occasionally delivered the sermon or homily at such services. Over the course of his authorship, he actually published thirteen of these "Discourses," only a few of which were actually delivered in churches.[42] In the preface to the last of these, Kierkegaard affirms that these

---

[41]Kierkegaard's discussion of worship on this point can be found in Kierkegaard, *Upbuilding Discourses*, 124-25.

[42]Recently Sylvia Walsh has collected all thirteen of these discourses, retranslating them and publishing them in one volume. See Søren Kierkegaard, *Discourses at the Communion on Fridays*, ed. and trans. Sylvia Walsh (Bloomington: Indiana University Press, 2011).

Communion discourses have a decisive importance for his authorship. He says that the authorship as a whole "points definitively to" and "gathers itself together in" these Discourses. In them the authorship "reaches its decisive point of rest" at the foot of the altar.[43]

Why does Kierkegaard see Communion as having such importance? One reason is that Communion requires confession and repentance, both of which are essential if sinful humans are to enjoy God's presence. However, equally important, Kierkegaard believes that in Communion Christ is really present to those who participate in faith. In a regular worship service, God's Word can be heard in the sermon, even though the words are those of the pastor. However, in the Communion service, even if the pastor speaks, the service is not about the words of the pastor. What the pastor says is only to help the communicant "pause on the way to the Communion table so that through the speaker's voice you yourself confess privately and secretly before God."[44] Nothing has any importance that does not direct us to hear God speaking to us through Christ's voice: "Today it is very particularly, is simply and solely, his voice that is to be heard. Everything otherwise done here is only for the purpose of concentrating the attention of the mind on this, that it is his voice that is to be heard."[45]

What does Christ say to us in communion?

It must be his voice that you hear when he says, Come here, all you who labor and are burdened—therefore his voice that invites you. And it must be his voice you hear when he says: This is my body. At the Communion table there is no speaking about him; there he himself is present in person; there it is he who is speaking—if not, then you are not at the Communion table. In the physical sense, one can point to the Communion table and say, "There it is," but, in the spiritual sense, it is actually there only if you hear his voice there.[46]

---

[43]See Sylvia Walsh's discussion of this in Walsh, "Introduction," in *Discourses*, 4-5. Kierkegaard's affirmation can also be found in the Hong edition of Kierkegaard's Writings. Søren Kierkegaard, *Without Authority*, ed. and trans. Howard V. Hong and Edna H. Hong (Princeton, NJ: Princeton University Press, 1997), 165. This volume contains the preface to the "Two Discourses at the Communion on Fridays" from 1849.

[44]Søren Kierkegaard, *Christian Discourses*, trans. and ed. Howard V. Hong and Edna H. Hong (Princeton, NJ: Princeton University Press, 1997), 271.

[45]Kierkegaard, *Christian Discourses*, 270.

[46]Kierkegaard, *Christian Discourses*, 271.

There is here an interesting juxtaposition: Christ is really present, but that presence is real to you only if you partake in faith, listening to God speak to you.

CONCLUSIONS

We have seen Kierkegaard's view of spirituality is thoroughly relational. To be spirit is to be related to God. All humans possess the capacity to recognize God as Lord through conscience. In one sense God is present to all, since, as St. Paul affirms, quoting a pagan philosopher, "In him we live and move and have our being." However, this generic human spirituality is a potentiality that must be actualized, as we passionately seek to realize our ethical ideals. Striving to do this should prepare us for Christian spirituality.

Christian spirituality arises out of the suffering and guilt that this generic human spirituality encounters and fosters. It offers new and powerful ways to enjoy the presence of God in Christ. Just as is the case for generic spirituality, Christian spirituality is not something given all at once but a process in which God's presence becomes more and more clear and intense. The Christian is called to live his or her life before Christ, who provides a way to God as the Pattern and the Redeemer, the one who points us to the Way and reconciles us to God even as we fail to be all God intended us to be.

BEYOND RESILIENCE, POSTTRAUMATIC GROWTH, AND SELF-CARE

A BIBLICAL PERSPECTIVE ON SUFFERING AND CHRISTIAN SPIRITUAL FORMATION

SIANG-YANG TAN

Two of my recent reviews—one coauthored with Melissa Castillo—addressed the current psychological literature on resilience, posttraumatic growth, and self-care and included a brief Christian or biblical perspective and critique on each of these significant topics.[1] This chapter summarizes these reviews and elaborates on sanctified or redemptive suffering as a crucial process of becoming more like Jesus in Christian spiritual formation.

---

[1]On resilience see, e.g., Donald Meichenbaum, *Roadmap to Resilience: A Guide for Military, Trauma Victims, and Their Families* (Clearwater, FL: Institute Press, 2012). On posttraumatic growth, see, e.g., L. G. Calhoun and R. G. Tedeschi, *Posttraumatic Growth in Clinical Practice* (New York: Routledge, 2013) and S. Joseph, *What Doesn't Kill Us: The New Psychology of Posttraumatic Growth* (New York: Basic Books, 2011). On self-care, see S. S. Canning, "Out of Balance: Why I Hesitate to Practice and Teach 'Self-Care,'" *Journal of Psychology and Christianity* 30 (2011): 70-74 and Siang-Yang Tan, *Counseling and Psychotherapy: A Christian Perspective* (Grand Rapids: Baker Academic, 2011). These have been reviewed by Siang-Yang Tan, "Resilience and Posttraumatic Growth: Empirical Evidence and Clinical Applications from a Christian Perspective," *Journal of Psychology and Christianity* 32 (2013): 358-64 and Siang-Yang Tan and Melissa Castillo, "Self-Care and Beyond: A Brief Literature Review from a Christian Perspective," *Journal of Psychology and Christianity* 33 (2014): 89-94.

RESILIENCE AND POSTTRAUMATIC GROWTH: A BRIEF SUMMARY[2]

The psychological literature on resilience and posttraumatic growth has grown significantly in the last decade or so.[3] Meichenbaum has defined resilience as "the capacity to adapt successfully in the presence of risk and adversity" and it includes the ability to "confront and handle stressful life events, grow and thrive in the face of challenges and adversities; bounce back and beat the odds; recover from or adjust to misfortune or change; endure traumatic events; [and] maintain a healthy outcome."[4] Richard Tedeschi and Lawrence Calhoun first used a related term "posttraumatic growth" to refer to positive changes reported by those who have gone through experiences of trauma and adversity, with the eventual outcome of greater well-being. It has also been termed *"benefit-finding, growth following adversity, personal transformation, stress-related growth, and thriving."*[5]

Although traumatic events (e.g., rape, sexual abuse, terrorist attacks, natural disasters, long-term sickness, major losses, and accidents) affect about 60 percent of the North American population in their lifetime and 20 percent in any one year, only up to 30 percent of them experience harmful effects such as developing posttraumatic stress disorder (PTSD) and other related adjustment problems. About 70 percent actually recover with resilience, and many eventually even experience posttraumatic growth or positive change after going through trauma or major life crises (usually many months later).

ELEMENTS OF RESILIENCE

Resilience and eventual posttraumatic growth require some time to occur after the initial traumatic experiences. Meichenbaum has delineated the following factors that impact people's response to adversities and trauma in their lives:

---

[2]See Tan, "Resilience."
[3]On resilience see, e.g., Meichenbaum, *Roadmap*; on posttraumatic growth, see, e.g., Calhoun and Tedeschi, *Posttraumatic Growth* and Joseph, *What Doesn't Kill Us.*
[4]Meichenbaum, *Roadmap*, 3.
[5]Joseph, *What Doesn't Kill Us*, 14.

- The availability of social relationships and their ability to avail themselves of social supports

- The extent of perceived personal control and use of energies and time on activities and circumstances in which they have some effect

- The extent to which they can have positive emotions and control negative affect. Those who daily experience a 3 to 1 ratio of positive emotions to negative ones tend to be resilient

- The ability to function with cognitive flexibility, using problem-solving and acceptance skills, depending on the situation

- The ability to be involved in activities that follow their priorities and values in life and for their future

- The type and number of social and emotional resources (guidance, empathy) as well as material resources (financial support) that are available to them

- The ability to face life's adversities and trauma, work through them, and share their struggles with others, instead of denying or avoiding negative emotions and pain[6]

Southwick and Charney, in their intensive study of 250 American prisoners of war from the Vietnam War who experienced solitary confinement and torture in their imprisonment up to eight years but who had lower than expected incidence of PTSD and depression years after their release, came up with the following prescription for a resilient life:

- Establish and nurture a supportive social network

- Engage in positive thinking and feelings

- Develop cognitive flexibility

- Develop a personal "moral compass" or shatterproof set of beliefs

---

[6]Meichenbaum, *Roadmap*, 6, from Tan, "Resilience," 358-59.

- Be altruistic
- Find a resilient model in a mentor or hero figure
- Learn to be adaptive in facing fears
- Develop active coping skills
- Have a sense of humor and laugh frequently
- Keep fit[7]

Meichenbaum also described several helpful strategies (including the above) for enhancing resilience in six major areas of fitness:

1. Physical fitness
2. Interpersonal fitness
3. Emotional fitness
4. Thinking fitness
5. Behavioral fitness
6. Spiritual fitness[8]

Similarly, Joseph has also described six signposts for facilitating post-traumatic growth, using a THRIVE model:

1. Taking stock
2. Harvesting hope
3. Re-authoring
4. Identifying change
5. Valuing change
6. Expressing change in action[9]

Meichenbaum has noted that the major religions of the world including Christianity, Judaism, Islam, Buddhism, and Hinduism all affirm

---

[7]M. Southwick and D. S. Charney, *Resilience: The Science of Mastering Life's Greatest Challenges* (West Nyack, NY: Cambridge University Press, 2012), in Meichenbaum, *Roadmap*, 12-13.
[8]Meichenbaum, *Roadmap*, 191-96.
[9]Joseph, *What Doesn't Kill Us*, 175-76.

that suffering is part and parcel of life, but they also teach that suffering can lead to growth or transformation as the eventual outcome.[10] Resilience and posttraumatic growth can therefore be the result of going through the pain of trauma and tragedy. While the Bible does support the view that people can grow through suffering, a Christian, biblical perspective on suffering and its relationship to posttraumatic growth or benefit-finding is actually more nuanced and paradoxical. Such a biblical perspective on sanctified or redemptive suffering and how it relates to Christian spiritual formation into deeper Christlikeness will be expanded and elaborated on later in this chapter. I have already briefly described a more biblical perspective on suffering and resilience and posttraumatic growth thus:

> However, a biblical or Christian perspective on suffering goes beyond affirming and emphasizing its potential benefits and blessings. Benefit-finding is not the ultimate meaning or end of human suffering. A deeper biblical view on suffering will also focus on knowing God and sharing in the fellowship of Christ's sufferings (Phil 3:10) in union and communion with him. Concrete benefits and blessings may not be apparent or clear but God is doing his deeper work of grace in our hearts and lives through redemptive and sanctified suffering, and in so doing reveals his greatest glory in and through us. . . . A biblical perspective on suffering must eventually be Christ-centered and cross-centered, but requiring also the power of His resurrection (Phil 3:10) and the help of the Holy Spirit as the Divine Comforter and Counselor (Jn 14:16-17).[11]

SELF-CARE AND BEYOND: A BRIEF SUMMARY[12]

Self-care is another important topic that continues to receive much attention in the psychological literature and research. As Tan and Castillo have pointed out in their recent review of self-care: "Self-care is crucial for the well-being of the counselor. It is also essential for the efficient, effective, and ethical practice of counseling, for the ultimate benefit and

---

[10]Meichenbaum, Roadmap, 7.
[11]Tan, "Resilience," 363.
[12]See Tan and Castillo, "Self-Care and Beyond," 90-95.

welfare of the client. . . . Self-care is not 'selfish care' or 'self-centered care.'"[13] Elsewhere I have emphasized:

> Self-care for the counselor, however, refers to healthy and wise strategies for taking good care of oneself as a counselor in order to manage stress well and prevent burnout. . . . It is . . . loving and wise to engage in proper self-care that eventually leads to the helping and healing of others.[14]

Various strategies are helpful for facilitating appropriate self-care for the counselor or minister. Norcross and Guy have described the following self-care strategies for psychotherapists and counselors:

1. Valuing the person of the psychotherapist

2. Refocusing on the rewards

3. Recognizing the hazards

4. Minding the body

5. Nurturing relationships

6. Setting boundaries

7. Restructuring cognitions

8. Sustaining healthy escapes

9. Creating a flourishing environment

10. Undergoing personal therapy

11. Cultivating spirituality and mission

12. Fostering creativity and growth[15]

Skovholt recommended the following self-care strategies for sustaining and nurturing the professional self of the therapist or counselor:

1. Avoiding the impulse toward grandiosity

2. Thinking long-term

---

[13]Tan and Castillo, "Self-Care and Beyond," 90.

[14]Tan, *Counseling and Psychotherapy*, 19.

[15]J. C. Norcross and J. D. Guy, *Leaving It at the Office: A Guide to Psychotherapist Self-Care* (New York: Guilford Press, 2007), xvii.

3. Putting together and actively applying an individual development method or plan

4. Cultivating professional self-understanding; creating a professional greenhouse (environment for growth) at work

5. Having leadership that facilitates balance between self-care and caring for others; drawing on professional social support from peers

6. Getting support from bosses, supervisors, and mentors

7. Learning how to be both playful and professional

8. Releasing emotions of distress through professional venting

9. Learning to be a "good enough practitioner"

10. Understanding the reality of early professional anxiety, which is pervasive

11. Reinventing oneself to increase excitement and reduce boredom

12. Dealing with ambiguous professional loss by minimizing it

13. Learning to refuse unreasonable requests[16]

Skovholt also listed the following ten activities for self-care for sustaining the personal self of the therapist or counselor:

1. Being with family

2. Training or education for job skills

3. Pursuing a hobby that is fun

4. Engaging in physical activity

5. Reading

6. Receiving supervision or consultation

7. Socializing at work

---

[16]T. M. Skovholt, *The Resilient Practitioner: Burnout Prevention and Self-Care Strategies for Counselors, Therapists, Teachers, and Health Professionals* (Needham Heights, MA: Allyn & Bacon, 2001), 206-7, 130-44. See also Tan, *Counseling and Psychotherapy*, 20.

8. Having time alone

9. Spending time with friends, partner, spouse

10. Taking a vacation[17]

As one more example of suggestions for self-care for the therapist or counselor, the following are recommendations explicated by Mahoney for therapist self-care in the context of conducting constructive psychotherapy:

1. Be gentle with yourself; honor your own process.

2. Get adequate rest.

3. Make yourself comfortable.

4. Move your body often.

5. Develop a ritual of transition for leaving work at the office.

6. Receive regular professional massages.

7. Cherish your friendship and intimacy with family.

8. Cultivate your commitment to helping; honor the privilege of our profession.

9. Ask for and accept comfort, help, and counsel (including personal therapy).

10. Create a support network among your colleagues.

11. Enjoy yourself.

12. Follow your heart and embrace your spiritual seeking.[18]

Tan and Castillo also provided a brief biblical perspective on self-care that affirms appropriate self-care for the Christian counselor or minister, just as Jesus took time off to rest and to be in prayer and solitude.[19]

---

[17]Skovholt, *The Resilient Practitioner*, 212.

[18]M. J. Mahoney, *Constructive Psychotherapy: A Practical Guide* (New York: Guilford Press, 2003), 260-61.

[19]Tan and Castillo, "Self-Care and Beyond"; see Siang-Yang Tan, *Full Service: Moving from Self-Serve Christianity to Total Servanthood* (Grand Rapids: Baker Books, 2006), 34; Siang-Yang Tan, *Rest: Experiencing God's Peace in a Restless World* (Vancouver, BC: Regent College Publishing, 2003).

However, they point out that a biblical perspective on self-care will critique the concept of self-care and go beyond it to trust in "God-care" for us and "we-care" in a loving community or the church for one another. They concluded,

> Beyond "self"-care—or beyond our abilities to care for ourselves—is God's desire to care for us through friendship with Christ and through friendships with others in Christian community. Beyond self-care is "God-care" for us, and "we-care" or "community-care" in the body of Christ for one another, where healing relationships, role-models, accountability, bearing one another's burdens, and other interdependent maturing aspects of spiritual formation promote health, growth, and resilience.[20]

Furthermore, Canning has biblically critiqued a view of self-care that emphasizes keeping one's life in "balance" all the time. She expressed her hesitation in teaching and practicing such "self-care" because from a biblical perspective we need to go beyond balanced self-care to stewardship and even sanctified suffering that may at times knock us out of balance and greatly stretch us.[21] We need to trust more in God's sovereign provision and grace for us, and therefore in "God-care" for us.[22] A deeper biblical perspective on self-care and beyond—which goes beyond resilience, posttraumatic growth, and self-care—includes a more substantial elaboration on sanctified suffering and its crucial role in Christian spiritual formation into greater Christlikeness. This is the topic we now will cover.

BEYOND RESILIENCE, POSTTRAUMATIC GROWTH, AND SELF-CARE: A BIBLICAL PERSPECTIVE ON SANCTIFIED SUFFERING AND CHRISTIAN SPIRITUAL FORMATION

There is much biblical teaching on the topic of suffering, including an emphasis on how we can grow spiritually and become more like

---

[20]Tan and Castillo, "Self-Care and Beyond," 93.
[21]Canning, "Out of Balance."
[22]Tan and Castillo, "Self-Care and Beyond."

Jesus through the trials and afflictions of our lives (e.g., see Rom 5:3-5; 8:18, 28-29; 2 Cor 4:16-18; Jas 1:2-4; 1 Pet 4:1-2, 12-13; 5:10). In recent years, the literature on suffering from a Christian, biblical perspective has grown.[23] Some of this literature will now be briefly reviewed and summarized.

Tada and Estes have compiled a list of thirty-six blessings or benefits, based on Scripture, that can come from the hand of God working through hardship and suffering. The following are some of them as mentioned by Tan:

1. God uses suffering to refine, perfect, strengthen, and keep us from falling (Ps 66:8-9; Heb 2:10).

2. Suffering allows the life of Christ to be manifested in our mortal flesh (2 Cor 4:7-11).

3. Suffering bankrupts us, making us dependent on God (2 Cor 12:9).

4. Suffering teaches us humility (2 Cor 12:7).

5. Suffering teaches us that God is more concerned with character rather than comfort (Rom 5:3-4; Heb 12:10-11).

6. Suffering teaches us that the greatest good of the Christian life is not the absence of pain but Christlikeness (Rom 8:28-29; 2 Cor 4:8-10).

---

[23]E.g., see R. Alcorn, *If God Is Good: Faith in the Midst of Suffering and Evil* (Colorado Springs: Multnomah Books, 2009); Larry Crabb, *Shattered Dreams: God's Unexpected Pathway to Joy* (Colorado Springs: WaterBrook Press, 2001); T. Keller, *Walking with God Through Pain and Suffering* (New York: Dutton, 2013); C. W. Morgan and R. A. Peterson, eds., *Suffering and the Goodness of God* (Wheaton, IL: Crossway, 2008); John Piper and Justin Taylor, eds., *Suffering and the Sovereignty of God* (Wheaton, IL: Crossway Books, 2006), especially Piper, "Suffering and the Sovereignty of God: Ten Aspects of God's Sovereignty over Suffering and Satan's Hand in It," 17-30; Piper, "The Suffering of Christ and the Sovereignty of God," 81-89; and Piper, "Why God Appoints Suffering for His Servants," 91-109; R. Rice, *Suffering and the Search for Meaning* (Downers Grove, IL: InterVarsity Press, 2014); J. E. Tada and S. Estes, *When God Weeps: Why Our Sufferings Matter to the Almighty* (Grand Rapids: Zondervan, 1997); T. Tchividjian, *Glorious Ruin: How Suffering Sets You Free* (Colorado Springs: David C. Cook, 2012); Gary Thomas, *Authentic Faith: The Power of a Fire-Tested Life* (Grand Rapids: Zondervan, 2002); C. Tiegreen, *Why a Suffering World Makes Sense* (Grand Rapids: Baker Books, 2006). See also Mother Teresa, *Come Be My Light* (New York: Doubleday, 2007) and P. Murray, *I Loved Jesus in the Night: Teresa of Calcutta—A Secret Revealed* (Brewster, MA: Paraclete Press, 2008).

7. Suffering can be a chastisement from God for sin and rebellion (Ps 107:17).

8. Obedience and self-control are learned through suffering (Ps 119:67; Rom 5:1-5; Heb 5:8).

9. Suffering strengthens and allows us to comfort others who are weak (2 Cor 1:3-11).[24]

Some of the blessings or benefits of suffering, from a biblical perspective, are therefore not always concrete or obvious in this life on earth. They may be blessings that are more spiritual in nature, unseen to the physical senses, or they may be blessings only actualized and experienced in heaven to come.

John Piper has also delineated several reasons for why God appoints suffering for his servants. They include the following:

1. Suffering deepens faith and holiness (2 Cor 1:8-9; Heb 5:8; 12:10).

2. Suffering makes your cup increase (Mt 5:11-12; Rom 8:18; 2 Cor 4:17-18).

3. Suffering is the price of making others bold (Jn 12:24; Phil 1:14).

4. Suffering fills up what is lacking in Christ's afflictions (2 Cor 1:5-6; Col 1:24).

5. Suffering enforces the missionary command to go (Lk 21:12-13; Acts 8:1; 11:19; cf. Mk 13:9).

6. The supremacy of Christ is manifest in suffering (Ps 63:3; Mt 5:11-12; Acts 5:41; Rom 5:2; 2 Cor 1:9; 12:9-10; Heb 10:34).[25]

Furthermore, Piper writes that "glad suffering shines brighter than gratitude," emphasizing that joy and love in our suffering glorifies God and impacts people and nations with true hope in God more than gratitude for the gifts we receive from God the giver.[26] In Piper's own words,

---

[24]Tada and Estes, *When God Weeps*, 232-40; Tan, *Full Service*, 77.
[25]Piper, "Why God Appoints," 91-109.
[26]Piper, "Why God Appoints," 108.

What proves that the giver is precious is the glad-hearted readiness to leave all his gifts to be with him. This is why suffering is so central in the mission of the church. The goal of our mission is that people from all nations worship the true God. But worship means cherishing the preciousness of God above all else, including life itself. It will be very hard to bring the nations to love God from a lifestyle that communicates a love of things. Therefore, God ordains in the lives of his messengers that suffering sever our bondage to the world. When joy and love survive this severing, we are fit to say to the nations with authenticity and power: hope in God.[27]

Piper also explicates well how hope in God is made visible, based on 1 Peter 3:15:

What Peter is saying is that the world should see a different hope in the lives of Christians—not a hope in the security of money or the security of power or the security of homes or lands or portfolios, but the security of "the grace that is coming to you at the revelation of Jesus Christ" (1 Pet 1:13, author's translation).[28]

Piper then focuses on how suffering is crucial in making our true hope in God visible to the world thus:

Therefore, God ordains suffering to help us release our hold on worldly hopes and put our "hope in God" (1 Pet 1:21). The fiery trials are appointed to consume the earthly dependencies and leave only the refined gold of "genuine faith" (1 Pet 1:7). . . . Therefore joy in suffering for Christ's sake makes the supremacy of God shine more clearly than all our gratitude for wealth.[29]

In another chapter in the excellent book *Suffering and the Sovereignty of God*, edited by Piper and Taylor, Piper describes ten aspects of God's sovereignty over suffering and Satan's hand in it. They include the following:

1. Let us celebrate that God is sovereign over Satan's Delegated World Rule.
2. Let us celebrate that God is sovereign over Satan's angels (demons, evil spirits).

---

[27]Piper, "Why God Appoints," 109.
[28]Piper, "Why God Appoints," 109.
[29]Piper, "Why God Appoints," 109.

3. Let us celebrate that God is sovereign over Satan's hand in persecution.

4. Let us celebrate that God is sovereign over Satan's life-taking power.

5. Let us celebrate that God is sovereign over Satan's hand in natural disasters.

6. Let us celebrate that God is sovereign over Satan's sickness-causing power.

7. Let us celebrate that God is sovereign over Satan's use of animals and plants.

8. Let us celebrate that God is sovereign over Satan's temptations to sin.

9. Let us celebrate that God is sovereign over Satan's mind-blinding power.

10. Let us celebrate that God is sovereign over Satan's spiritual bondage.[30]

While it is very helpful to hold on to the sovereignty of God over our suffering and Satan's hand in it, it can still be particularly painful and devastating for us when we experience shattered dreams in our lives. However, Larry Crabb has described shattered dreams as God's unexpected pathway to joy. Based on the book of Ruth and the story of Naomi, he concludes with the following essential lessons of brokenness:

> Lesson 1—The good news of the gospel is not that God will provide a way to make life easier. . . . He will make our lives better. We will be empowered to draw closer to God and to love others well . . . to glorify God. Lesson 2—When God seems most absent from us, He is doing His most important work in us. Lesson 3—Bad times provide an opportunity to know God that blessings can never provide.[31]

Years earlier, A. W. Tozer described a similar process that he termed "the ministry of the night" thus:

> To do His supreme work of grace within you, He will take away from your heart everything you love most. Everything you trust in will go from you. Piles of ashes will lie where your most precious treasures used to be . . . slowly you will discover God's love in your suffering. . . . You will feel and understand the ministry of the night; its power to purify, to detach, to humble, to destroy the fear of death, and what is more important to you at the moment, the fear

---

[30]Piper and Taylor, *Suffering and the Sovereignty of God*, especially Piper, "Suffering and the Sovereignty of God: Ten Aspects," 19-30.

[31]Crabb, *Shattered Dreams*, 155, 157, 159.

of life. And you will learn that sometimes pain can do what even joy cannot, such as exposing the vanity of earth's trifles and filling your heart with longing for the peace of heaven.[32]

Another similar but more comprehensive concept that has become well-known in the Christian spiritual formation literature is what St. John of the Cross has described as "the dark night of the soul." As Richard Foster has pointed out, the dark night (see Is 50:10) is meant to draw us closer to God and to set us free, and therefore it is not a destructive, primitive, or bad thing. It may include experiences of dryness, aloneness, or even lostness, leading to the removal of any overdependence on the emotional life.[33]

It is well known that Mother Teresa of Calcutta actually experienced a very prolonged and unusual true dark night of the soul in her own spiritual life for about fifty years, shortly after she founded the Missionaries of Charity until her death in 1997.[34] She apparently had a brief period of respite from her dark night ten years into it (in 1958) during a Mass conducted in the cathedral in Calcutta when she experienced an extraordinary illumination. For a short while, her long darkness, pain of loss, and loneliness disappeared and she was filled with love and joy untold instead, in an unbroken union of love.[35] In her long dark night, Mother Teresa experienced the absence and blankness of God, subjectively feeling unwanted, unloved, alone, empty, and dark deep in her soul, often crying out "My God" or "Where is Jesus?"[36] She was mystically sharing in the deepest passion of the fellowship of Christ's sufferings (Phil 3:10), and yet was able to still love God and others, being his light to the poorest of the poor, the unwanted and unloved and rejected lepers and others in Calcutta, India, deeply feeling what they felt, and how Jesus felt for them.

---

[32]A. W. Tozer, *That Incredible Christian* (Beaverlodge, AB: Horizon House, 1977), 122, 124.

[33]See R. J. Foster, *Celebration of Discipline*, rev. ed. (San Francisco: HarperSanFrancisco, 1988), 102-4.

[34]See Mother Teresa, *Come Be My Light*.

[35]Murray, *I Loved Jesus*, 52.

[36]See Mother Teresa, *Come Be My Light*, 1-2, 307.

However, her very prolonged experience of the dark night of the soul is unique and not typical of most dark night experiences that are usually of shorter duration.

In all of these experiences of suffering, whether it be shattered dreams, the ministry of the night, or the dark night of the soul, a common element in all of them is that of brokenness from a biblical perspective. Psalm 51:16-17 states: "You do not delight in sacrifice, or I would bring it; you do not take pleasure in burnt offerings. My sacrifice, O God, is a broken spirit; a broken and contrite heart you, God, You will not despise" (NIV). Such biblical brokenness, holy and healthy, is precious to God and essential for us in Christian spiritual formation into deeper Christlikeness. It involves coming to the end of ourselves and learning to utterly depend on God and surrender to him, embracing the reality that we can do absolutely nothing without Christ (Jn 15:5). Nelson has helpfully differentiated between voluntary and involuntary brokenness. Voluntary brokenness involves intentional submission to God, revolving around the practice of the traditional spiritual disciplines as behaviors of brokenness.[37] Such traditional spiritual disciplines or behaviors of brokenness, following Richard Foster and Dallas Willard, include the behaviors of abstinence (solitude, silence, fasting, simplicity, chastity, sacrifice, and secrecy), and disciplines of activity (study, prolonged prayer, celebration, service, fellowship, confession, and submission).[38] Involuntary brokenness happens to us and occurs when we least expect it, with experiences such as "health issues, financial distress, relationship turmoil, job disruption, dream frustrations, aging milestones, and periods of spiritual and emotional dryness."[39]

The traditional spiritual disciplines as behaviors of brokenness can help us to maintain voluntary brokenness if they are practiced in the power of the Holy Spirit and by God's grace.[40] However, they can also

---

[37]A. E. Nelson, *Embracing Brokenness: How God Refines Us Through Life's Disappointments* (Colorado Springs: NavPress, 2002), 105.

[38]Nelson, *Embracing Brokenness*, 108-16.

[39]Nelson, *Embracing Brokenness*, 104.

[40]Siang-Yang Tan and D. H. Gregg, *Disciplines of the Holy Spirit* (Grand Rapids: Zondervan, 1997).

be potentially dangerous if they are practiced by self-effort in the sinful nature or false self (or legalistically) because they can harm our spiritual life and growth in Christ by producing self-righteousness, self-sufficiency, and spiritual pride. Gary Thomas has therefore described another category of spiritual disciplines that he calls "authentic disciplines" that are akin to involuntary brokenness experiences mentioned by Nelson.[41] They include the disciplines of selflessness, waiting, suffering, persecution, social mercy, forgiveness, mourning, contentment, sacrifice, hope, and fear, which are mostly initiated outside of us and therefore are such a crucial or vital addition to the traditional spiritual disciplines. As Thomas puts it,

> They turn us away from human effort—from men and women seeking the face of God—and turn us back toward God seeking the face of men and women. . . . God brings them into our life when he wills and as he wills. . . . This is a God-ordained spirituality, dependent on his sovereignty. . . . There's no pride left when God takes me through a time of suffering. There is no self-righteousness when I am called to wait. There is no religiosity when I am truly mourning. This is a spirituality I can't control, I can't initiate, I can't bring about. It is a radical dependence on God's husbandry. All I can do is try to appreciate it and learn from it.[42]

Ultimately, the authentic disciplines initiated or sent by God lead to *"learning to love with God's love and learning to serve with God's power."*[43]

The apostle Paul listed and described the various and many trials and afflictions he suffered in his life and ministry as a servant of Jesus Christ, including imprisonment; beatings and floggings; shipwrecks; dangers of all kinds (e.g., bandits, persecutions); extreme labor and toil; sleeplessness; hunger and thirst; and the daily pressure from concern for all the churches (2 Cor 1:3-11; 4:7-12; 11:16-33). He also struggled with "a thorn in his flesh" that was not removed, but grace was given him daily, and he experienced how God's power is perfected in weakness, so that

---

[41]Thomas, *Authentic Faith*, 7.
[42]Thomas, *Authentic Faith*, 14-15.
[43]Thomas, *Authentic Faith*, 12.

when he was weak he really was strong in God's power and grace
(2 Cor 12:7-10). He even learned how to comfort others in their trials and
sufferings with the comfort he received from God in his own afflictions
and sufferings (2 Cor 1:3-4). The extent to which Paul and his colleagues
suffered and were stretched even beyond their own endurance is clearly
stated in 2 Corinthians 1:

> We do not want you to be uninformed, brothers and sisters, about the
> troubles we experienced in the province of Asia. We were under great
> pressure, far beyond our ability to endure, so that we despaired of life itself.
> Indeed, we felt we had received the sentence of death. But this happened
> that we might not rely on ourselves but on God, who raises the dead.
> (2 Cor 1:8-9 NIV)

A deeper biblical perspective on such sanctified or redemptive suffering and its crucial role in Christian spiritual formation in becoming
more like Jesus, therefore, focuses especially on a Christ-centered and
cross-centered mystical sharing in the passion and fellowship of Christ's
sufferings (Phil 3:10), as Mother Teresa and the apostle experienced. It
does not make benefit-finding the ultimate end or outcome of suffering,
especially if benefits or blessings are defined more concretely as limited
to good outcomes on earth, or worse still, as Tchividjian has pointed out,
if benefit-finding refers to the "Oprah-fication of suffering" that makes
self-improvement and personal gain the ultimate end of suffering.[44]
Instead, a truly biblical perspective on suffering emphasizes outcomes
such as brokenness, humility, spiritual formation or growth into deeper
Christlikeness, and God's power being made perfect in weakness
(2 Cor 12:9-10). As Packer recently put it, weakness is the way in life with
Christ as our strength.[45] It does not focus on outcomes such as greater
self-reliance and independence, or self-improvement and personal gain,
and therefore it goes beyond resilience and posttraumatic growth, and
even self-care to "God-care" and "we-care," where we both learn to rely
on God and not on ourselves (2 Cor 1:9) and we learn to live and suffer

[44]Tchividjian, *Glorious Ruin*, 104-5.
[45]J. I. Packer, *Weakness Is the Way: Life with Christ Our Strength* (Wheaton, IL: Crossway, 2013).

so that others may be blessed (see 2 Cor 1:5-6; Col 1:24; 1 Thess 1:5-6; 2 Tim 2:10) and God be glorified (1 Cor 10:31).

Sanctified suffering, allowed or sent by God in his sovereignty and control of all things, is ultimately for the display of "the greatness of the glory of the grace of God."[46] Tiegreen has similarly asserted that the main reason why a suffering world makes sense in the context of a fallen, sinful world is because it reveals the character and glory of God.[47] However, there are different types of suffering and people with different temperaments who suffer, but there is a need for all of us, according to Keller, to be involved in walking, weeping, trusting, praying, thinking, thanking, loving (in community) and forgiving (and reconciling), and hoping, as we learn to walk with God through pain and suffering—because of the sovereignty of God and the suffering of God.[48]

CONCLUSION

The biblical views on suffering that have been reviewed in this chapter do provide some rich answers to why God allows us to suffer, but mystery and paradox still remain as we face the pain of our suffering in this fallen, sinful world and try to create meaning and experience growth through adversity and affliction.[49] Ultimately, we learn to surrender to God and trust him in his love and grace to transform us by the power of the Holy Spirit—the Comforter and Counselor par excellence (Jn 14:16-17)—and make us more like Jesus through sanctified and redemptive suffering, even if concrete benefits or blessings on earth are not evident. Sometimes the benefits or blessings of such sanctified redemptive suffering will only be fully realized and experienced in heaven to come. As Piper has pointed out, suffering is ultimately for the display of "the greatness of the glory of the grace of God."[50] However, suffering does not automatically make us better people in Christ; it can also make us bitter people if we do not

---

[46]Piper, "Suffering of Christ," 89.
[47]Tiegreen, *Why a Suffering World Makes Sense*.
[48]Keller, *Walking with God*.
[49]Rice, *Suffering and the Search for Meaning*.
[50]Piper, "Suffering of Christ," 89.

respond in appropriate ways. We need to rely on the Holy Spirit and God's grace to respond to suffering in our lives in constructive and appropriate ways, with the help of a caring and loving community, in order to become better people and not bitter people, in Christlikeness. Ultimately, we all need to learn and experience the truth of John 15:5, so that we will be able to affirm from the core of our being, "without Christ, we can do nothing,"[51] and we are "formed for the glory of God,"[52] as Jonathan Edwards emphasized.

In concluding this chapter, a biblical perspective on suffering will also not make suffering the ultimate end or virtue of life. The ultimate end of life is eternal life and joy in Christ now (Jn 10:10; 15:11; 17:3; cf. Ps 16:11) in the kingdom of God on earth and forever in heaven to come (including the New Earth), where there will be no more suffering or pain (Rev 21:4).[53] While suffering is a crucial process in Christian spiritual formation in becoming more like Jesus, it is not the only one. We can also be transformed into deeper Christlikeness through other processes such as contentment (Phil 4:11-13), thanksgiving (1 Thess 5:18), prayer (1 Thess 5:17; cf. Phil 4:6-7), and rejoicing in the Lord (Phil 4:4; 1 Thess 5:16), celebrating and enjoying him and his blessings (see 1 Tim 6:17).

---

[51]K. Strobel, *Metamorpha: Jesus as a Way of Life* (Grand Rapids: Baker Books, 2007), 250.

[52]K. Strobel, *Formed for the Glory of God: Learning from the Spiritual Practices of Jonathan Edwards* (Downers Grove, IL: InterVarsity Press, 2013).

[53]E.g., see Ellen T. Charry, *God and the Art of Happiness* (Grand Rapids: Eerdmans, 2010); Dallas Willard, *The Divine Conspiracy* (New York: HarperSanFrancisco, 1998); Dallas Willard, *Living in Christ's Presence* (Downers Grove, IL: InterVarsity Press, 2014). See also James M. Houston, *Joyful Exiles* (Downers Grove, IL: InterVarsity Press, 2006).

SEEKING THE TROPOLOGICAL IMPORT OF PSALM 35

ELLEN T. CHARRY

Psalm 35

¹ Contend, O LORD, with those who contend with me; fight against those who fight against me!

² Take hold of shield and buckler, and rise up to help me!

³ Draw the spear and javelin against my pursuers; say to my soul, "I am your salvation."

⁴ Let them be put to shame and dishonor who seek after my life. Let them be turned back and confounded who devise evil against me.

⁵ Let them be like chaff before the wind, with the angel of the LORD driving them on.

⁶ Let their way be dark and slippery, with the angel of the LORD pursuing them.

⁷ For without cause they hid their net for me; without cause they dug a pit for my life.

⁸ Let ruin come on them unawares. And let the net that they hid ensnare them; let them fall in it—to their ruin.

⁹ Then my soul shall rejoice in the LORD, exulting in his deliverance.

¹⁰ All my bones shall say, "O Lᴏʀᴅ, who is like you? You deliver the weak from those too strong for them, the weak and needy from those who despoil them."

¹¹ Malicious witnesses rise up; they ask me about things I do not know.

¹² They repay me evil for good; my soul is forlorn.

¹³ But as for me, when they were sick, I wore sackcloth; I afflicted myself with fasting. I prayed with head bowed on my bosom,

¹⁴ as though I grieved for a friend or a brother; I went about as one who laments for a mother, bowed down and in mourning.

¹⁵ But at my stumbling they gathered in glee, they gathered together against me; ruffians whom I did not know tore at me without ceasing;

¹⁶ they impiously mocked more and more, gnashing at me with their teeth.

¹⁷ How long, O Lᴏʀᴅ, will you look on? Rescue me from their ravages, my life from the lions!

¹⁸ Then I will thank you in the great congregation; in the mighty throng I will praise you.

¹⁹ Do not let my treacherous enemies rejoice over me, or those who hate me without cause wink the eye.

²⁰ For they do not speak peace, but they conceive deceitful words against those who are quiet in the land.

²¹ They open wide their mouths against me; they say, "Aha, Aha, our eyes have seen it."

²² You have seen, O Lᴏʀᴅ; do not be silent! O Lord, do not be far from me!

²³ Wake up! Bestir yourself for my defense, for my cause, my God and my Lord!

²⁴ Vindicate me, O Lᴏʀᴅ, my God, according to your righteousness, and do not let them rejoice over me.

²⁵ Do not let them say to themselves, "Aha, we have our heart's desire." Do not let them say, "We have swallowed you up."

²⁶ Let all those who rejoice at my calamity be put to shame and confusion; let those who exalt themselves against me be clothed with shame and dishonor.

²⁷ Let those who desire my vindication shout for joy and be glad, and say evermore, "Great is the Lᴏʀᴅ, who delights in the welfare of his servant."

²⁸ Then my tongue shall tell of your righteousness and of your praise all day long. (NRSV)[1]

---

[1]All Scripture quotations in this chapter follow the NRSV unless otherwise noted.

PRESENTING PROBLEM

The psalms labeled as imprecations may be Christianly troubling because they seek retribution against those who have harmed the speaker when an offer of forgiveness and the reestablishment of relationship is what Christians would prefer to find. Psalm 35 is one of the stronger imprecations, in which the speaker spends himself decrying the contempt he has experienced and asking God to shame those who have scorned him. The poem tells us that such reprisal is warranted by the untoward behavior of ruffians who seek the pious speaker's life (be it literally or psychologically). The theme is sustained through its concluding hope that the speaker's opponents experience shame, confusion, and dishonor (Ps 35:26) just as he has. On the other hand, the complainant wants the opposite for his supporters: joy and gladness (Ps 35:27) in order to proclaim God's righteousness publicly (Ps 35:18, 28). The goal is not revenge for its own sake but that retributive justice may prevail to God's credit.

Here is a seemingly perfect portrait of one who feels disrespected and asks God to dishonor those who have insulted him. Like other imprecatory psalms and verses of psalms, the aggrieved does not consider taking action against his foes himself—perhaps he is not in any position to do so—but implores God to do so on his behalf. Even at its rawest, the psalmist seeks retaliation only indirectly. No psalm advocates direct action against those who harm the speaker. On the contrary, even though it may hurt Christian ears longing for a reconciliatory moment, the Psalter offers a notable theological departure from the tit-for-tat policy of retaliatory revenge as a deterrent for bad behavior found in the following texts:

> When people who are fighting injure a pregnant woman so that there is a miscarriage, and yet no further harm follows, the one responsible shall be fined what the woman's husband demands, paying as much as the judges determine. If any harm follows, then you shall give life for life, eye for eye, tooth for tooth, hand for hand, foot for foot, burn for burn, wound for wound, stripe for stripe. (Ex 21:22-25)

Anyone who maims another shall suffer the same injury in return: fracture for fracture, eye for eye, tooth for tooth; the injury inflicted is the injury to be suffered. One who kills an animal shall make restitution for it; but one who kills a human being shall be put to death. (Lev 24:19-21)

If a malicious witness comes forward to accuse someone of wrongdoing, then both parties to the dispute shall appear before the LORD, before the priests and the judges who are in office in those days, and the judges shall make a thorough inquiry. If the witness is a false witness, having testified falsely against another, then you shall do to the false witness just as the false witness had meant to do to the other. So you shall purge the evil from your midst. The rest shall hear and be afraid, and a crime such as this shall never again be committed among you. Show no pity: life for life, eye for eye, tooth for tooth, hand for hand, foot for foot. (Deut 19:16-21)

SYMPATHETIC PERSPECTIVES

In his work on revenge and forgiveness, evolutionary social psychologist Michael McCullough argues that both revenge and forgiveness are adaptive mechanisms that were so successful in addressing specific problems that they became ego-syntonic. The desire for retaliation deters interpersonal and social harm while forgiveness effectively preserves valuable relationships despite those harms.[2] On this evolutionary view, it seems that the revenge sought from God in Psalm 35 hopes to establish or impose standards of civility in Israel, and that is a good thing in the long-term. The poet is not interested in the care and nurture of interpersonal relationships in the short-term but in inculcating social reciprocity in the body politic because he appreciates the ruinous social consequences of angry contempt (Ps 35:11-18). The challenge the poet poses to us is how to deal constructively with scorn.

Far later Western Christians, schooled to desire forgiveness, may overlook the destructive power of contempt that the hope of early forgiveness and reconciliation may obscure. The issue here then is not a hard choice between revenge and forgiveness, wrong and right, but a

---

[2]M. E. McCullough, *Beyond Revenge: The Evolution of the Forgiveness Instinct* (San Francisco: Jossey-Bass, 2008).

subtler question of how to deal with the dysfunction wrought by contempt when people honestly feel misunderstood and disrespected. Wanting to be vindicated in such situations is not untoward because vindication will restore the integrity and confidence of the complainant and encourage her to continue in the good path she is following.

At the same time, to be called to account for sneering is a long-term gain for society if it results in personal growth. The trick is how to manage the dynamic so that both parties emerge from the encounter edified. The pastoral challenge of the scenario is that the wounded not emerge from the incident by becoming smug and that the scorners not emerge from it untouched. The angry rhetoric here may be stronger than is helpful—especially in the opening three verses of this psalm that call God to arms against the scoffers—but people with fire in the belly are often given to hyperbole. Christian theology is certainly no exception to that generalization!

In Psalm 35, like all the imprecatory psalms, invoking God as the agent of retribution for the humiliated speaker enables the speaker to express his hurt safely in the presence of those who empathize with him (God and his supporters, Ps 35:27). Evidently the parties to the dispute cannot talk to each other, and pouring his heart out to God and his listening audience are safe outlets for the speaker's unstable emotions. Dominick Hankle suggests that imprecatory psalms may be therapeutic in counseling when handled well.[3] When used to cling to anger and hurt, they may support unhealthy emotions, but when employed judiciously they can provide for catharsis and a way beyond pathological grief and anger, leaving God to resolve complicated situations.

SEEKING TO BE UNDERSTOOD

While the initial triplet of verses asks God to make war against the speaker's foes (Ps 35:1-3), the second triplet (Ps 35:4-6) makes clear that

---

[3]D. D. Hankle, "The Therapeutic Implications of the Imprecatory Psalms in the Christian Counseling Setting," *Journal of Psychology & Theology* 38, no. 4 (2010): 275-80.

the real interest of the speaker is not to harm his opponents physically but to edify them by having them experience the shame they have caused. God will vindicate him by flummoxing his adversaries (Ps 35:8). Foiling them is not extrinsic to their behavior toward the speaker—although verse 8 could be asking for extrinsic punishment. Yet the thrust of the psalm is to have the speaker's foes learn to stop their bad behavior by experiencing the shame and embarrassment that they have imposed on him. He wants God to ensnare them in the very net in which they ensnared him (Ps 35:7-8). For the most part, and this may be significant, the speaker wants his tormentors to understand what he is experiencing and to reflect on their role in causing harm so that they learn from it.

Perhaps part of the motivation behind this perspective on contempt is that divine chastisement is likely to be more effective than chastisement from the one hurt. In the latter case, the reproach is more likely to fail because being rebuked by one whom one has hurt may arouse defensiveness rather than the self-reflection needed for change, while being corrected by an independent source (here, God) is more likely to be accepted and reflected upon. The dynamics here call for psychological perspicacity.

PSALM 35 AS A PRIVATE LITTLE WAR

Psalm 35 repeats the cry for retribution previously heard in Psalms 7, 12, and 28. Psalmic poetry in Jeremiah 18:18-23 and Jeremiah 20:10-13, with the same themes and tone as this psalm, prompted the Antiochene theologian Theodore of Mopsuestia (ca. 350–428) to attribute Psalm 35 to Jeremiah, albeit as David's prophetic anticipation of what Jeremiah would later write, of course. The suggestion has merit even today.

The Older Testament's support for retribution has, of course, often been contrasted with Christianity's interest in divine mercy. The slightly later Antiochene theologian Theodoret of Cyrus (ca. 393–457) shared the concern. He cautions readers not to be misled:

I beseech those reading [Psalm 35] not to incur even the slightest harm from the prayer of the righteous man or make it the occasion for curses against one's enemies, but realize that the inspired author was adopting the way of life sanctioned by the Law, not by the Gospels. . . . Looking at this difference, therefore, realize what is in keeping with the Law, and what with grace. In particular, it was not to deliver a curse that David said this; rather, in inspired fashion he foretold what would clearly come to be. . . . Even he did not take vengeance of those who wronged him.[4]

Theodoret is pointing out that David is leaving chastisement of those who engage in untoward behavior to God and not taking matters into his own hands. This is an especially important tropological point for societies lacking effective judicial systems where tribal loyalties tempt people to take revenge, inciting round after round of tribal vendettas.[5] Recognizing a rupture between the morality of the text and later Christian moral sensibility, Theodoret advises Christians to wait patiently for God to act as and when he will. In the meantime, it is appropriate to urge God to act in accord with the justice proper to his character and perhaps to the situation at hand so that all may be edified.

As suggested above, it would be shortsighted to oppose the psalms' focus on retributive justice with a later focus on mercy. While Christians are wont to stress divine mercy and forgiveness as chief traits for human emulation, divine wrath is never far from Western Christian concern and is often articulated in terms of the divine sanction (evident in Matthew, John, and Revelation) to stimulate fear of God in order to arouse recoil from sin, assuming that what constitutes "sin" is recognized by those who commit it.

The centrality of the themes of debt and retributive justice in second-millennium Western Christian theology beginning with Anselm's *Cur Deus Homo* (although partly adumbrated by Augustine) attest the desire

---

[4]Theodoret, *Theodoret of Cyrus: Commentary on the Psalms* (Washington, DC: Catholic University of America Press, 2000), 216-17.
[5]McCullough recounts the story of the five martyrs of the Ecuadorean rainforest whose deaths converted the Waorani (Huaorani) to Christianity by allowing themselves to be murdered by those to whom they witnessed with offers of friendship (January 8, 1956). McCullough, "Beyond Revenge," 213-15.

for standards of law and order in a Europe struggling its way beyond what
we once called the Dark Ages that followed the collapse of Mediterranean
civilization in the fifth century. As Anselm well knew, the challenge in
dealing with offended and offender is not to insist on choosing mercy over
retribution but to employ both astutely and effectively for the well-being of
the whole body within which the parties to the problem are held.

PSALM 35 AS A PUBLIC MATTER

Recognizing that the poet has set what might be read as a private little
war between two or a few individuals in the public space occupied by
God and the speaker's friends leads to a further perspective on this and
perhaps other imprecatory or lament psalms more generally. These have
often been read as personal complaints about soured personal relationships. Yet there is another angle from which to view them. Although
whatever has transpired between the parties has undoubtedly hurt the
speaker, it could be that the encounter speaks to a larger issue: the position
of those faithful to God ridiculed by those Israelites who apostatized, as
was rampant during the divided monarchy. When he began to rule, Hezekiah undertook the cleansing of the house of the Lord to reclaim the
ancestral faith of David (2 Chron 29–31). He sent emissaries throughout
the north as well his own kingdom to urge people to come to Jerusalem
for Passover. The chronicler reports that the mission to the north was not
very successful and the missionaries were met with contempt ("they
laughed them to scorn, and mocked them," 2 Chron 30:10). The word *l'g*,
to mock or scorn, is used by both the chronicler and this poem (Ps 35:16).[6]
That is, those faithful to God are derided by those who should be
worshiping God alongside them.

More evidence can be brought to strengthen the case for this public
perspective on the poem, but it is sufficient here to explore how such an
interpretation might be pastorally helpful by casting the imprecation in a
fresh light. The contempt of which the speaker complains would not then

---

[6]‎(אֶלְעֲנֵי מָעוֹג Ps 35:16) that the Chronicler uses to describe the experience of Hezekiah's emissaries
‎(וּמַלְעִגִים 2 Ch 30:10).

be personal but theological. In mocking God's prophets or Hezekiah's emissaries, the adversaries are mocking God, and the psalmist is asking God to vindicate himself because he is being rejected by precisely those who should be worshiping him. Yet further, if, as I am persuaded, the Psalter as a whole insists on Israel's faithful worship of God as an outreach tool to make God known among the nations—as King Cyrus recognized when he sent the exiles home with financial support to rebuild Jerusalem—the psalmist's plea for vindication is at the same time deeply personal.

Yet for God to forgive Israel's apostasy would not quite be appropriate either. For God to forgive and reconcile with his own people who pointedly reject him would be strange, for it would imply that God accepts paganism. This would undermine belief in the universality of the one God that is the bedrock belief on which Israel's mission to the gentiles is predicated. Indeed, it is the foundation of Israelite religion, Judaism, and Christianity. Psalm 78 points to the difficult position Israel has put God in. Punishment does not seem to deter Israel's apostasy, but neither does God's guidance and care endear him to them. God is frustrated. Psalm 78 seems to stop rather than conclude with the selection of David as God's shepherd of the people. The poet knows that the tortured story is unfinished.

Just to press this interpretation one step further, when people are sneered at for pursuing a just but unpopular cause, it is difficult not to take the scorn personally and to hold fast to the mission dispassionately. If this psalm or at least part of it is a cry of frustration at the failure to bring Israel back to God, or some analogous event, the complainant might be plagued by doubts about how well-prepared he was for his mission, how well he carried it out, or how he might have done it better because ultimately, he feels himself accountable to God for the failure of the mission as witnessed by the scorn heaped upon him.

CONCLUSION

In brief, the tropological sense of Psalm 35 depends on how we read it. If we read it as a personal complaint about a private little war, its tropological value is in cultivating self-restraint and inviting a third party (in this case, God) to take our case. It does not countenance a Stoic attitude that such abuse should not be allowed to bother us. By giving the matter over to God, the complainant recuses himself from taking action against his opponent(s), thus protecting them from his hot anger while being able to express it in a "safe space": prayer. By venting the hurt and anger verbally he prevents the incident from expanding into what could become a tribal vendetta.

If, however, we read this poem against the religious situation in Israel where the speaker feels marginalized because he worships God amid many Israelites who have abandoned God for other gods and the speaker is wearied at the slender results of his effort to bring them "home," its tropology is quite different. In that case, the poet is disclosing the misery of one called to a difficult mission that one pursues with integrity yet is foiled, and he struggles with anger, defeat, frustration, and disappointment at having failed in his appointed task. On this view, the cry is to be liberated from the onerous mission while knowing that that would be to abandon God, which he cannot do. In his frustration he tells God that he [God] will have to do more to rebuke his people to stop the paganism in Israel, for his messenger is exhausted. Perhaps the take-away for us here is to know our limits even when charged with a mission we feel passionately about. The speaker persevered too long until he burnt himself out, at which point he almost became a danger to others. Yet even at that point, he prevented himself from harming others. This rich psalm has much to teach us about Scripture interpretation and the freedom of the text, about theology's effects on psychological well-being, and about directing negative emotions in a God-ward way. It can strengthen us to endure scorn and rejection for principled reasons. It can help us understand the challenge of spiritual development and more. May the psalms ever teach us who we are, reveal to us why we do what we do, and deepen our ability to love well.

PART THREE

PSYCHOLOGICAL

INSIGHTS

FOR A

THEOLOGY OF

SPIRITUAL

FORMATION

ON SPECKS AND PLANKS

PSYCHOTHERAPY, SPIRITUAL FORMATION, AND MORAL JUDGMENT

EARL D. BLAND

Addressing Christian spiritual formation, the late Dallas Willard once quipped, "We have multitudes of professing Christians who may be ready to die, but obviously are not ready to live, and hardly get along with themselves, much less with others."[1] While certainly not unique among faith communities, in some ways this is a remarkable statement given the ethic of loving-kindness so essential to the Christ's message. Yet if you've spent any amount of time around Christians, you realize the truth of his assertion and how Willard's ecclesial diagnosis typifies much of the church through history. Moreover, those of us with any sensitivity to the pain that results when we treat each other poorly are often aware of our culpability; we sometimes act in ways that we know, upon reflection, perpetuate the problem Willard identifies. Perhaps, hopefully, we feel some tugging to take responsibility to lessen our duplicity and move toward greater understanding and acceptance in our collective

---

[1]Dallas Willard, "Spiritual Formation in Christ: A Perspective on What It Is and How It Might Be Done," *Journal of Psychology and Theology* 28 (2000): 254.

community. Toward this end—a little different than many conversations about Christianity and psychology—I want to explore this very real human problem, how we get along, and bypass more distant ideas about theory or theology. To use L. Rebecca Propst's "particularistic approach," which argues that "integration models derive from practice rather than precede it," and following the experience near or phenomenological slant of my psychoanalytic self-psychological training, I would like to let the problem of troubled and conflicted relational communities set the agenda for how we approach the conversation between Christianity and psychology.[2] In an even narrower gaze I have chosen a specific relational dynamic, interpersonal moral judgment, as the pathway for the dialogue between depth psychological principles and practices and the traditions of Christian formation.

The title of this chapter alludes to the well-known—much used and abused—passage in Matthew where Christ instructs that before we judge the speck or flaws of another, we should first remove the plank or major flaw from our eye so that we can see clearly (Mt 7:1-5). The use of hyperbole in this passage is interesting because it seems stylistically incompatible with what we typically expect when we read Scripture, but it turns out Christ was not exaggerating or being sarcastic, just metaphorical. Obviously, Jesus was not talking about all judgments, such as the capacity to evaluate or distinguish between better or worse courses of action. He was addressing judgmental condemnation, our tendency to sometimes treat others with moral disapproval, to censure them and create distance, like when we condemn a house because it's no longer fit to inhabit.[3] The metaphor expresses something akin to outrage, as Christ finds our tendency toward duplicity and self-righteous fault finding difficult to tolerate.[4] He echoes

<hr>

[2]L. Rebecca Propst, "Therapeutic Conflict Resolution and the Holy Trinity," in *Limning the Psyche: Explorations in Christian Psychology*, ed. R. C. Roberts and M. R. Talbot (Grand Rapids: Eerdmans, 1997), 58-59.
[3]C. L. Blomberg, *Matthew*, The New American Commentary, vol. 22 (Nashville, TN: B & H, 1992); M. J. Wilkins, *Matthew*, The NIV Application Commentary (Grand Rapids: Zondervan, 2004).
[4]M. Simonetti, ed., *Matthew 1-13*, Ancient Christian Commentary on Scripture, vol. 1a (Downers Grove, IL: InterVarsity Press, 2001).

this sentiment in an analogous parable of the unforgiving servant (Mt 18:21-35). In this story, a servant who was forgiven much refuses to extend the merciful spirit of his master to those who were indebted to him. The unmerciful servant is labeled "wicked" (Mt 18:32 NIV) because of his failure to reflect on his own good fortune and enlarge this spirit of generosity and mercy within his community.[5] This difficulty is common in relationships. Our tendency to focus on others' problems or failures is often a distraction and defense against dealing with how we contribute to relational disharmony.

One of the key challenges to overcoming condemnation and judgmentalism is the task of dealing with difference. As Christians, our history is replete with arguments and schisms caused by our very human tendency to distrust, judge, condemn, and demean those who believe or practice their life/faith differently. Sometimes even slight variations are enough to spark considerable communal and intersubjective distress. Interestingly, when Jesus outlines his thoughts on the judgment and condemnation of others (Mt 7:1-5), his corrective remedy is self-examination. In essence we must understand and remediate our own subjective organization before we attempt to speak into the life of another. However, this does not appear to be an invitation for solipsistic rumination. The instruction to "first take the plank out of your own eye, and then you will see clearly to remove the speck from your brother's eye" (Mt 7:5) cannot be taken in isolation from the rest of Matthew's Gospel, which is preoccupied with embedded discipleship as a relational process of serving each other within a community that seeks to "learn Jesus."[6] Further, Scripture as a whole—think about Paul's metaphor of interdependent body systems (1 Cor 12) or John's assertion that Christians are identified by the expression of relational love (Jn 13:35)—aligns itself with the notion that spiritual formation is a relational endeavor. We learn in our families and communities how to

---

[5] All Scripture quotations in this chapter follow the NIV unless otherwise noted.
[6] L. T. Johnson, *Living Jesus: Learning the Heart of the Gospel* (New York: HarperSanFrancisco, 1999), 158.

face our contradictions and darkness so that we may become better followers of Christ.[7] Willard crystalizes the idea here by suggesting that
the Christian's first order of business is to "begin with ourselves."[8] We
know ourselves and engage in adequate and principled self-reflection
within a context rich in relational engagements, something Stanley
Grenz referred to as an "ecclesial self."[9] Expanding the notion that
relationships are critical to healthy self-development, Grenz positions
the self within the eschatological horizon of God's kingdom, one free of
condemnation (Rom 8:1) and striving toward a community whose
model is the relationally entangled Trinity.

Developmentally we might think of relational ways of being that encourage honest self-examination such as empathy and specifically the
mentalization of affect and behavior.[10] *Mentalization* is a relatively new
moniker that refers to the developmental capacity to form a theory of
mind (understanding subjective mental states and the social understanding that others have minds that may think and feel differently). The
capacity to understand the meaning of one's own and other's subjective
feeling states and their linkage to various behaviors, perceptual
tendencies, and memories is a critical developmental achievement. To
develop properly, the type of relational connection needed for adequate
mentalization or subjective self-reflection must contain sufficiently
structured care, empathy, attunement, and love. Self-reflection demands
a relational connection, an almost twinship experience, where one can
be fully known by another who is intentionally engaged and committed
to one's growth and flourishing. Most find these relational connections
with families, friends, and mentors. Sufficiently nurturing and attuned

---

[7]F. L. Shults and S. J. Sandage, *Transforming Spirituality: Integrating Theology and Psychology* (Grand Rapids: Baker Academic, 2006).

[8]Dallas Willard, *The Great Omission: Reclaiming Jesus's Essential Teachings on Discipleship* (New York: HarperSanFrancisco, 2006), 225.

[9]Stanley Grenz, *The Social God and the Relational Self: A Trinitarian Theology of the Imago Dei* (Louisville, KY: Westminster John Knox, 2001), 312.

[10]P. Fonagy and A. Bateman, eds., *Handbook of Mentalizing in Mental Health Practice* (Arlington, VA: American Psychiatric Publishing, 2012); P. Fonagy, G. Gergely, E. Jurist, and M. Target, *Affect Regulation, Mentalization, and the Development of the Self* (New York: Other Press, 2004).

parents and caregivers foster the implicit and explicit capacity to read the emotional states of self and others, leading to the understanding of intentions at both conscious and unconscious levels. These intersubjective processes appear critical in the formation of secure attachments necessary for interpersonal safety and security.[11] In essence our capacity to understand the minds of other people, to form a theory of the intentions behind their actions, and to make judgments about both internal and external motivational processes takes shape within a rich and dynamic intersubjective field that cannot be divorced from our own development of these same capacities—most critical for our purposes, the ability to self-reflect.[12]

The intersubjective reciprocal nature of psychological development is essential to keep in mind as we think about how we form our innate potential and intersubjective aptitude for social understanding, judgment, and intimate relational engagements. The relational quality and sociocultural context of our developmental experiences shapes our moral thinking as both implicit and explicit emotional experiences both bind us to others and blind us from our in-group tendency to exclude and vilify others who we deem wrong or distasteful.[13] In sum, the metacognitive ability to judge others and ourselves is a developmental achievement that emerges from the embodied reciprocal relational exchanges embedded within sociocultural contexts, including religious and spiritual traditions. No doubt essential for the development of community, interpersonal judgment is a normal and necessary human capacity but one that is prone to self-serving justifications.

Although we could talk about many contributors to moral condemnation, addressing the problem through the intersubjective lens of

---

[11]K. Lyons-Ruth, "The Interface Between Attachment and Intersubjectivity: Perspective from the Longitudinal Study of Disorganized Attachment," *Psychoanalytic Inquiry* 26 (2006): 595-616.

[12]I. Brinck and R. Liljenfors, "The Developmental Origin of Metacognition," *Infant and Child Development* 22 (2013): 85-101; R. Liljenfors and L. G. Lundh, "Mentalization and Intersubjectivity Towards a Theoretical Integration," *Psychoanalytic Psychology* 32 (2015): 36-60.

[13]J. Haidt, *The Righteous Mind: Why Good People Are Divided by Politics and Religion* (New York: Pantheon Books, 2012).

psychotherapy as it is experienced in the lives of patients and revealed in the clinical setting reveals two important considerations of the Matthew passage. First, judgmental condemnation is a common human propensity, with an insidious quality that, when experienced, hampers psychological and spiritual growth; blocks intimacy and relational connectedness; and perpetuates experiences of exclusion, aggression, and injustice. Although this is a major problem for our current civil discourse, it is perhaps most damaging in the moment-to-moment relational exchanges of everyday people in the course of daily living. Intimate relationships are especially vulnerable because this is where we are most apt to experience our uncensored self, where fears, aggression, shame, and guilt evoke and provoke responses of judgment and denunciation. As both conscious and unconscious motivational states act to hide and disavow our defensive judgments and justifications, humility and even humanity are lost to the cacophony of distancing strategies such as the focus on personal rights, binary moral categories, literalist dogma, attribution error, and self-enhancing biases.[14] In other words, despite deep convictions to the contrary, Christians often get defensive when angry, project blame, and exclude based on arbitrary preferences. The self-evident ubiquity of these tendencies leads to the second reason for focusing on this problem. In agreement with Willard, the process of spiritual formation is less about the pursuit of memorable spiritual experiences and more about the actualization of Christ's image in the daily, granular relational moments we all have.[15] Spiritual formation does not pursue the control of actions; it is the pursuit of a relational reality, which by its very nature regulates self-experience. In other words, spiritual formation is a whole-person engagement that has particular outcomes in mind, all of which are an anathema to interpersonal judgment and condemnation. For Willard, when we become Christian "we stand in a new reality where

---

[14]E. Pronin, T. Gilovich, and L. Ross, "Objectivity in the Eye of the Beholder: Divergent Perceptions of Bias in Self Versus Others," *Psychological Review* 111 (2004): 781-99.

[15]Willard, *Great Omission*; Dallas Willard, *Knowing Christ Today: Why We Can Trust Spiritual Knowledge* (New York: HarperCollins, 2009).

condemnation is simply irrelevant."[16] Pursuing the Spirit-filled life involves an "abandonment of all defensiveness . . . (which) includes a willingness to be known in our most intimate relationships for who we really are" because condemnation is an embodied expression of inner states that stifle the expression of Christ where we revile people with our actions.[17] Willard's trajectory forces us to consider whom we visit, talk or eat with, who receives our charity or respect, and a host of other embodied actions that selectively reflect our moral judgments. We mind the tilt of our judgment as it emerges from our family history, culture, and faith tradition where the power of accepted normality smooths over particularities and implicitly organizes our perceptual field and the meanings we ascribe to difference and newness.

As clinicians we have a deep ethical responsibility to encounter our traditions by expanding awareness to the way theory, economic status, culture, and religious tradition operate at an unconscious or implicit level in shaping our encounters with patients.[18] Jones argues that psychologists should be comfortable explicitly stating their religious and philosophical leanings both to contextualize their perspectives and to lessen the likelihood of blatant bias and unconscious partisan judgments.[19] For example, I emerged from the mid to late twentieth century Wesleyan Holiness movement and its expression in the Pentecostal Assemblies of Canada. Drinking deeply from the Pentecostal cup with a chaser of Baptist fundamentalism, spiritual formation in my tradition was emotive, behavioral, and tenuous. I was supposedly given clear markers about what it meant to be a true Christian, and for much of my developmental years I was pretty sure I could tell who was a Christian

---

[16]Dallas Willard, *The Divine Conspiracy: Rediscovering Our Hidden Life in God* (New York: HarperSanFrancisco, 1998), 227.

[17]Dallas Willard, *Renovation of the Heart* (Colorado Springs: NavPress, 2002), 195.

[18]B. D. Strawn, R. Wright, and P. Jones, "Tradition-Based Integration: Illuminating the Stories and Practices That Shape Our Integrative Imaginations," *Journal of Psychology and Christianity* 33 (2015): 300-310; R. Wright, P. Jones, and B. Strawn, "Tradition-Based Integration," in *Christianity & Psychoanalysis: A New Conversation*, Earl D. Bland and B. D. Strawn, eds. (Downers Grove, IL: IVP Academic, 2014), 37-54.

[19]Stanton L. Jones, "A Constructive Relationship for Religion with the Science and Profession of Psychology: Perhaps the Boldest Model Yet," *American Psychologist* 49 (1994): 184-99.

and who wasn't—even through times when I felt my own standing in jeopardy. I am also a clinical psychologist with psychoanalytic training and consider my theoretical geography reflective of the contemporary psychoanalytic traditions—most notably that of self psychology. Each of these powerful influences has shaped my moral emotions and cognition, playing a role in both implicit and explicit acts of clinical assessment and judgment. The irreducible subjectivity of these traditions is most keenly displayed in the formation of transference judgments and reactions within the psychotherapeutic process.[20] In other words, I cannot escape the formative experience of my tradition with its mixture of error and truth. To highlight these issues as they arise in the context of psychotherapy, I will turn to a brief examination of integration issues and the specific psychological contexts of moral judgment or condemnation that may arise in psychotherapy. I follow this with a clinical case example to demonstrate the qualitative aspects of psychotherapeutic and relational processes that temper or reduce judgmentalism and increase relational harmony.[21]

SPIRITUAL FORMATION, PSYCHOTHERAPY, AND JUDGMENTALISM

A generous and collaborative approach to spiritual formation and psychotherapy includes the following assumptions: First, Christian formation is the progressive movement toward a true image of Christ as he is revealed in Scripture and experienced in Christianity both in its broad cultural expression (i.e., the civic acknowledgment of Christianity—public prayers, holidays, etc.) and more specifically in the particularities of different faith traditions. Second, spiritual formation necessarily involves an encounter with God's divine personhood both in its transcendent reality and immanent quality. Third, knowledge (of all sorts) is inseparable from the knower. Not that knowledge can't be shared or

---

[20]Strawn et al., "Tradition-Based Integration"; Wright et al., "Tradition-Based Integration."
[21]K. J. Gergen, R. Josselson, and M. Freeman, "The Promises of Qualitative Inquiry," *American Psychologist* 70 (2015): 1-9.

have a degree of objectivity or transcendence, I simply mean that for humans, what we know shapes and is shaped by our embodied experience. Fourth, the therapeutic dialogue is, at all times, intersubjective or relational, clinical, ethical (read *moral*), cultural, embodied, and spiritual. Even if we don't explicitly acknowledge these factors it does not mean they are inoperable. Finally, as I have argued elsewhere, the process of depth psychotherapeutic work—like those found in psychoanalysis and psychoanalytic psychotherapy—can make a powerful contribution to spiritual formation.[22]

Historically, the integrative literature in psychology and Christianity has wrestled with the degree to which Christian principles and methodologies need explicit recognition or usage in the psychotherapeutic process and to what degree spiritual formation and psychological development overlap.[23] Taking shape within the larger modernist discussion of how science relates to religion, this conversation is robust and ongoing.[24] So many different contributions from philosophy, theology, and psychology have been proposed that it is impossible to present a reasonable summation in the current context.[25] Comprising

---

[22]Earl D. Bland and B. D. Strawn, eds., *Christianity & Psychoanalysis: A New Conversation* (Downers Grove, IL: IVP Academic, 2014).

[23]D. N. Entwistle, *Integrative Approaches to Psychology and Christianity: An Introduction to Worldview Issues, Philosophical Foundations and Models of Integration*, 2nd ed. (Eugene, OR: Cascade Books, 2010); S. P. Greggo and T. A. Sisemore, eds., *Counseling and Christianity: Five Approaches* (Downers Grove, IL: IVP Academic, 2012); E. L. Johnson, ed., *Psychology and Christianity: Five Views*, 2nd ed. (Downers Grove, IL: IVP Academic, 2010); Stanton L. Jones and Richard E. Butman, *Modern Psychotherapies: A Comprehensive Christian Appraisal*, 2nd ed. (Downers Grove, IL: IVP Academic, 2011); M. R. McMinn, *Psychology, Theology, and Spirituality in Christian Counseling*, rev. ed. (Carol Stream, IL: Tyndale House Publishers, 1996).

[24]A. E. Bergin, "Values and Religious Issues in Psychotherapy and Mental Health," *American Psychologist* 46 (1991): 394-403; Jones, "A Constructive Relationship."

[25]For influential examples see J. D. Carter and S. B. Narramore, *The Integration of Psychology and Theology* (Grand Rapids: Zondervan, 1979); E. L. Johnson, *Foundations for Soul Care: A Christian Psychology Proposal* (Downers Grove, IL: IVP Academic, 2007); M. R. McMinn and C. D. Campbell, *Integrative Psychotherapy: Toward a Comprehensive Christian Approach* (Downers Grove, IL: IVP Academic, 2007); R. C. Roberts, *Spiritual Emotions: A Psychology of Christian Virtues* (Grand Rapids: Eerdmans, 2007); R. C. Roberts and M. R. Talbot, eds., *Limning the Psyche: Explorations in Christian Psychology* (Grand Rapids: Eerdmans, 1997); Siang-Yang Tan, *Counseling and Psychotherapy: A Christian Perspective* (Grand Rapids: Baker Academic, 2011); E. L. Worthington, *Coming to Peace with Psychology: What Christians Can Learn from the Psychological Sciences* (Downers Grove, IL: IVP Academic, 2010).

numerous issues and theoretical slants, an enduring subtext in all of these writings is the question of how spiritual or Christian formation processes actually work in the psychotherapy relationship. At times this debate has become strident, but for the sake of clarifying my position, I want to acknowledge that explicit usage of Christian principles/ methodologies can be important and often very helpful in therapeutic work. However, it does not necessarily correlate that such practices produce greater Christlikeness and a progressive movement towards greater virtue. Absent deep and connective relational engagement that encourages the exploration of both conscious (explicit) and unconscious (implicit) psychological processes, I would argue that use of prayer, Scripture, and other Christian practices are limited in their effectiveness.[26] Because I am primarily interested in therapeutic realities that are most likely to have transformative effects, I want to stress, in line with research investigating the mechanisms of therapeutic action and change, that unconscious relational processes are critical in the effectiveness of psychotherapy.[27] While some views place heavy emphasis on the conscious recognition of Christian realities in psychotherapy, I want to suggest that, although providing a helpful framework for change, heavy reliance on explicit use of Christian language and techniques may sometimes blind both therapist and patient to unconscious enactments that operate to undermine lasting change. For example, consider divided self-states that actively seek to avoid depth engagement of painful affects such as shame and guilt. Prone to interventions that seek to suppress undesirable behavior in the short term, sometimes these interventions are limited in their effectiveness because of the collusive avoidance between therapist and patient of the very affect states that create the problem for which patients seek help.[28] If

---

[26]See E. L. Worthington, E. L. Johnson, J. N. Hook, and J. D. Aten, eds., *Evidence-Based Practices for Christian Counseling and Psychotherapy* (Downers Grove, IL: IVP Academic, 2013).

[27]The Boston Change Process Study Group, *Change in Psychotherapy: A Unifying Paradigm* (New York: W. W. Norton, 2010).

[28]Earl D. Bland, "The Divided Self: Courage and Grace as Agents of Change," *Journal of Psychology and Christianity* 28 (2009): 326-37; A. Goldberg, *Being of Two Minds: The Vertical Split in Psychoanalysis and Psychotherapy* (Hillsdale, NJ: The Analytic Press, 1999).

the goal is transformation of the whole human, the aping of Christ is not a sufficient target unless it also mimics a deep relational engagement with the world as exemplified in the person of Christ.[29] Consequently, spiritual formation processes become evident in the outcome of psychotherapeutic practice and the question within Christian psychology becomes this: To what degree does psychotherapy encourage the actualization of virtue at levels beyond the alleviation of symptoms? This is not the embracing of a utilitarian ethic or the diminishment of symptom relief. Very simply, all roads to change are not equal; how we change is fundamental to the outcome.

We must acknowledge that even the criteria we use for sensing how God works can be blinded by our expectations, preferences, and traditions. In the process of forming and transforming ourselves into a community free of condemnation, we may need to enlarge our vision to include the unconscious defensive and self-preserving motivations that hamper our ability to see clearly into the life of another. As Christ so aptly demonstrated in his rebuke of first-century Jewish culture, the act of judgmental condemnation rarely feels condemning to the persons who pass judgment; they are blinded to their own culpability by the self-justified "plank" that is unconsciously maintained, sometimes with the guise of theological, cultural, or behavioral orthodoxy. Although psychotherapy is not the only context where transformative intentional relationships can develop, at its best psychotherapy embodies a relational stance that is most hospitable to such connections. Done well, a depth psychotherapeutic relationship allows for the emergence of problematic psychological and relational organizing principles and patterns that foster harmful judgment and condemnation. Although difficult to navigate, it is within these relational enactments that deep mutual examination and understanding of the patient's particular struggles allows each to consider alternative ways of being—ones that reflect a more Christ-like grounded, humble, free, and confident expression of self.

---

[29]J. Zimmerman, *Incarnational Humanism: A Philosophy of Culture for the Church in the World* (Downers Grove, IL: IVP Academic, 2013).

But how does this work specifically? How can the psychotherapeutic enterprise accomplish this Christian call to remove the plank
from your own eye? I propose four domains of therapeutic exploration that encourage the formation of new relational experiences and
have the potential to wither the negative influence of judgmentalism.
Consideration of these factors may be woven into the ongoing
therapeutic dialogue. The domains to consider are defensive self-
righteousness; certitude, self-cohesion, and fragmentation; exclusion;
and projected self-loathing.

Defensive self-righteousness. Many deeply held religious or moral
convictions are associated with intense emotional valence, which intensifies the commitment to traditions and thought patterns that play
key roles in identity formation and the stability of self-experience. In
most areas of human endeavor, differences in these convictions lead
to spirited and persistent debate and hopefully, but clearly not always,
these boundaries and distinctions add diversity and variety to shared
lives and communities. In contrast, judgmental condemnation that
emanates from rigid belief structures serves as defensive avoidance
and distancing from unacceptable thoughts, wishes, or memories of
past behavior. In psychoanalytic parlance this is sometimes referred
to as reaction formation—the unconscious defensive process that
allows one to maintain distance from undesirable emotions or
impulses by adopting an exaggerated stance directly opposing the
objectionable inner state. Denying one's vulnerability to undesirable
behaviors or intentions and castigating similar weaknesses in others
cloaks unconscious shame and guilt and extends the reaction formation process to include the projection of punishment and exclusion
onto the condemned person. Examples are plentiful and run from the
banal—gossiping to a friend about how much another person gossips;
to the egregious—persons with inherited wealth who know they have
not worked for what they have yet consciously or unconsciously equate
poverty with laziness and may endorse or implicitly act to maintain
sociocultural structures that lead to poverty. But Jesus saved some of

his harshest words for the defensively self-righteous: "Woe to you, teachers of the law and Pharisees, you hypocrites! You are like white-washed tombs" (Mt 23:27). The essence of his rebuke was not about the content of the pharisaical judgment, but the duplicitous hypocrisy "you appear to people as righteous but on the inside you are full of hypocrisy and wickedness" (Mt 23:28). In psychotherapy, addressing and teasing out the defensive qualities of entrenched judgmental positions is sometimes a dicey enterprise and runs the risk of placing the therapist under similar condemnation. Because hypocrisy avoids the experience of shame by presenting a preferred image of self rather than a true image, most self-righteous patients struggle with depth therapeutic inquiry because it threatens to unmask the internal contradictions that have previously been successful by "subverting the accuracy of other's appraisal, which forms a necessary condition for reflective self-awareness."[30] Accessing the sometimes rigid, sometimes fragile defensive self-righteous must include therapeutic processes that seek relational intimacy, safety, and transparency of motives, where disavowed self-experience can be revealed absent the threat of humiliating shame.[31]

Certitude, self-cohesion, and fragmentation. Intransigent moral judgments often act as bulwarks against fragmentation of self-experience. Here I am referring to the binding effects of certitude—not only in its ability to bind a person to a particular community, but in its self-cohesive properties that protect against feeling states that threaten to cause emotional and existential instability. Most readily demonstrated in the wake of trauma, judgmental certitude as a buffer against fragmentary self-states is clearly highlighted in the work of Doris Brothers.[32] For Brothers, trauma consists of a shattering self or

---

[30]R. C. Naso, "Beneath the Mask: Hypocrisy and the Pathology of Shame," *Psychoanalytic Psychology* 24 (2007): 113-25.

[31]Bland, "Divided Self"; A. Goldberg, *Errant Selves: A Casebook of Misbehavior* (Hillsdale, NJ: The Analytic Press, 2000).

[32]Doris Brothers, *Toward a Psychology of Uncertainty: Trauma-Centered Psychoanalysis* (New York: The Analytic Press, 2008); Doris Brothers, "Traumatic Attachments: Intergenerational Trauma,

relational experience and the effort to restore some solidification to the sense of self. Especially when the trauma is isolated from relational validation or a relational home, inflexible patterns of certitude emerge, and victims often seek external systems whose expectations and boundaries provide reasonable explanations for their chaos.[33] The shelter against a fragmentation of self-experience and the unpredictable existential dread that follows trauma is to answer these questions of uncertainty by forming clear expectations and defense against the unknown. Inconsistent or alternative, more flexible ways of being are not just split from conscious consideration; they are imbued with scorn as they contain the projected and dissociated aspects of self (weakness, terror, shame, etc.). Uncertainty, fear, anxiety, suffering, and mourning are disavowed and minimized. Alternative ways of being, which contain unacceptable and unconscious wishes and fears, are seen as evil, distorted, and "of the world." Because trauma is always complex, self-recovery through the reduction of chaos and uncertainty frequently necessitates a simplification in one's responses to the various uncertainties of life. In addition, dissociation of traumatic emotional states such as shame, terror, rage, or loss are never voiced or validated in the context of intimate relating. "Traumatic attachments," to use Brothers's term, speaks not to the categorical nature of attachments (disorganized, avoidant, secure, etc.) but to tone of relational engagements and the level of inflexibility and dissociative processes that lead to rigid and constrictive perceptual and reasoning processes that are resistant to change.[34] These simplified rigid certainties "often lie at the heart of traumatized attachments that organize the lives of traumatized parents and their children."[35] Traumatized parents are often unable to tolerate differences in their children as experiences of sameness are

Dissociation, and the Analytic Relationship," *International Journal of Psychoanalytic Self Psychology* 9 (2014), 3-15.

[33]R. Stolorow, *Trauma and Human Existence: Autobiographical, Psychoanalytic and Philosophical Reflections* (New York: The Analytic Press, 2007).

[34]Brothers, "Traumatic Attachments," 3.

[35]Brothers, "Traumatic Attachments," 7.

sought as a buffer against uncertainty. Disavowed and dissociated shame, loss, fear, anger, and dread move stealthily through generations in what Lorrain Cates calls insidious emotional trauma where suffering persists in the absence of "felt recognition."[36] Reflective self-awareness is missing and self-states of "imperceptible emotional pain" permeate life experience.[37]

Exclusion. In many ways judgment and condemnation evolve in the absence of knowing the other who may not be recognized as similar. Reinforcing a psychology of exclusion, relational distancing acts to decrease anxiety from the intersubjective threat one feels when the difference of someone else's story (history, traditions, beliefs) provokes fear, shame, guilt, or other dysregulating emotional states. Volf defines exclusion as the severing of human bonds or the eradication of connection that sustains reciprocal human relations.[38] Interdependence requires a level of self-other distinction where difference is seen and separation is allowed within the mutually validating binds of community. Exclusion, on the other hand, mutes the validity of difference and erases interdependent separateness. The inferior other is either assimilated into self-sameness or subjugated. Long seen as the more painful aspect of prejudice and discrimination, exclusion has been described as enacting a projective identification process whereby the people experienced as other are maintained in their underprivileged or ignorant state by processes that are unconsciously preserved through selective inattention to the nuanced contextual factors that often perpetuate and maintain the condition of the other.[39] Think about processes of institutional racism and sexism or socially accepted micro-aggressions that perpetuate power, class, race, and status differences.[40] As Taylor remarks, "The great challenge of this

---

[36]Lorrain Cates, "Insidious Emotional Trauma: The Body Remembers . . .," *International Journal of Psychoanalytic Self Psychology* 9 (2014): 38.

[37]Cates, "Insidious," 38.

[38]M. Volf, *Exclusion and Embrace* (Nashville, TN: Abingdon Press, 1996).

[39]N. Altman, *The Analyst in the Inner City: Race, Class, and Culture Through a Psychoanalytic Lens*, 2nd ed. (New York: Routledge, 2010).

[40]D. W. Sue, "Race Talk: The Psychology of Racial Dialogues," *American Psychologist* 68 (2013): 663-72.

century, both for politics and for social science, is that of understanding the other."[41] In psychotherapy the road to replacing condemnation with understanding requires patience and the slow but persistent undoing of implicit understandings that distort the reality of the other—for both patient and therapist. This only happens, however, when we allow ourselves to be challenged and questioned by what is different in the other's life, which confronts us with our own peculiarity, but hopefully a less distorted view of life's realities. Sorenson described his understanding of this recognition process as requiring kenosis (self-emptying), a therapeutic virtue that enfolds alterity; "the 'me' and 'not-me' end up being more related than I first guessed."[42] Taylor expands on this idea by using Hans Gadamer's notion of the "fusion of horizons."[43] The horizon that is distinct when seen from different points of view can fuse when one or both parties undergo a shift. This mutual horizon extends to allow new ways of creating meaning or perceiving in the world. Requiring openness to the text of different traditions allows for diverse narratives and perspectives to question us, to challenge our therapeutic assumptions that are embedded within a Western, scientific, largely Caucasian culture.[44] Patients hope to experience their therapist as looking for the most accurate understandings of him or her—not to diminish the essence of difference to convenient categories or attributes, or to minimize the importance of difference—but to create space for a comprehensive account of who they are and what is needed. Reimer and Dueck call for therapists who create space to understand their patients as created in the image of God, to wait for the patients to respond rather than forcing assimilation to their expert judgment. Allowing the difference to exist in tension without excluding or moving away invites the judgmental patient into the self of the therapist and vice versa—what Volf calls "closing."[45] The

[41]C. Taylor, *Dilemmas and Connections* (Cambridge, MA: Belknap Harvard, 2011), 24.
[42]R. L. Sorenson, *Minding Spirituality* (Hillsdale, NJ: The Analytic Press, 2004), 17.
[43]Taylor, *Dilemmas*, 30.
[44]K. Reimer and A. Dueck, "Inviting Soheil: Narrative and Embrace in Christian Caregiving," *Christian Scholar's Review* 35 (2006): 205-20.
[45]Volf, *Exclusion and Embrace*.

construction of a joint narrative accesses the connective relational capacities so essential for defusing judgmental condemnation.

Projected self-loathing. To close our discussion on domains of
therapeutic exploration regarding judgmental condemnation, I want to
highlight a less comprehensive defensive posture that often hampers a
patient's ability to take in empathy and love. Here I refer to some of my
patients who find empathy or care destabilizing. Because of the admixture
of neglect, abuse, and humiliation characteristic of some patients' developmental history, they come to experience caring relationships as an
untenable reawakening of thwarted relational longings. Most of their
past experience has involved the suppression of needs for care and
nurturance. The inherent caring and concern of therapeutic relationships is accompanied by unconscious dread of pain, sorrow, and loss.
Internally the patient's anxiety diminishes the impact of the therapist's
(or any person's) wish to provide love and care. Conversely, the newly
awakened relational hope is fragile and the patient's capacity for self-
empathy is tentatively dictated by the empathy he or she feels from the
therapist. When the patient experiences a relational rupture or disruption
of empathy, they may retreat into defensive posturing that allows for
self-protection by minimizing a desire and need for relational connection.
Although this can take various forms, I want to highlight how this can
occur when therapists are experienced as different from the patient
regarding various beliefs and attitudes, or when the therapist voices a
contradictory view or even has a different perspective about a person
toward whom the patient feels anger and condemnation, such as an
offending spouse, an abusive parent, or a wayward child. The difference
in perspective can be experienced as a relational disjunction and threatening to the patient's self-organization because the therapist, in a sense,
is experienced as in cahoots with the enemy, a threatening enemy. In
these moments of empathic rupture or failure, therapists repair the relational breach with an extended flow of empathy regarding the cause of
the breach and the activation of painful emotions. Two areas remain
open for investigation: the therapist's own error, and the self-deficit or

emotional arrangement that maintains the patient's vulnerability to collapse in the face of disappointment and difference. Critical here is the realization that judgmental condemnation from this domain can be considered projected internalized material (self-loathing), which is difficult for the patient to experience. In other words, the interruption of empathy activates a variety of disavowed emotion states such as anxiety, shame, or guilt. Intolerable to hold in an ambivalent tension with anger and disappointment, all painful emotions are expelled in the form of judgment and condemnation toward others, including therapists who may be experienced as no longer trustworthy.

CASE DISCUSSION

To conclude I want to underscore some of the previous theoretical insights in light of clinical material. The complex relational dynamics surrounding judgment and condemnation in this case study allow us to examine the nuances and difficulty of change. The case also invites us to become emotionally involved with the realities of change in the context of faith traditions and relational difference.

William is a forty-five-year-old man who was referred for individual treatment by a colleague. William was referred to me, in part, because my colleague (and perhaps William as well) thought I would understand his more conservative theological leanings that seemed to be causing conflict in the marriage—especially his reaction to what he experienced and believed to be his wife's inappropriate behavior at work. William's wife Emily travelled significantly and when on the road she would occasionally go out with her colleagues. When he saw pictures that were posted on social media he found her behavior and dress to be morally suspect. He did not trust or like her colleagues, whom he saw as not supporting their marriage and leading his wife to compromise her value as his wife and the expectations of her religious faith. At the time I first met with William, Emily's offenses had largely stopped in deference to his concerns, but memories and various feelings of hurt, jealousy, and anger remained active because Emily continued to travel and would complain that her job just wasn't as fun anymore. Anxiety was clearly present in the early months of our work together as we talked about his struggle to get his wife to understand the egregious nature of her actions. He also resisted pressure he felt from his marital therapist to reframe her actions using less morally laden terms (e.g., developmental longings or expanding her sense of self). For William this "psychobabble" trivialized the intensity of his subjective distress and misconstrued self-evident moral standards. Anger was also present for William and typically expressed by sardonic disdain towards those people whose morals and value choices influenced his wife. He argued that there actually was a preferable way to live life, which he attempted to follow: hard work, frugality, family focus, and devotion to his Catholic Christian faith. In my reactions to William I was struck by what seemed like an incongruity between the hard line (I sometimes used the word *harsh*) he was drawing in relation to his wife and an otherwise pleasant disposition. Although admittedly a bit too focused on work, William was conscientious, curious, reasonable, and kind in most areas of his life. He did not diminish his own self-interest but was principled and did not seem to advance himself at the expense of others. For instance, he would often talk about standing up for his employees, that it was his duty to get them raises and to protect them by providing a challenging yet rewarding work environment. In contrast, I was struck how he would sometimes speak about Emily in a disconnected manner that lacked affection, grace, or understanding to what she described as her struggle for some relational connections in her work environment. Emily (who experienced significant grief in her life over not having children) had struggled to find a career she felt fit her, and when she landed her current job, she felt she finally fit in the world of work. Emily had returned to graduate school to increase her prospects when William was promoted to a partner position in his architectural firm and had significantly less time to spend with her. While William understood her desire for a career, he was admittedly jealous and angry at what he experienced to be his wife's intentionally hurtful behavior. We talked about his tendency to overwhelm her with logic and go into debate mode that would fluster and dominate her—leading her to respond with capitulation or ignoring. His anger at her was, at times, palpable as he refused to be married to someone with "those kind of values." Beyond primary concern, he and his wife struggled to open up any topic that include feeling states, ambivalent wishes, conflicting ideas, or anything that was difficult to resolve quickly.

William's anxiety was significant, as he did not know how to be open to ways of being that he perceived as fundamentally different from his values. Although his wife was also a conservative Catholic, he found her desire to participate in some social actions deplorable. He would diatribe about relativistic values and how these were not the actions of a good Catholic wife; when pushed, he admitted to his embarrassment that his wife might not be the modest, conservative person he had married. William disparaged the idea that her actions might be part of a phase of life developmental striving to expand her sense of self. Did she dupe him? Did she lie to him about who she really was when they got married? William's disappointment and frustration would get so intense that he considered divorce and wondered if he could remain with a woman who did not share his values.

Immediately the transference centered on his referral to me as a person who was going to help him be more liberal and open or accepting of his wife. While this was not my goal, his perception was not a complete projection as I did want him to be more open and accepting of his wife and I did not agree with some of his conclusions, especially times when he could become harsh and exclusionary. William expressed a tenor of wariness toward me, and he viewed my desire to analyze motives for his beliefs and attitudes with suspicion. However, as we settled into the work, I had the lingering notion that as much as William verbally stated his dislike of this loose-feminized-emotional-find-yourself "psychoanalytic bullshit," he enjoyed our discussions and seemed to like me being interested in him. I certainly enjoyed William; he was bright, engaging, humorous, playful, and ironic. An architect and mathematician by training, he would listen to me with careful precision and analysis to see if there were logical flaws in my statements. He strongly reacted to generalized statements that he saw as revealing relativism, acceptance of immoral behavior, and even soft psychological words like agency or finding your true self would provoke laughter and some sarcastic comment. He would playfully mock me as I asked about his feelings—"oh you want to know my feelings about that" in an exaggerated tone. In his more irritated moments he would mordantly indicate—"oh you probably want me to talk about that feeling shit," glancing at the clock to see if the session was near ending. Although this may seem evidence of a derogatory stance, I did not experience these statements as aggressive devaluation. In fact, it seemed that we could banter a bit about the nature of our work—my focus on feelings, his attempts to avoid emotional conversation—and came to understand these statements as somewhat affectionate, the repartee of two people who cared for each other and the work we were doing even if the tolerances were different.

William did respond with some relief when I assured him that in matters of spousal behavior it was perfectly acceptable to talk about the limits of his tolerance and, while he could do this without guilt, perhaps it was his approach that was off-putting. We engaged in various conversations about being able to state his limits and how to talk about their differences, I expressed my thought that he was probably coming across harsh in his communication. He reported that Emily would complain about his rigidity and demands for unanimity, but he found these accusations unfair and misleading. Exploring this further revealed hurt and fear that were masked by his anger. He attempted to soften with his wife: "You just can't do those things, and I don't want you to want to do those things." When he did soften and clarify, Emily agreed and stated that although she did not perceive the events the same way he did, she would not participate in the objectionable activities again. What became apparent, however, was a strong distrust of feeling states—he had no use for them—his sarcastically mocking continued until I was able to convince him to consider emotions as information that might be useful to him in his interactions with others. This lead to several sessions in which he would report back to me how he had thought about his feelings and used them as knowledge and how it had actually helped him avoid some sticky situations at work, but he would continue to resist any consideration of empathy with his wife's feelings. He met with suspicion any suggestion that his reactions to his wife's behavior were because he and his wife had different perspectives but that they could also arrive at the same moral endpoint from different directions—"you're taking her side." Even my wondering what it might be like to be his wife provoked an anxious glare. Our work had always hinted that his current marital difficulty might have something to do with his early years, and our work intensified as we began to focus around the notion of feelings and how his hurt and anger at his wife may be echoing rather distant losses and vulnerabilities of his childhood and adolescence.

William was the middle of eight children born to a third-generation Mexican American family; his father was the youngest of eleven and the only one to surpass the rather poor, blue-collar existence of his south Texas rural family. Steeped in the Catholic traditions, four emotional/relational self-states were dominant in William's home: predictability (consistent provision, care, and nurture for most of life's necessities); anger (bickering and fighting with siblings and parents); disconnected recognition (the recognition of family and loyalty to the family); and sarcastic affection (any connective efforts were housed in mocking sarcasm, which he enjoyed and continued to use). Everyone had strong opinions and vulnerability, sensitivity, or uncertainty were derided and rarely modeled. Christian faith was important and provided a strong moral center to the family. William entered college strongly considering the priesthood but later changed his mind and went into architecture. He met his wife while in college and was drawn to her because of the similarities in their values and life sensibilities. He also saw her as a woman who was not showy or frivolous. Early in their dating relationship William experienced some ambivalence on her part due to the lingering presence of Emily's previous boyfriend. He talked about this as significant due to a fear that he was repeating an earlier failed relationship in high school. Eventually his anxiety about her commitment was resolved enough, and they married soon after college.

As we became more comfortable exploring these connections, William's anger towards his wife actually increased: he was not to blame for the marital problems; her actions were immoral and inappropriate for a Christian marriage; he was not being rigid, he was being steadfast; he was not closed-minded, he was resolute. He felt the pressure from his marital therapist, his wife and, at times, me as almost ganging up on him. He even took to quoting Psalms that referred to the wicked clamoring to overtake him. The confusing piece here was that there was clear evidence that his wife shared his same values, did not want to divorce, and in general, believed what he believed. However, any attempt to deconstruct his stance angered him and hardened his resolve. At one point, because we were actually dealing with offenses that had occurred over three years prior, I asked William why he could not forgive his wife for her past actions and accept that she was in agreement with him about what it meant to have a good Christian marriage. His response was that she had never apologized—a fact that his wife disputed. His problem, according to her, was that he didn't like that she didn't agree with his negative evaluation of her actions or intentions and that they differed in the specifics of her questionable behavior. This of course got us exploring what he meant by apologizing. For William, the problem was not her apology but her contrition. Emerging from his Catholic tradition, contrition is an important concept in the process of forgiveness and eventual absolution. In contrast to my more Protestant emphasis on the primacy of God's grace as the critical factor in repentance, Catholic teaching emphasizes the contrite heart as essential to receiving grace and eventual reconciliation. As I considered this concept further, I was able to understand what might be partially interfering with William's ability to be more gracious with his wife. Let us go into a little more detail.

Contrition emerges from the Latin *contrition*—a breaking of something hardened. It is defined explicitly by the Council of Trent as "a sorrow of soul and a hatred of sin committed, with a firm purpose of not sinning in the future."[46] Although the word itself is not frequent in Scripture, we can think of David's lament in Psalm 51 as a prototypical contrite heart. Aquinas states, "Since it is requisite for the remission of sin that a man cast away entirely the liking for sin which implies a sort of continuity and solidity in his mind, the act which obtains forgiveness is termed by a figure of speech 'contrition.'"[47] Further, there are four qualities to the process of contrition. First, it must be interior; contrition must be real and sincere sorrow of heart, not merely an external manifestation of repentance. Second, it must be supernatural; contrition ought to be prompted by God's grace and aroused by motives that spring from faith, not merely natural motives or to avoid some undesired outcome like the loss of fortune, esteem, or a marriage. Third, it must be universal; contrition must involve the desire to avoid all sin and the seeking of repentance for all of one's sins. Fourth, it must be sovereign; contrition involves the firmness of will to not sin despite what evil may befall a person in the future—a steadfastness, if you will, to persevere in one's commitment to not sin whatever the circumstances.[48]

We spent a few sessions talking about how he might approach his wife with this renewed request for an apology, along with the full explanation of how her actions hurt him. He really doubted her trustworthiness, and he was afraid that if she still wanted to hang out with coworkers during her business trips, they would subtly seduce her

---

[46]J. Waterworth, ed. and trans., "The Council of Trent: The Fourteenth Session," in *The Canons and Decrees of the Sacred and Oecumenical Council of Trent* (London: Dolman, 1848), 92-121, Hanover Historical Texts Project, para. 5, https://history.hanover.edu/texts/trent/ctl4.html.
[47]As cited in E. Hanna, "Contrition," in *The Catholic Encyclopedia*, ed. K. Knight (New York: Robert Appleton Company, 1908), 4, par. 2, www.newadvent.org/cathen/04337a.htm.
[48]Hanna, "Contrition."

away from their covenantal relationship. After some significant prepa-
ration William was able to make this request of his wife, and in gracious
response to his appeal William's wife sincerely apologized for how she
had hurt him and stated that she had no desire to wound him in the
future. This act of contrition had a significant impact on William's
mood, and for the next several sessions he relaxed and reported feeling
more at ease and trusting of his wife. At one point we even considered
spacing out our sessions more, but then a serious breach occurred that
infuriated William, which lead to significant distress for Emily, myself,
and their marriage therapist.

On a visit home to see her family, Emily was eating out with a friend
and ran into an old boyfriend who joined them for dinner and drinks.
While Emily was open about this and she did not see it as a problem at
all, William was angry and felt duped. He had forgiven his wife for
previous acts of indiscretion and now she was doing it again; this time
he felt it was purposeful. I was also somewhat baffled by Emily's un-
empathic justifications. The relational nuances and entanglements that
emerged from this incident were numerous and serious; both contem-
plated divorce at the return of old defensive patterns of relating. In our
work, William returned to significant experiences of anger: he wanted
his marriage to work but would not tolerate more hurtful behavior
from his wife, especially because she was justifying herself and trying
to convince him that he was just uptight. As we talked, it became clear
that William's anger was not helping him communicate effectively with
his wife; he kept resorting to rational moral justifications, something
his wife experienced as dominating and controlling. By this time
William and I were very familiar with how his anger and rational debate
was a cover for more tender emotions of hurt, fear, longing, and disappointment. As we worked to access these more vulnerable self-states,
William fought me. He would delay talking about painful topics until
the end of sessions and in a playful repartee we would use the clock as
a gauge for how long we would immerse ourselves in the intimate discussion of feelings. As we struggled to articulate his inner world,

William wanted to remember the specifics of how I phrased his feelings. I was captured by the tragedy of his dilemma. Raised to cloak relational longing and needs in emotionally distant trappings of argument or sarcasm, William was terrified to discuss the fear of losing his wife, his difficulty trusting that she wanted to be with him, and the disappointment and hurt that she did not treasure her faith in a manner similar to him. We also slowly began to discover that his arguments about moral relativism and how his wife needed to admit her wrongness were not only calls from his Catholic tradition for a contrite spirit, they protected him from the intimate vulnerability of sharing his feelings of fear and longing. Framing her infractions in the language of moral certitude bypassed his terror of risking full disclosure. Slowly, tentatively, as William and I were able to sit with his lack of trust, fear of being hurt, and uncertainty of being wanted, he began taking small risks with his wife.

SUMMARY DISCUSSION

Because Christian formation is an embodied, walked out, relational process, I believe our experience of change or transformation must pass through or be marked by another.[49] In other words, the movement toward imaging Christ is not a solitary endeavor and requires the connective experience of involved relationship to progress. In addition, Christian formation at its most fundamental addresses the everyday relational processes that help or hinder our ability to live in a community of faith, love, and justice.

My work with William is a fascinating experience not only for its exploration of the meaning of burdensome moral judgment but also in highlighting the particularities of a person's moral stance as it emerges within the context of one's psychological development and Christian tradition. The severity of William's judgment of his wife

---

[49]Change must pass through another: H. Kohut, "Forms and Transformations of Narcissism," *Journal of the American Psychoanalytic Association* (1966): 243-72; change must be marked by another: Fonagy et al., *Affect Regulation*.

enacted a defense against the longing and fear of his own need for intimate connection and the co-opting of particular moral judgments to reinforce a preferred relational distance. But that is not all it was. It is important to recognize that William's suspicion of the psychoanalytic method is not without merit. As a mode of inquiry and method of promoting change, psychoanalysis often avoids explicit declaration of its tendency to reduce moral preferences to psychological and emotional processes. While seeking authenticity, psychoanalysis is prone to an emotive relativism and egoism that is counter to the ethical imperatives of many faith traditions. Yet it need not be so, as Taylor pointed out; relativism and self-centered egoism are debasements of an ethic of authenticity that seeks the expression of who one truly is within the context of an ongoing relational world.[50] The goal for William and me was not to assuage his authentic value construals but to increase and delimit his articulation within the relational context in a manner that would be most conducive to his finding common ground with Emily.

However, the implicit morality within the contemporary psychoanalytic work is not the only player.[51] Contrary to the myth that clinical practice often perpetuates, we therapists of any stripe do not operate from a morally neutral stance, and those of us who are Christian must understand the mutuality of our engagement in the construction of what it means to form a Christian and the entanglement of joint pursuits as our own traditions mix and interpenetrate those of our patients. Where I was looking for more grace, William needed sorrow and contrition; my invitation and pursuit of a more authentic emotional engagement activated anxiety, but also helped to free his ability to express his desires in a way that his wife could appreciate. I needed to respect his moral positions as meaningful, a display of deeply held

---

[50]C. Taylor, *The Ethics of Authenticity* (Cambridge, MA: Harvard University Press, 1991).

[51]P. Cushman, *Constructing the Self, Constructing America: A Cultural History of Psychotherapy* (Boston: Da Capo Press, 1995); D. Burston and R. Frie, *Psychotherapy as Human Science* (Pittsburgh, PA: Duquesne University Press, 2006); S. Buechler, *Clinical Values: Emotions That Guide Psychoanalytic Treatment* (Hillsdale, NJ: The Analytic Press, 2004).

convictions, and he to accept the hidden emotional vulnerability underlying the onerous tone of his moral positions. As we created space for each other, enough to allow difference and tension without losing connection, I became a little bit Catholic with William, and he became a little bit of a psychologist with me.

QUEEN OF THE VIRTUES AND KING OF THE VICES

GRACED GRATITUDE AND DISGRACED INGRATITUDE

ROBERT A. EMMONS

Gratitude is a human quality with unusual power, so much so that it would not be an overstatement to say that the good life is impossible without it. As the "moral memory of mankind,"[1] gratitude makes life better for self and others. Awareness of its importance raises inescapable big questions: How gratefully or ungratefully will each of us live our own lives? Why will we choose to do so and what effects will this have on ourselves and those around us? Writing in the *Notre Dame Journal of Law, Ethics, and Public Policy*, Elizabeth Loder noted, "Gratitude affects how a person conceives the world and expects others to behave. It increases interpersonal receptivity. It seeps into one's being and affects all dispositions pervasively."[2] Throughout history, the concept of gratitude

---

Some content in this chapter has been developed separately as Robert A. Emmons, "Queen of the Virtues? Gratitude as a Human Strength," *Reflective Practice: Formation and Supervision in Ministry* 32 (2012), http://journals.sfu.ca/rpfs/index.php/rpfs/article/viewFile/59/58.

[1]Georg Simmel, *The Sociology of Georg Simmel* (New York: The Free Press, 1950).

[2]R. E. Loder, "Lawyers and Gratitude," *Notre Dame Journal of Law, Ethics, and Public Policy* 20 (2006): 176.

has been central to society running smoothly, being a mainstay of philosophical and religious accounts of living, leading it to be deemed not only "the greatest of the virtues, but the parent of all others."[3]

The act of praising God flows nearly automatically from acknowledging and recognizing the many gifts that he bestows and is a hallmark of what it means to participate fully in human flourishing by living in right relation to him. Without this awareness, it is impossible to truly flourish no matter in what other ways a person appears to be living well. This is not to say that secularists have no concept of gratitude, for they surely do. Yet there is something distinctive in seeing the world through a lens of Christian gratitude.

Feelings of gratitude can be powerful, overcoming its possessor with an intensity that rivals any other human emotion. It was this feeling of being overwhelmed with gratitude that the Catholic Saint Ignatius of Loyola was well familiar with. His prayer life was said to be so intense that during Mass he often had to pause as his eyes filled with tears and he could not see. After a while the constant tearing began to adversely affect his eyes. He sought a special papal dispensation to relieve him of some devotional duties so that his health might be preserved. In his spiritual diary he wrote, "Because of the violent pain that I felt in one eye as a result of the tears, this thought came to me: If I continue saying Mass, I could lose this eye, whereas it is better to keep it."[4] It is this intensity of gratitude that led a contemporary philosopher to proclaim that "gratitude is the most pleasant of the virtues and most virtuous of the pleasures."[5]

How do these extraordinary claims regarding the power and promise of gratitude fare when scientific lights are shined on them? Can gratitude live up to its billing? In this chapter I review the growing database on

[3]R. A. Emmons and C. A. Crumpler, "Gratitude as a Human Strength: Appraising the Evidence," *Journal of Social and Clinical Psychology* 19 (2000): 56-69.
[4]W. W. Meissner, *To the Greater Glory: A Psychological Study of Ignatian Spirituality* (Milwaukee, WI: Marquette University Press, 1999).
[5]A. Comte-Sponville, *A Small Treatise of the Great Virtues*, trans. C. Temerson (New York: Metropolitan Books, 2001).

gratitude and human flourishing, explore mechanisms by which gratitude promotes flourishing, and conclude by discussing issues in the cultivation of gratitude. My discussion is placed in the context of spiritual formation and factors that must be taken into account for a Christian person to effectively grow in gratitude.

WHAT IS GRATITUDE?

Gratitude is a positive, moral emotion that people experience when they receive direct benefits or gestures of caring support from others. As a morally compelling emotion, it motivates recipients of aid to express appreciation toward benefactors and reciprocate in some normatively appropriate way. However, gratitude goes beyond mere reciprocity because it also motivates people to help strangers. A declaration of appreciation for some act of kindness may thus function as a reliable signal of a person's inclination to cooperate with others in everyday exchanges. Thus, communities that hope to maintain cooperative relations are likely to institute clear prescriptive norms for expressing gratitude. Individuals who express gratitude when they receive benefits are rewarded in various ways. In turn, those who fail to express gratitude may suffer reputational penalties. Ungrateful people are likely to be perceived as both low in competence because they required assistance and low in warmth because their ingratitude violates cooperative norms and these perceptions arouse intense feelings of contempt.[6]

Vertically, religions have long viewed gratitude as central to the human-divine relationship. As long as people have believed in a Supreme Being, believers have sought ways to express gratitude and thanksgiving to this being, their ultimate giver. In monotheistic traditions God is conceived of as a personal being that is the source of goodness and the first giver of all gifts, to whom much is owed. Gratitude is the basic response to the perception and reception of divine grace, the feeling that one has received gifts and benefits beyond those that are expected, deserved, or earned. As a Christianly imbued way of being, it arises when a believer reflects on God's intervention in history

---

[6]M. E. McCullough, M. B. Kimeldorf, and A. D. Cohen, "An Adaptation for Altruism: The Social Causes, Social Effects, and Social Evolution of Gratitude," *Current Directions in Psychological Science* 17 (2008): 281-85.

or in the life of that individual, providing or doing for them that which they never could have done or provided for themselves. In the most general sense, grateful affect comes from the recognition that creation is a gift of God and not a right, privilege, or accident, occurring when the mind is turned toward contemplation of God's incomprehensible goodness. Recognizing God's provision of benefits and responding with grateful emotion is one of the most common religious dispositions that Christian people are encouraged to develop. With gratitude there is amplification, strengthening, and deepening of the entire awareness of life.

Though the concept of a personally transcendent God is not relevant in nontheistic traditions, gratitude retains its spiritual nature with gratitude primarily as an interpersonal ethic. The terms "cosmic" or "transpersonal gratitude" are sometimes used to depict this form of gratitude. This fundamental spiritual quality to gratitude that transcends religious traditions is aptly conveyed by Frederick Streng: "In this attitude people recognize that they are connected to each other in a mysterious and miraculous way that is not fully determined by physical forces, but is part of a wider, or transcendent context."[7] This spiritual core of gratefulness is essential if gratitude is to be not simply a tool for narcissistic self-improvement. True gratefulness rejoices in the other. It has as its ultimate goal reflecting back the goodness that one has received by creatively seeking opportunities for giving. The motivation for doing so resides in the grateful appreciation that one has lived by the grace of others, a grace that is neither earned nor deserved.[8] In this sense, the spirituality of gratitude is opposed to a self-serving belief that one deserves or is entitled to the blessings that he or she enjoys. Rather, it is knowing the grace by which one lives, itself a profound spiritual realization.

---

[7]F. J. Streng, "Introduction: Thanksgiving as a Worldwide Response to Life," in *Spoken and Unspoken Thanks: Some Comparative Soundings*, ed. J. B. Carman and F. J. Streng (Dallas, TX: Center for World Thanksgiving, 1989), 1-9.

[8]Compare another discussion of this material in Robert A. Emmons and Robin Stern, "Gratitude as a Psychotherapeutic Intervention," *Journal of Clinical Psychology: In Session* 69, no. 8 (2013): 846-55.

FINDINGS FROM THE SCIENCE OF GRATITUDE

Examinations of gratitude in the history of ideas come from a number of perspectives—philosophy, theology, and political economy, to name a few. Not to be outdone, the tools and techniques of modern science have recently been brought to bear on understanding the nature of gratitude and why it is important for human health and happiness. A scientific perspective can provide an evidence-based approach to understanding how and in what ways gratitude brings benefits into the life of the practitioner.

Gratitude is foundational to well-being and mental health throughout the life span. From childhood to old age, accumulating evidence documents the wide array of psychological, physical, and relational benefits associated with gratitude. In the past few years, there has been a tremendous increase in the accumulation of scientific evidence showing the contribution of gratitude to psychological and social well-being. Clinical trials indicate that the practice of gratitude can have dramatic and lasting positive effects in a person's life. It can lower blood pressure; improve immune function; promote happiness and well-being; and spur acts of helpfulness, generosity, and cooperation. Additionally, gratitude reduces lifetime risk for depression, anxiety, and substance abuse disorders.[9]

Based on Erika Rosenberg's hierarchical levels of affective experience, gratitude has been identified as a trait, emotion, and mood.[10] The grateful disposition can be defined as a stable affective trait that would lower the threshold of experiencing gratitude. As an emotion, gratitude can be understood as an acute, intense, and relatively brief psychophysiological

---

[9]M. E. McCullough, S. D. Kilpatrick, R. A. Emmons, and B. D. Larson, "Is Gratitude a Moral Affect?," *Psychological Bulletin* 127 (2001): 249-66; R. A. Emmons and M. E. McCullough, "Counting Blessings Versus Burdens: An Experimental Investigation of Gratitude and Subjective Well-Being in Daily Life," *Journal of Personality and Social Psychology* 84 (2003): 377-89; J. J. Froh, W. J. Sefick, and R. A. Emmons, "Counting Blessings in Early Adolescents: An Experimental Study of Gratitude and Subjective Well-Being," *Journal of School Psychology* 46 (2008): 213-33. See discussion of these ideas in a different context in Robert A. Emmons, "Why a Positive Psychology of Gratitude Needs Original Sin," *Christian Psychology* 8, no. 1 (2014): 16-19.

[10]E. L. Rosenberg, "Levels of Analysis and the Organization of Affect," *Review of General Psychology* 2 (1998): 247-70.

reaction to being the recipient of a benefit from another. Last, as a stable mood, gratitude has also been identified to have a subtle, broad, and longer-duration impact on consciousness.[11] Gratitude is not just a transient emotion, but it is also a virtue. Grateful people are more prone to the emotion, are prone to respond with gratitude to a wider range of beneficent actions, and are more likely to notice beneficence on the part of others—in particular more likely to respond to it with the emotion of gratitude rather than with alternative emotions like resentment, shame, or guilt. Grateful people are likely to agree with statements such as "It's important to appreciate each day that you are alive," "I often reflect on how much easier my life is because of the efforts of others," and "For me, life is much more of a gift than it is a burden." Items such as these come from personality questionnaires designed to measure trait levels of gratitude—in other words, to identify people who are by nature grateful souls.

Both state and dispositional gratitude have been shown to enhance overall psychological, social, and physical well-being. For example, gratitude involves and encourages more positive social interactions, in turn making people better adjusted and accepted by people around them, and finally leading to well-being. Since the emergence of gratitude research over the past decade, the two main measures that have been widely administered to measure dispositional gratitude are the 6-item Gratitude Questionnaire[12] and the 44-item Gratitude, Resentment, and Appreciation Test or the GRAT.[13] Dispositional gratitude is a generalized tendency to first recognize and then emotionally respond with thankfulness, after attributing benefits received through benevolence to an external moral agent. The 44-item GRAT includes the three dimensions of trait gratitude: resentment, simple appreciation,

---

[11]M. E. McCullough, J. Tsang, and R. A. Emmons, "Gratitude in Intermediate Affective Terrain: Links of Grateful Moods to Individual Differences and Daily Emotional Experience," *Journal of Personality and Social Psychology* 86 (2004): 295-309.

[12]McCullough et al., "Gratitude."

[13]P. C. Watkins, D. L. Grimm, and L. Hailu, "Counting Your Blessings: Grateful Individuals Recall More Positive Memories," presented at the 11th Annual Convention of the American Psychological Society, Denver, CO, June 1998.

and social appreciation. Other measures to assess gratitude include personal interviews, rating scales, and other self-report measures such as free response and personal narratives.[14]

Dispositional gratitude has been shown to uniquely and incrementally contribute to subjective well-being and contribute to benefits above and beyond general positive affect. Dispositional gratitude has also been found to be positively associated with prosocial traits such as empathy, forgiveness, and willingness to help others.[15] For example, people who rated themselves as having a grateful disposition perceived themselves as having more prosocial characteristics, expressed by their empathetic behavior and emotional support for friends within the last month.

People with stronger dispositions toward gratitude tend to be more spiritually and religiously minded. Not only do they score higher on measures of traditional religiousness, but they also scored higher on non-sectarian measures of spirituality that assess spiritual experiences (e.g., sense of contact with a divine power) and sentiments (e.g., beliefs that all living things are interconnected) independent of specific theological orientations. Although the absolute magnitude of the correlations between gratitude and religion/spirituality are not large, the extant evidence suggests that spiritually or religiously inclined people have a stronger disposition to experience gratitude than do their less spiritual/ religious counterparts. Watkins and colleagues found that trait gratitude correlated positively with intrinsic religiousness and negatively with extrinsic religiousness. The authors suggest that the presence of gratitude may be a *positive* affective hallmark of religiously and spiritually engaged people, just as an absence of depressive symptoms is a *negative* affective

---

[14]R. A. Emmons, M. E. McCullough, and J. Tsang, "The Assessment of Gratitude," in *Positive Psychological Assessment: A Handbook of Models and Measures*, ed. S. J. Lopez and C. R. Snyder (Washington, DC: American Psychological Association, 2003), 327-41.

[15]P. C. Watkins et al., "Gratitude and Happiness: Development of a Measure of Gratitude, and Relationships with Subjective Well-Being," *Social Behavior and Personality* 31 (2003): 431-52; A. M. Wood, S. Joseph, and J. Maltby, "Gratitude Uniquely Predicts Satisfaction with Life: Incremental Validity Above the Domains and Facets of the Five Factor Model," *Personality and Individual Differences* 45 (2008): 49-54.

hallmark of spiritually and religiously engaged people. They likely see benefits as gifts from God, "as the first cause of all benefits."[16]

Additional research has examined trait gratitude in religious contexts or gratitude felt toward God. A nationwide survey found that people who have no religious preference or who have not attended church services recently are twice as likely to skip traditional Thanksgiving holiday observances compared to people who are active religiously.[17] Krause found that gratitude felt toward God reduced the effect of stress on health in late-life adults.[18] Using data from a longitudinal nationwide survey, Krause and colleagues further uncovered a linkage between "congregational cohesiveness" and gratitude toward God.[19] Gratitude toward God was measured by modifying the Gratitude Questionnaire to make reference to God (e.g., "I have so much in life to be thankful to God for"; "I am grateful to God for all he has done for me"). Perceptions of cohesiveness (a belief that personal values are shared by church members) predicted an increase in feelings of gratitude toward God over time leading the researchers to conclude that church attendance influences gratitude indirectly through congregation-based emotional support. Using the same data set, Krause found that gratitude toward God mediated the effect of financial strain on depression in late-life adults.[20] Financial stress had a greater impact on depression for older adults lower in gratitude, whereas the negative effects of financial strain on depressive symptoms were eradicated for older adults who were more grateful. Gratitude directed toward God adds unique variance in predicting

---

[16]R. A. Emmons and T. E. Kneezel, "Giving Thanks: Spiritual and Religious Correlates of Gratitude," *Journal of Psychology and Christianity* 24 (2005): 140-48.

[17]Marianne Smallwood, "For Those Who Don't Celebrate Thanksgiving," Huffington Post, www .huffingtonpost.com/marianne-smallwood/for-those-who-dont-celebrate-thanksgiving _b_8648310.html.

[18]N. Krause, "Gratitude Toward God, Stress, and Health in Late Life," *Research on Aging* 28 (2006): 163-83.

[19]N. Krause and C. G. Ellison, "The Doubting Process: A Longitudinal Study of the Precipitants and Consequences of Religious Doubt in Older Adults," *Journal for the Scientific Study of Religion* 48 (2009): 293-312.

[20]N. Krause, "Religious Involvement, Gratitude, and Change in Depressive Symptoms over Time," *International Journal for the Psychology of Religion* 19 (2009): 155-72.

happiness and life satisfaction above and beyond general trait gratitude.[21] Last, dispositional gratitude was found to contribute to greater stress resiliency in a small sample of Presbyterian clergy.[22]

Another empirical approach to religious gratitude is to examine themes of thankfulness and gratitude in personal prayer content. In a study of prayer in the lives of college students, prayers of thanksgiving were the second most common type of prayer, following petitionary appeals.[23] Another study looking at prayer found that prayers of thanksgiving were negatively related to depression and anxiety and positively related to greater hope in patients with rheumatoid arthritis.[24] Prayers of praise and thankfulness were rated as the second most effective form of prayer in coping with personal difficulties. A bidirectional relationship between gratitude and prayer has been demonstrated. Grateful people spend more time in prayer, and frequent prayer has been shown to increase gratefulness.[25]

A number of studies have examined the effects of experimentally based gratitude interventions. In one of the first studies examining the benefits of experimentally induced grateful thoughts on psychological well-being in daily life, the experimenters focused on gratitude in relation to three conditions: gratitude provoking experiences, hassles, and neutral life events.[26] As expected, the gratitude condition led to overall well-being as revealed by fewer health complaints and a more positive outlook toward life. Participants in the gratitude condition also reported fewer

---

[21]D. H. Rosmarin et al., "Grateful to God or Just Plain Grateful? A Comparison of Religious and General Gratitude," *The Journal of Positive Psychology* 4 (2011), doi.org/10.1080/17439760.2011.596557.

[22]C. Lee, "Dispositional Resiliency and Adjustment in Protestant Pastors: A Pilot Study," *Pastoral Psychology* 59 (2010): 631-40.

[23]J. P. McKinney and K. G. McKinney, "Prayer in the Lives of Late Adolescents," *Journal of Adolescence* 22 (1999): 279 90.

[24]S. P. Laird et al., "Measuring Private Prayer: Development, Validation, and Clinical Application of the Multidimensional Prayer Inventory," *The International Journal for the Psychology of Religion* 14 (2004): 251-72.

[25]N. M. Lambert et al., "Can Prayer Increase Gratitude?," *Psychology of Religion and Spirituality* 3 (2009): 139-49.

[26]Emmons and McCullough, "Counting Blessings"; Robert A. Emmons, *Thanks! How the New Science of Gratitude Can Make You Happier* (New York: Houghton-Mifflin, 2007).

physical health problems and also rated their life to be better compared to participants in the hassles and neutral conditions. Furthermore, in a study examining the contribution of gratitude in daily mood over twenty-one days, gratitude was strongly associated with spiritual transcendence and other positive affective traits (e.g., extraversion).[27] In the past few years, a number of laboratory and research-based intervention studies have also been examining the positive impact of gratitude induced activities (e.g., the gratitude visit, gratitude letter) on psychological well-being in both healthy and clinical samples.[28]

In these studies, participants in the gratitude condition are provided instructions similar to the following: "We want to focus for a moment on benefits or gifts that you have received in your life. These gifts could be simple everyday pleasures, people in your life, personal strengths or talents, moments of natural beauty, or gestures of kindness from others. We might not normally think about these things as gifts, but that is how we want you to think about them. Take a moment to really savor or relish these gifts, think about their value, and then write them down every night before going to sleep." A wide range of experiences sparked gratitude: cherished interactions, awareness of physical health, overcoming obstacles, and simply being alive, to name a few. This instructional set was in contrast with comparison conditions asking those in other randomly assigned groups to chronicle their daily travails or hassles or to reflect on ways in which they were better off than others.

In daily studies of emotional experience, when people report feeling grateful, thankful, and appreciative, they also feel more loving, forgiving, joyful, and enthusiastic. These deep affections appear to be formed through the discipline of gratitude. In this regard, it is interesting that the Greek root of the word enthusiasm, *enthousiasmos*, means "inspired by or

---

[27]M. E. McCullough, J. Tsang, and R. A. Emmons, "Gratitude in Intermediate Affective Terrain: Links of Grateful Moods to Individual Differences and Daily Emotional Experience," *Journal of Personality and Social Psychology* 86 (2004): 295-309.

[28]S. L. Kerr, A. O'Donovan, and C. A. Pepping, "Can Gratitude and Kindness Interventions Enhance Well-Being in a Clinical Sample?," *Journal of Happiness Studies* 16 (2014), doi: 10.1007 /s10902-013-9492-1.

possessed by a god." Importantly, this data showing that gratitude is correlated with beneficial outcomes is not limited to self-reports. Notably, the family, friends, partners, and others that surround them consistently report that people who practice gratitude seem measurably happier and are more pleasant to be around. Grateful people are rated by others as more helpful, more outgoing, more optimistic, and more trustworthy.[29]

The benefits of gratitude were further confirmed in another study that compared the efficacy of five different interventions that were hypothesized to increase personal happiness and decrease personal depression.[30]

In a random-assignment, placebo-controlled internet study, a gratitude intervention (writing and delivering a letter of thankfulness to someone who had been especially helpful but had never been properly thanked) was found to significantly increase happiness and decrease depression for up to one month following the visit. Results indicated that "participants in the gratitude visit condition showed the largest positive changes in the whole study." Thus the benefits of gratitude do not appear to be limited to the self-guided journal-keeping methodology utilized by Emmons and McCullough.[31]

WHY IS GRATITUDE GOOD? EXPLORING MECHANISMS

How does one account for the psychological, emotional, and physical benefits of gratitude? Gratitude implies a recognition that it is possible for other agents to act toward us with beneficial, selfless motives. A number of possible explanations have been suggested; however not all of them have been fully investigated. In the next section, we examine five explanations for the relation between gratitude and well-being.

Gratitude increases spiritual awareness. The idea of gratitude has appeal far beyond Christian discourse. Many world religions commend gratitude as a desirable human trait, which may cause spiritual or

---

[29]M. E. McCullough, R. A. Emmons, and J. A. Tsang, "The Grateful Disposition: A Conceptual and Empirical Topography," *Journal of Personality and Social Psychology* 82, no. 1 (2002): 112-27.
[30]M. E. P. Seligman, T. A. Steen, N. Park, and C. Peterson, "Positive Psychology Progress: Empirical Validation of Interventions," *American Psychologist* 60 (2005): 410-21.
[31]Emmons and McCullough, "Counting Blessings."

religious people to adopt a grateful outlook.[32] Upon recognition of God's provision of benefits, humans respond with grateful affect, and gratitude is one of the most common religious feelings that believers in virtually all spiritual traditions are encouraged to develop. When contemplating a positive circumstance that cannot be attributed to intentional human effort, such as a miraculous healing or the gift of life, spiritually inclined people may still be able attribute these positive outcomes to a human or non-human agent (viz., God or a higher power) and thus, experience more gratitude. Third, spiritually inclined people also tend to attribute positive outcomes to God's intervention, but not negative ones.[33] As a result, many positive life events that are not due to the actions of another person (e.g., pleasant weather, avoiding an automobile accident) may be perceived as occasions for gratitude to God, although negative events (e.g., a long winter, an automobile accident) would likely *not* be attributed to God. This attributional style, then, is likely to magnify the positive emotional effects of pleasant life events. Being grateful to a Supreme Being and to other people is an acknowledgment that there are good and enjoyable things in the world to be enjoyed in accordance with the giver's intent. Good things happen by design. If a person believes in the spiritual concept of grace, they believe that there is a pattern of beneficence in the world that exists quite independently of their own striving and even their own existence. Gratitude thus depends upon receiving what we do not expect to receive or have not earned or receiving more than we believe we deserve. This awareness is simultaneously humbling *and* elevating.

Gratitude promotes physical health. Some of the benefits of gratitude for mental health may result from gratitude's ability to enhance physical health functioning. A growing number of studies have reported physical

---

[32]J. B. Carman and F. J. Streng, eds., *Spoken and Unspoken Thanks: Some Comparative Soundings* (Cambridge, MA: Harvard University Press, 1989); R. A. Emmons and C. A. Crumpler, "Gratitude as a Human Strength: Appraising the Evidence," *Journal of Social and Clinical Psychology* 19 (2000): 56-67.

[33]M. B. Lupfer et al., "Making Secular and Religious Attributions: The Availability Hypothesis Revisited," *Journal for the Scientific Study of Religion* 33 (1994): 162-71; M. B. Lupfer, D. Tolliver, and M. Jackson, "Explaining Life-Altering Occurrences: A Test of the 'God-of-the-Gaps' Hypothesis," *Journal for the Scientific Study of Religion* 35 (1996): 379-91.

health benefits of gratitude, and these relations have been largely independent of trait negative affect.[34] Gratitude interventions have been shown to reduce the bodily complaints, increase sleep duration and efficiency, and promote exercise.[35] Experimental research suggests that discrete experiences of gratitude and appreciation may cause increases in parasympathetic myocardial control, lower systolic blood pressure, as well as improve more molar aspects of physical health such as everyday symptoms and physician visits.[36] McCraty and colleagues found that appreciation increased parasympathetic activity—a change thought to be beneficial in controlling stress and hypertension—as well as "coherence" or entrainment across various autonomic response channels.[37] Therefore, there might be some direct physiological benefits to frequent experience of grateful emotions. These findings provide a link between positive emotions and increased physiological efficiency, which may partly explain the growing number of correlations documented between positive emotions, improved health, and increased longevity.

Gratitude maximizes the good. Gratitude maximizes enjoyment of the pleasurable in our lives. A well-established law in the psychology of emotion is the principle of adaptation. People adapt to circumstances both pleasant and unpleasant. Our emotion systems like newness. Unfortunately for personal happiness, adaptation to pleasant circumstances occurs more rapidly than adaptation to unpleasant life changes. This is why even a major windfall, such as a huge pay raise, tends to impact happiness for only a mere few months. Once the glow fades, we return to the same happiness level we had before. Psychologists call this

---

[34]P. Hill, M. Allemand, and B. W. Roberts, "Examining the Pathways Between Gratitude and Self-Rated Physical Health Across Adulthood," *Personality and Individual Differences* 54 (2013): 92-96.

[35]A. M. Wood, S. Joseph, J. Lloyd, and S. Atkins, "Gratitude Influences Sleep Through the Mechanism of Pre-Sleep Cognitions," *Journal of Psychosomatic Research* 66 (2009): 43-48.

[36]R. McCraty and D. Childre, "The Grateful Heart: The Psychophysiology of Appreciation," in *The Psychology of Gratitude*, ed. R. A. Emmons and M. E. McCullough (New York: Oxford University Press, 2004), 230-55; R. W. Shipon, "Gratitude: Effect on Perspectives and Blood Pressure of Inner-City African-American Hypertensive Patients," Temple University, 2007, *Dissertation Abstracts International: Section B: The Sciences and Engineering*, 68 (3-B): 1977, 35; Hill et al., "Examining the Pathways."

[37]McCraty and Childre, "The Grateful Heart."

phenomenon hedonic adaptation. The only thing that can change it and prolong the increase in happiness is gratitude. Gratitude promotes the savoring of positive life experiences and situations, so that the maximum satisfaction and enjoyment is derived from one's circumstances. In helping people not take things for granted, gratitude may recalibrate people's "set points" for happiness—our baseline levels of happiness that appear to be primarily innate, driven by one's genes.[38]

Gratitude protects against the negative. Gratitude also mitigates toxic emotions and states. Nothing can destroy happiness more quickly than envy, greed, and resentment. The German moral philosopher Balduin Schwarz identified the problem when he said, "the ungrateful, envious, complaining man . . . cripples himself. He is focused on what he has not, particularly on that which somebody else has or seems to have, and by that he tends to poison his world."[39] Grateful people tend to be satisfied with what they have, and so are less susceptible to such emotions as disappointment, regret, and frustration. Moreover, in the context of material prosperity, by maintaining a grateful focus, a person may avoid disillusionment and emptiness. The sense of security that characterizes grateful people makes them less susceptible to needing to rely on material accomplishments for a stable sense of self.

Gratitude strengthens relationships. Perhaps most important of all is that gratitude strengthens and expands relationships. It cultivates a person's sense of interconnectedness, both to others and to God. People who keep gratitude journals report feeling closer and more connected to others, are more likely to help others, and are actually seen as more helpful by significant others in their social networks. Gratitude is the "moral memory of mankind," wrote noted sociologist Georg Simmel. One just needs to try to imagine human relationships existing without gratitude. By way of contrast, ingratitude leads inevitably to a confining,

---

[38]P. C. Watkins, *Gratitude and the Good Life: Toward a Psychology of Appreciation* (New York: Springer, 2014).

[39]S. Schwarz, *Values and Human Experience: Essays in Honor of the Memory of Balduin Schwarz* (New York: P. Lang, 1999).

restricting, and "shrinking" sense of self. Emotions like anger, resentment, envy, and bitterness tend to undermine happy social relations. But the virtue of gratitude is not only a firewall of protection against such corruption of relationships; it contributes positively to friendship and civility, because it is both benevolent (wishing the benefactor well) and just (giving the benefactor his due, in a certain special way). We also have evidence that people who are high on dispositional gratitude, the chronic tendency to be aware of blessings in life, have better relationships, are more likely to protect and preserve these relationships, are more securely attached, and are less lonely and isolated. People who have an easier time conjuring up reasons to be grateful are less likely to say that they lack companionship or that no one really knows them well. Our innate longing for belonging is strengthened when we experience and express heartfelt gratitude. Gratitude takes us outside ourselves where we see ourselves as part of a larger, intricate network of sustaining relationships, relationships that are mutually reciprocal.

OVERCOMING OBSTACLES TO GRATITUDE

Research has proven that gratitude is essential for happiness, but modern times have regressed gratitude into a mere feeling instead of retaining its historic value, a virtue that leads to action. Just as great philosophers such as Cicero and Seneca conclude in their writings, gratitude is an action of returning a favor and is not just a sentiment. By the same token, ingratitude is the failure to both acknowledge receiving a favor and refusing to return or repay the favor. Just as gratitude is the queen of the virtues, ingratitude is the king of the vices. People who are incapable of or unwilling to acknowledge benefits that others have conferred upon them are highly scorned in most traditional conceptions of human social life. Generosity should evoke thankfulness, but many of us can probably think of times when either our own benefaction was met afterwards with coldness and resentment, or perhaps when we resented and avoided someone who had been generous to us. Any discussion of gratitude has to reckon with the reality of ingratitude.

Given its magnetic appeal, it is a wonder that gratitude might be rejected. Yet it is. If we fail to choose it, by default we choose ingratitude. Millions make this choice every day. Why? Provision, whether supernatural or natural, becomes so commonplace that it is easily taken for granted. We believe the universe owes us a living. We do not want to be beholden. Losing sight of protection, favors, benefits, and blessings renders a person spiritually and morally bankrupt. It would be hard to improve upon the words of Abraham Lincoln: "We have grown in numbers, wealth and power, as no other nation ever has grown. But we have forgotten God. We have forgotten the gracious Hand which preserved us in peace, and multiplied and enriched and strengthened us; and we have vainly imagined, in the deceitfulness of our hearts, that all these blessings were produced by some superior wisdom and virtue of our own."[40]

DISGRACED INGRATITUDE

Perhaps the most famous instance of ingratitude in Scripture is found in the New Testament Gospel of Luke.

> Now on his way to Jerusalem, Jesus traveled along the border between Samaria and Galilee. As he was going into a village, ten men who had leprosy met him. They stood at a distance and called out in a loud voice, "Jesus, Master, have pity on us!"
>
> When he saw them, he said, "Go, show yourselves to the priests." And as they went, they were cleansed.
>
> One of them, when he saw he was healed, came back, praising God in a loud voice. He threw himself at Jesus' feet and thanked him—and he was a Samaritan.
>
> Jesus asked, "Were not all ten cleansed? Where are the other nine? Has no one returned to give praise to God except this foreigner?" Then he said to him, "Rise and go; your faith has made you well." (Lk 17:11-19 NIV)

---

[40]Abraham Lincoln, "Proclamation Appointing a National Fast Day," March 30, 1863, abraham lincolnonline.org/lincoln/speeches/fast.htm.

Jesus instructs the ten to show themselves to the priests who, as the public health officials of the day, hold the authority to pronounce them clean and fit to return to society. Cured of their contagious condition and their dignity restored, they get their old lives back. They are literally brought back from the dead. One would expect overwhelming expressions of gratitude. Yet only one returned to express thanksgiving for being healed. The parable appears to remind us of just how common ingratitude is, how easy it is to take blessings for granted, and how gratitude is dependent upon unmerited favors. The parable also conveys another very powerful truth: that Jesus' giving did not depend upon expected gratitude. He heals all ten, knowing full well that only one will return and give thanks.

Were the others ungrateful? Perhaps they were just forgetful. After all, given back their dignity, they were no doubt in a hurry to return to their families and old lives. Contemporary research, though, paints a more complicated picture of ingratitude. People who are ungrateful tend to be characterized by an excessive sense of self-importance, arrogance, vanity, and an unquenchable need for admiration and approval. Narcissists reject the ties that bind people into relationships of reciprocity. They expect special favors and feel no need to pay back or pay forward. Given this constellation of characteristics, being grateful in any meaningful way is beyond the capacity of most narcissists. Without empathy, they cannot appreciate an altruistic gift because they cannot identify with the mental state of the gift-giver. Narcissism is a spiritual blindness; it is a refusal to acknowledge that one has been the recipient of benefits freely bestowed by others. A preoccupation with the self can cause us to forget our benefits and our benefactors or to feel that we are owed things from others and therefore have no reason to feel thankful. Ignatius Loyola wrote that ingratitude is a forgetting of the graces, benefits, and blessings received, and as such it is the cause, beginning, and origin of all evils and sins. Gratitude is grace; ingratitude is disgrace.

Why is ingratitude such a profound moral failure? The principle of reciprocity, upon which human societies are based, states that one has an obligation to help others who have helped us, while at the same time not harming others who have helped us. Directing ingratitude toward our benefactor is a way of inflicting harm upon that person. The moral rule underlying reciprocity is violated when one is not grateful for the benefit received. While occasionally each of us respond to a benefit in a manner that may be interpreted as an ungrateful response by our benefactor, there is clearly a psychological disturbance in the personality that habitually responds to benefits with indifference, resentment, or ingratitude. This is a flagrant violation of natural law.

THE TRUEST APPROACH TO LIFE

Is there an antidote to ingratitude? Gratitude is often prescribed as the remedy for the exaggerated deservingness that marks narcissistic entitlement. But what enables gratitude in the first place?

According to Mark T. Mitchell, professor of political science at James Madison University,

> Gratitude is born of humility, for it acknowledges the giftedness of the creation and the benevolence of the Creator. This recognition gives birth to acts marked by attention and responsibility. Ingratitude, on the other hand, is marked by hubris, which denies the gift, and this always leads to inattention, irresponsibility, and abuse.[41]

In gratitude and humility, we turn to realities outside of ourselves. We become aware of our limitations and our need to rely on others. In gratitude and humility, we acknowledge the myth of self-sufficiency. We look upward and outward to the sources that sustain us. Becoming aware of realities greater than ourselves shields us from the illusion of being self-made, being here on this planet by right—expecting everything and owing nothing. The humble person says that life is a gift to be grateful for, not a right to be claimed. Humility ushers in a grateful response to life.

Humility is a key to gratitude because living humbly is the truest approach to life. Humble people are grounded in the truth that they need

---

[41]M. T. Mitchell, "Ingratitude and the Death of Freedom," in *New Threats to Freedom*, ed. A. Bellow (West Conshohocken, PA: Templeton Press, 2011), 181-88.

others. We all do. We are not self-sufficient. We did not create ourselves. We depend on parents, friends, our pets, God, the universe, and yes, even the government, to provide what we cannot provide for ourselves. Seeing with grateful eyes requires that we see the web of interconnection in which we alternate between being givers and receivers. The humble person says that life is a gift to be grateful for, not a right to be claimed.

Humility is profoundly countercultural. It does not come easily or naturally, particularly in a culture that values self-aggrandizement. It requires the sustained focus on others rather than self, or as the Jewish proverb states, humility is limiting oneself to an appropriate space while leaving room for others.[42] Thinking about oneself is natural; humility is unnatural. Perhaps this is why gratitude is counterintuitive. It goes against our natural inclinations. We want to take credit for the good that we encounter. This self-serving bias is the adult derivative of childhood egocentricity.

Reining in entitlement and embracing gratitude and humility is spiritually and psychologically liberating. Formation in gratitude requires recognizing that life owes me nothing and all the good I have are gifts. It is not getting what we are entitled to. Recognizing that everything good in life is ultimately a gift is a fundamental truth of reality and it is humility makes that recognition possible. The humble person says, "How can I not be filled with overflowing gratitude for all the good in my life that I've done nothing to merit?" The realization is that all is gift is freeing, and freedom is the very foundation upon which gratitude is based. True gifts are freely given and require no response. Jesus was free to withhold the gift of healing and he did not demand the other nine who were healed return to express gratitude. The one who did return exercised his freedom as well. Gratitude sets us free. A sense of personal freedom may be one of the most important effects of practiced gratitude.[43]

---

[42]Alan Morinis, *Everyday Holiness: The Jewish Spiritual Path of Mussar* (Durban, South Africa: Trumpeter, 2008).

[43]Some material in this section was previously published in Robert Emmons, "What Must We Overcome as a Culture or as Individuals for Gratitude to Flourish?," Big Questions Online, November 11, 2013, www.bigquestionsonline.com/2013/11/11/what-must-overcome-culture-individuals-gratitude-flourish.

GRATITUDE FREES US FROM OURSELVES

Despite all of the benefits that living a grateful life can bring, gratitude can be hard and painful work. It does not always come easily or naturally. Grateful states, along with their numerous benefits, can remain theoretical concepts that are transient and unpredictable experiences in the majority of people's lives. The feeling of gratitude is too often dependent on the ordering of external events, rather than being a basic orientation toward life itself. People may find it relatively easy to feel happily grateful when life proceeds according to plan—however, people rarely sustain such energizing feelings as a norm in the midst of their ordinary daily lives. It is too easy to shunt aside, overlook, or take for granted the basic gifts of life. At the other end of the spectrum, a tragedy or crisis can often elicit feelings of grateful relief that the situation did not turn out worse than it might have or incite feelings of gratitude for escaping a potentially life-threatening event. Research has shown that people often and easily fall prey to old patterns of self-centered, unappreciative thought and action soon after the event has passed.

Because of numerous obstacles, gratitude, at least initially, requires discipline. So this is the paradox of gratitude: while the evidence is clear that cultivating gratitude in our life and in our attitude to life makes us happier and healthier people, more attuned to the flow of blessings in our lives, it is still difficult. Practicing gratitude is easier said than done. A number of evidence based-strategies, including journaling and letter writing, have proven effective in creating sustainable gratefulness. At this point we step back to see what general features these strategies share. In many respects, then, gratitude can be thought of as a mindfulness practice that leads to a greater experience of being connected to life and awareness of all of the benefits available.

One of the first steps is attention. Attention is noticing and becoming aware of blessings that we normally take for granted. It is tuning into the many reasons for gratitude that already exist in our lives. Simultaneously, directing our attention this way in a focused manner blocks thoughts and perceptions that are inimical to gratitude, such as feelings of exaggerated deservingness or perceptions of victimhood. Focusing techniques that enhance attentiveness (such as mindfulness meditation) will be effective in increasing one's appreciation for the simple blessings of life and in banishing incompatible thoughts from consciousness.

Then there is remembering. Grateful people draw upon positive memories of being the recipients of benevolence. This is why religious traditions are able to so effectively cultivate gratitude—litanies of remembrance encourage gratitude, and religions do litanies very well. The Scriptures, sayings, and sacraments of faith traditions inculcate gratefulness by drawing believers into a remembered relationship with a Supreme Being and with the members of their community.

Much of what we have learned about gratitude has been gleaned through quantitative psychological studies and is not the result of studying gratitude as it occurs moment to moment within everyday life but, rather, has involved laboratory experiments, surveys, and questionnaires. These traditional methods have limitations. Gratitude letters, gratitude journals, and other reflective gratitude exercises can be readily incorporated into various social media platforms that may enhance their efficacy and to capture moments of thankfulness that might otherwise be missed using traditional assessment methods.

I recently compared the effectiveness of a gratitude app (the "gratitude tree") with the gratitude letter and visit exercise.[44] In this experiment, 414 students were given choice of using a gratitude app for seven days or writing three different letters to people whom they had never properly taken the time to thank. Following the practice, they answered questions related to ease, enjoyment, and the effectiveness of the two different methods. Although the app was perceived as easier and more enjoyable, writing the letter caused participants to think more about others, made them realize how dependent they were on others, and led them to want to give back more to others than did those who used the app. The letter,

---

[44]R. A. Emmons, "Tweeting Blessings: Using Social Media to Communicate Gratitude," paper presented at the Annual Convention of the American Psychological Association, Washington, DC, August 2014.

in other words, produced the outward focus that gratitude requires, whereas engaging with the gratitude tree app did not. This does seem consistent with the belief that trying to be grateful by intentionally engaging in a gratitude-based activity may backfire. A preoccupation with our performance can actually hinder our performance.[45] By making it all about ourselves, the focus is on how we are doing. But gratitude, by its very nature, is an external focus. Gratitude is an apprehension of receiving a gift or benefit from a source external to the self. Self-focused attention prevents a proper perspective that results in gratitude. Practices that direct our attention to the ways in which we have been supported and sustained by others are conducive to gratitude because they help us to transcend our self-focus.

CONCLUSION

A commitment to building a life fashioned out of gratitude is one solution to the problem of how to achieve fullness in one's life.[46] Gratitude is fundamental to the spiritual life because it is in gratitude that we become aware of our limitations and our need to rely on others and our Creator. In gratitude we acknowledge the myth of self-sufficiency. We look outward and upward to the sources that sustain us. Becoming aware of realities greater than ourselves shields us from the illusion of being self-made, being here on this planet by right—expecting everything and owing nothing. The thankful person says that life is a gift to be grateful for, not a right to be claimed. This realization ushers in a grateful response to life. Gratitude is therefore the truest approach to life. We are receptive beings, dependent on the help of others, on their gifts and their kindness. As such, we are called to gratitude. If we choose to ignore this basic truth, we steer ourselves off course.

Modern psychology has placed great emphasis upon individual autonomy and self-sufficiency. Gratitude requires, however, that we affirm

---

[45]T. Tchividjian, *One-Way Love: Inexhaustible Grace for an Exhausted World* (Colorado Springs: David C. Cook, 2013).
[46]C. A. Taylor, *A Secular Age* (Cambridge, MA: Harvard University Press, 2007).

our dependency on others and recognize that we need to receive what we cannot provide for ourselves. Until we acknowledge this dependence, gratitude remains a potentiality at best, and we are unable to capitalize on its promises and potential. When embraced, gratitude's essence can be construed not only from behaviors that are measurable, but from ways of living that are both pathways for aspiring to the good life and passages for attaining it.

RELATIONAL SPIRITUALITY, DIFFERENTIATION, AND MATURE ALTERITY

STEVEN J. SANDAGE, DAVID R. PAINE, AND JONATHAN MORGAN

This is the true meaning of . . . listening for the genuine in another. Such an experience cannot become a dogma—it has to remain experiential all the way. It is a probing process trying to find the opening into another. And it requires exposure, sustained exposure. One of the great obstacles to such exposure is the fact of segregation. The religious experience as I have known it seems to swing wide the door, not merely into Life but into lives.

HOWARD THURMAN,
THE LUMINOUS
DARKNESS (1965)

Howard Thurman (1889–1981) was a pastor, practical theologian, and social activist whose writings display a rich integration of spiritual formation, psychology, intercultural awareness, and commitment to social justice. The quote in the epigraph comes from the turbulent civil rights era in a book in which Thurman combines an interdisciplinary account of the evils and psychological toxicity of racism and segregation with an understanding of the central role of mature alterity in Christian spiritual formation. For Thurman, spirituality included a process of seeking to understand the perspectives and experiences of others, grounded in a relationship with God secure enough to "swing wide the door" of one's heart and mind.

Howard Thurman, *The Lumnous Darkness: A Personal Interpretation of the Anatomy of Segregation and the Ground of Hope* (New York: Harper & Row, 1965), 111.

In this chapter, we offer a brief overview of a differentiation-based relational model of spirituality and transformation that has been articulated in depth elsewhere, and then we focus on interdisciplinary conceptual frameworks and empirical findings related to a key dimension of that model—alterity. We suggest that alterity (or ways of relating to otherness) involves psychological and spiritual dynamics of relationality that can promote integrative spiritual formation. Alterity can also be anxiety-provoking, and alterity anxiety can both inhibit or facilitate spiritual transformation depending upon several dynamics we consider below. We will also offer a thesis building upon Thurman and several other theorists that mature, well-differentiated, and humble alterity is a necessary dimension of Christian spiritual maturity.

RELATIONAL SPIRITUALITY

Spirituality is a contested term that is defined in many ways, so we will first summarize what we mean by *spirituality*. We start by building upon the work of Hill and Pargament, who offered a descriptive and psychological definition of spirituality as the "search for the sacred," highlighting the active quest of humans to discover the Divine or Ultimate Truth within their particular contexts.[1] Shults and Sandage adapted this definition to fit an integrative relational framework by defining relational spirituality as "ways of relating to the sacred."[2] Humans relate to God and the sacred in a variety of ways (e.g., submission, angry complaint, warm-hearted contemplation, avoidance, purposeful collaboration, terror). We find an emphasis on relational spirituality helpful for several reasons.

First, within Christian traditions, a relational view of spirituality is consistent with Trinitarian theology and the understanding that God

---

[1]P. C. Hill and K. I. Pargament, "Advances in the Conceptualization and Measurement of Religion and Spirituality," *Psychology of Religion and Spirituality* 1 (2008): 3-17.

[2]F. L. Shults and S. J. Sandage, *Transforming Spirituality: Integrating Theology and Psychology* (Grand Rapids: Baker Academic, 2006). Also see T. W. Hall, "Christian Spirituality and Mental Health: A Relational Spirituality Paradigm for Empirical Research," *Journal of Psychology and Christianity* 23 (2004): 66-81.

always exists in relationship. God as Trinity exemplifies differentiated relationality, that is, separate persons existing in intimate and cooperative relationship.[3] Some models or folk understandings of spiritual formation seem to employ a view of spirituality as a substance one would have more or less of (e.g., "getting my tank filled at church" or "He is not a very spiritual person"). However, our commitment to Trinitarian and relational theologies suggests the value of conceptualizing spirituality in relational ways rather than viewing spirituality as simply a quantity of an inner substance or essence of an individual.

Second, a focus on relationality also fits our theoretical orientation within social science. Many social science theorists across various models construe the self as constituted in and through relationships.[4] This relational view of selfhood can readily be integrated with relational views of theological anthropology or personhood. The growing field of interpersonal neurobiology has provided evidence that our limbic brains are imprinted with relational templates that move us toward familiar relational patterns, that is, unless there is a limbic transformation.[5] Psychological research has also validated the earlier theories of many psychoanalysts that relational experiences, particularly attachment-based experiences, can shape templates used in forming God images and theological beliefs.[6] For example, those who have an insecure style of attachment are more likely to have difficulty experiencing God as consistently and warmly present compared to those with a secure style of attachment. Many different contemporary models of psychotherapy also emphasize relationality and contextualization in contrast to an earlier modernistic or Cartesian view of the

---

[3]J. O. Balswick, P. E. King, and K. S. Reimer, *The Reciprocating Self: Human Development in Theological Perspective* (Downers Grove, IL: InterVarsity Press, 2005).

[4]S. Chen, H. C. Boucher, and M. P. Tapias, "The Relational Self Revealed: Integrative Conceptualization and Implications for Interpersonal Life," *Psychological Bulletin* 132 (2006): 151-79.

[5]L. Cozolino, *The Neuroscience of Psychotherapy: Healing the Social Brain*, 2nd ed. (New York: W. W. Norton, 2010). T. Lewis, F. Amini, and R. Lannon, *A General Theory of Love* (New York: Vintage, 2000).

[6]P. Granqvist, M. Mikulincer, and P. R. Shaver, "Religion as Attachment: Normative Processes and Individual Differences," *Personality and Social Psychology Review* 14 (2010): 49-59. Hall, "Christian Spirituality."

de-contextualized individual subject.[7] All of these developments in social science and psychotherapy can be brought into productive integrative conversation with the relational ontology that is central to Christian theology and our understanding of a Christian model of spiritual formation and change.

Third, a relational approach to spirituality can also utilize the psychological lens of human development to consider distinctive ways of relating to sacred. In our model of relational spirituality, we have also found it useful to differentiate spiritual well-being and spiritual maturity at the levels of both theory and research measurement. We have suggested growth toward developmental maturity often involves a stressful, crucible-like process with periodic reductions in spiritual well-being as deconstructive processes lead to a systemic reorganization toward more complex ways of relating with the sacred. Spiritual writers have used various metaphors besides a crucible for these challenging periods of deconstruction—valley, desert, dark night of the soul. Deconstruction does not always lead to spiritual transformation, but we believe transformation is nearly always preceded by an increase in existential anxiety. Spiritual maturity involves working through crucible-like integrity dilemmas and struggles to ultimately integrate spiritual maturity with relatively consistent well-being.

Conversely, some maintain immature forms of spiritual well-being by utilizing defense mechanisms like denial or repression rather than facing difficult realities either within the self (e.g., guilt or ambivalence) or in the world (e.g., consciousness of racism or poverty) or both. William James described a religious temperament of "healthy-mindedness" in which the person focused exclusively on the sunny side of life and remained oblivious to suffering in the world. More recently, this has been described as "illusory spiritual health" or "spiritual bypassing." It is possible for some to stay in homogeneous spiritual

---

[7]J. C. Norcross, *Psychotherapy Relationships That Work: Evidence-Based Responsiveness*, 2nd ed. (New York: Oxford University Press, 2011). Also see Boston Change Process Study Group, *Change in Psychotherapy: A Unifying Paradigm* (New York: W.W. Norton, 2010).

enclaves that prevent exposure to diversity or troubling levels of suffering and oppression.

Fourth, a relational approach to spirituality can also be useful for understanding pathological forms of spiritual development that inhibit growth and maturity. For example, narcissism is a trait that can interfere with the relational virtues of Christian spiritual maturity, such as gratitude, compassion, humility, and forgiveness.[8] Those who are high in narcissistic forms of relating to the sacred may self-report special insights and intense levels of closeness with God; however, interpersonal data will often reveal struggles with entitlement, conflict resolution, or dogmatism. This can be an important consideration for Christian communities. Narcissistic leaders may seem gifted but can do significant damage to the spiritual formation of persons under their influence.[9] Others struggle with forms of relational spirituality that are more chronically shame-prone or hold relational assumptions of rejection and persecution from both God and others. In some cases, this reflects the influence of trauma on limbic templates and might be perpetuated by fear-based or non-integrative approaches to theological teaching and spiritual formation.

Finally, our relational orientation includes an emphasis on relational dialectics in spiritual formation. While there are many ways of relating to the sacred, two primary dialectical themes are spiritual dwelling and spiritual seeking, drawing on concepts from Wuthnow's sociology of religion.[10] Spiritual dwelling involves relatively stable ways of relating to the sacred, while spiritual seeking involves questing toward new ways of relating with the sacred. Spiritual seeking can be part of crucible-like processes that are stressful and destabilizing but may ultimately lead to spiritual transformation and more integrated

[8]S. J. Sandage and S. P. Moe, "Narcissism and Spirituality," in *The Handbook of Narcissism and Narcissistic Personality Disorder: Theoretical Approaches, Empirical Findings, and Treatment,* ed. W. K. Campbell and J. Miller (New York: John Wiley & Sons, 2011), 410-20.
[9]S. J. Sandage and M. G. Harden, "Relational Spirituality, Differentiation of Self, and Virtue as Predictors of Intercultural Development," *Mental Health, Religion, & Culture* 14 (2011): 819-38.
[10]Robert Wuthnow, *After Heaven: Spirituality in America Since the 1950s* (Berkeley and Los Angeles: University of California Press, 1998).

forms of spiritual dwelling. It is also possible for individuals or communities to seek to maintain a spiritual dwelling that lacks complexity. This may lead to spiritual complacency or developmental arrest. While some faith communities emphasize either the stability of dwelling within spiritual commitments or the open process of spiritual seeking and questing, we have come to see spiritual dwelling and seeking as an ongoing dialectical process within spiritual formation. In research with seminary students, we found general linear trends toward both increased internalization of faith commitment and increased spiritual questing during seminary.[11] This mature capacity to integrate internalized commitments and authentic openness to new understanding is partially captured in the notion of differentiation of self, which we describe below.

DIFFERENTIATION OF SELF

Differentiation of self (DoS) is a form of relational selfhood that involves the developmental capacity to balance (a) cognitive and emotional functioning and (b) autonomy and connection in relationships.[12] Those who are high in DoS are self-aware with a healthy sense of identity and also generally effective in the self-regulation of emotions. Interpersonally, they can manage independence and solitude while also able to connect with others in close relationships. Bonhoeffer spoke to this dialectic in saying the person who cannot be alone is not ready for community, and the person who cannot be in community is not ready to be alone. Those who are low in DoS tend to struggle with emotional reactivity and use emotional cutoff (distancing) or fusion (enmeshment) to manage interpersonal stress. Families, groups, and congregations can also differ in collective levels

---

[11]Ian T. Williamson and Steven J. Sandage, "Longitudinal Analyses of Religious and Spiritual Development Among Seminary Students," *Mental Health, Religion, & Culture* 12 (2009): 787-801.

[12]Elizabeth A. Skowron and Thomas A. Schmitt, "Assessing Interpersonal Fusion: Reliability and Validity of a New DSI Fusion with Others Subscale," *Journal of Marital and Family Therapy* 29 (2003): 209-22; Brian Majerus and Steven J. Sandage, "Differentiation of Self and Christian Spiritual Maturity: Social Science and Theological Integration," *Journal of Psychology & Theology* 38 (2010): 41-51.

of DoS. More differentiated systems tend to do better in tolerating the anxiety of within-group differences and to show more resilience in adapting to stress and change. DoS involves the mature capacity to value both unity and diversity similar to the apostle Paul's teaching in 1 Corinthians 12.

In our empirical studies with Christian graduate-level students at Bethel Seminary, DoS has been positively associated with a wide range of spiritual formation factors, including spiritual well-being, spiritual maturity, interpersonal forgivingness, hope, humility, gratitude, meditative prayer, intercultural competence, and social justice commitment.[13] DoS has statistically accounted for the connections between several spiritual formation variables. For example, DoS has mediated the positive relationship between interpersonal forgivingness and mental health in two studies.[14] DoS also mediated the negative relationship between spiritual well-being and negative emotion in a sample of distressed students, supporting the self-regulatory function of DoS as part of spirituality.[15] We have discussed these connections between DoS, well-being, and spirituality in other places, but we want to focus in the remainder of this chapter on the role of DoS in relational spirituality that promotes healthy and mature alterity.

[13]P. J. Jankowski and S. J. Sandage, "Meditative Prayer, Gratitude, and Intercultural Competence: Empirical Test of a Differentiation-Based Model," *Mindfulness* 5 (2014): 360-72. S. J. Sandage, S. Crabtree, and M. Schweer, "Differentiation of Self and Social Justice Commitment Mediated by Hope," *Journal of Counseling and Development* 92 (2014): 67-74. S. J. Sandage and M. G. Harden, "Relational Spirituality, Differentiation of Self, and Virtue as Predictors of Intercultural Development," *Mental Health, Religion, & Culture* 14 (2011): 819-38. S. J. Sandage and P. J. Jankowski, "Spirituality, Social Justice, and Intercultural Competence: Mediator Effects of Differentiation of Self," *International Journal of Intercultural Relations* 37 (2013): 366-74.

[14]S. J. Sandage and P. J. Jankowski, "Forgiveness, Spiritual Instability, Mental Health Symptoms, and Well-Being: Mediation Effects of Differentiation of Self," *Psychology of Religion and Spirituality* 2 (2010): 168-80.

[15]P. J. Jankowski and S. J. Sandage, "Spiritual Dwelling and Well-Being: The Mediating Role of Differentiation of Self in a Sample of Distressed Adults," *Mental Health, Religion, & Culture* 15 (2012), doi: 10.1080/13674676.2011.579592.

THEORIES OF ALTERITY

Relational spirituality is not contained within the individual and therefore necessarily involves otherness. Many traditions view God or the sacred as "other" relative to humans, and certainly this is true in Christianity. Virtually all spiritual traditions raise the question of how the individual ought to engage with others. Sandage and Shults suggested, "One important test of spirituality is the impact on alterity."[16] As mentioned above, *alterity* refers to how individuals relate to otherness. In this section, we engage with the insights of contemporary theorists of alterity that inform our understanding of the association between relational spirituality and responses to otherness.

Emmanuel Levinas is one of the most influential phenomenological philosophers of the twentieth century. He is well-known for his ethics based in a conception of alterity or otherness. Levinas believed that the foundation of ethics is grounded in human relationships and that the wellspring of moral action is an encounter with another person.[17] For Levinas, the other is not knowable and cannot be reduced to any categories that might be imposed by the subject. Therefore, a person will experience the other as distant yet benevolent. He writes, "The Other precisely reveals himself [sic] in his alterity not in a shock negating the I, but as the primordial phenomenon of gentleness."[18] Though others may present themselves in a spirit of gentleness, the encounter is inherently disruptive. A Levinasian theorist describes the other as potentially unsettling, "The vulnerability of the other makes me vulnerable, traumatizes me, takes me hostage, puts me in a state of suffering where all I can do is offer my crust of bread, my hope from empty hands."[19] Levinas asserts that subjects encountering the other are beset with an ethical demand to assume responsibility for the

---

[16]S. J. Sandage and F. L. Shults, "Relational Spirituality and Transformation: A Relational Integration Model," *Journal of Psychology & Christianity* 26 (2007): 262.

[17]E. Levinas, *Totality and Infinity: An Essay on Exteriority* (Netherlands: Springer, 1961).

[18]Levinas, *Totality*, 150.

[19]D. Orange, *The Suffering Stranger: Hermeneutics for Everyday Clinical Practice* (New York: Routledge, 2011), 63.

other's needs. The "face" of the other evokes a primordial emotion of connection within which the ethical demand is inherent. Levinas downplays the primacy of conscious choice in responding to this call. He insisted that the truly ethical response is found in a passive receptivity to our fundamental responsibility.

Levinas's insights have influenced ethical perspectives in the helping professions. For example, though Levinas was skeptical of psychoanalysis as an institution, a number of psychologists have endeavored to apply his theories to clinical practice. Orange describes several principles of what she calls a "Levinasian therapeutics." Clinicians adhering to this approach (a) welcome clients in a spirit of simplicity, humility, and patience; (b) refrain from judging whether clients "deserve" hospitality; (c) avoid clinical violence in the form of undue labeling and the imposition of cultural categories; and (d) accept responsibility for attending to the client's needs while downplaying relational reciprocity. Orange asserts that the ethical demand inherent to encountering the client requires therapists to suspend their needs for mutuality and control in the therapeutic relationship.[20] Dueck and Reimer have offered some similar applications of Levinas to psychology from a Christian perspective and with more attention to cultural diversity.

While Levinas has had a profound influence on our understanding of benevolent responses to otherness, some of his assertions have been called into question by other theorists of alterity. One point of criticism focuses on Levinas's insistence that the others are "absolutely other" in that they are irreducible to categories imposed by the self.[21] Ricoeur asserts that for Levinas "the other represents absolute exteriority with respect to an ego defined by the condition of separation. The other, in this sense, absolves himself of any relation."[22] Benjamin develops a nuanced psychoanalytic theory of intersubjectivity that challenges the

---

[20]Orange, *Suffering Stranger*.

[21]J. Benjamin, *Shadow of the Other: Intersubjectivity and Gender in Psychoanalysis* (New York: Routledge, 1998).

[22]P. Ricoeur, *Oneself as Another* (Chicago: The University of Chicago Press, 1992), 188-89.

idea of "absolute exteriority." She asserts, like Levinas, that alterity must be acknowledged so that the other is not reduced to a projection of the self. However, perceiving an individual to be totally other allows the possibility for the self to repudiate and exclude the other. In a less afflicting sense, it also permits the other to be patronized. They may be viewed as a project that stands to benefit from the salubrious or "rescuing" effects of contact with the self.

For Benjamin, a balance must be found between recognizing otherness and apprehending points of similarity and convergence. She asserts that a healthy relationship to alterity requires that we occupy the dynamic space between understanding the other as different and understanding the other as an ego, a subject that shares in our human condition. If others are absolutely other, they are not subjects but objects to be assimilated, repudiated, or manipulated at the will of the self. We find it hard to exclude that which is the same but are free to exclude that which is totally other. For Benjamin, inclusion rests at the heart of an ethical alterity and is predicated on the recognition of similarity as well as distance. Such an orientation is compatible with differentiation of self (DoS) described above. Benjamin's intersubjectivity may be understood as intrapersonally and interpersonally differentiated. That is, she asserts the need for a harmonious self who (a) tolerates the tension evoked by the difference and similarity of the other and (b) maintains a sense of selfhood within the context of an intimate encounter.

A theological companion to the work of Benjamin is that of Miroslav Volf. Volf asserts that the question of alterity is an inextricable component of any solid understanding of social realities. He asserts the need for recognizing distance and having adequate respect for otherness. He writes, "Belonging without distance destroys."[23] However, he also asserts that benevolent responses to otherness must incorporate differentiated identification with the other. Volf recognizes the existence of strong cultural divides and acknowledges the presence and

---

[23]M. Volf, "Exclusion and Embrace: Theological Reflections in the Wake of 'Ethnic Cleansing,'" *Journal of Ecumenical Studies* 29 (1992): 230-48, 236.

potential for seemingly intransigent conflicts between self and other. To address the divisions between individuals, he provides a theological basis for the assertion that the self is ultimately connected with the other on an intimate level.

First, he establishes the principle that others should be loved by us as they are loved by God. We are connected in that we are all created and loved by God. Volf writes, "The exclusion of the other is an exclusion of God."[24] Then he articulates a second point of identification: the shared legacy of sin before God. For Volf, we find similarity in that we are all sinners who fall short of our ultimate end, to love and serve God and others. While the others are distant in many ways, they are close in God's love and shared iniquity. Volf draws on Christian theology to affirm that these similarities are at the ontological heart of the self. "Why should I embrace the other? The answer is simple: because the others are a part of my own true identity. I cannot live authentically without welcoming the others . . . for I am created to reflect the personality of the triune God."[25] The perspectives of both Benjamin and Volf offer a theory of alterity that seeks balance between the distance and intimacy of the other and promotes a differentiated form of relationality in which alterity is neither minimized nor idealized.

Another point of contention in Levinas may be found in his implication that the traumatic encounter with the other necessarily calls for a benevolent response. Whatever the ontological nature of this call, it is clear that encounters with otherness do not always elicit compassion and understanding. Benjamin agrees with the Levinasian view that an encounter with the other is a disruptive, sometimes traumatic event that can make us aware of our limitations. She writes, "The world exposes us to the different others who, not only in their mere existence as separate beings reflect our lack of control, but who also threaten to evoke in us what we have repudiated in order to protect the self."[26]

---

[24]Volf, "Exclusion and Embrace: Theological Reflections," 241.
[25]Volf, "Exclusion and Embrace: Theological Reflections," 248.
[26]Benjamin, *Shadow*, 95.

However, as was alluded to earlier, she recognizes that this disruption can have negative consequences. First, the other may be perceived as a threat that must be excluded or harmed. Second, one may wish to assimilate the other; that is reducing them to the fixed categories of the self, thereby negating their distinct identity. Finally, the self may become so overwhelmed by the presence of the other that they allow themselves to be consumed and their own identity negated. Meeting the other is not always positive. Benjamin argues that these pitfalls may be avoided if the self is able face and accept the paradoxical distance and intimacy of the other.

Volf also recognized the peril of encountering the other. Similar to Benjamin, he asserts that excluding and negating the other are attempts to re-center the self, thus avoiding the dread of self-negation.[27] Additionally, legitimate transgressions may cause the self to experience the other as violent, oppressive, and pernicious. For Volf, there are several ways the self may address this problem, allowing for inclusion of the other. From a theological frame, one may re-center oneself in the love of Christ, thus making room for loving the other. One may expand this Christian view to include other forms of ultimate meaning that call for a re-centering of self. Volf also champions the need for humility in assessing the nature of the other. He writes, "We need more adequate judgment based on a distinction between legitimate 'differentiation' and illegitimate 'exclusion' and made with humility that counts with our proclivity to misperceive and misjudge."[28]

Levinas's perspective on alterity is not altogether distant from these views. It can be asserted that Levinas was not inattentive to the subjectivity of the other or the potential for deleterious encounters. He asserted that recognizing the face or humanity of the other is a wellspring of the social justice demand to give and serve.[29] He was also no stranger to the

[27]M. Volf, *Exclusion and Embrace: A Theological Exploration of Identity, Othernness, and Reconciliation* (Nashville, TN: Abingdon Press, 1996), 70.

[28]Volf, *Exclusion*, 68.

[29]E. Levinas, *Ethics and Infinity* (Pittsburgh, PA: Duquesne University Press, 1985).

callousness with which the self can meet the other, having experienced imprisonment in the Nazi death camps firsthand. We like to think of Benjamin and Volf as sharpening some of Levinas's foundational points to create space for differentiated aspects of lived experience that Levinas may have been less focused upon. Levinas emphasized the ethical imperative to care for the other, which is rooted in something other than rationality. Drawing upon ethical roots in the Hebrew Bible, he emphasized the ontological nature of that call, similar to the way Thurman draws upon Christian traditions. The others we have discussed in this section offer an understanding of the practical implications of that call, given the need to negotiate intimacy and otherness. In doing so, they provide insights on what constitutes an inclusive and differentiated alterity.

Levinas perceives our experience of the face of the other as the foundation of ethics. This is compatible with Ricouer's conception of solicitude (benevolent concern for the other) as essential to a just ethic.[30] Ricouer understands ethical intention "as aiming at the good life with and for others, in just institutions."[31] This is distinguished from morality, which is defined as the expression of this aim in terms of norms, obligations, and duties of action. Benevolent alterity is comprised of both (a) differentiated perceptions of self and others, and (b) an ethical orientation to the good and socially just moral action. Recent empirical studies have explored the psychological and ethical or moral dimensions of alterity in association with relational spirituality with particular focus on constructs such as intercultural sensitivity and social justice. To these studies we turn in the next section.

EMPIRICAL RESEARCH ON ALTERITY
AND RELATIONAL SPIRITUALITY

The theoretical perspectives on alterity from philosophy, relational psychoanalysis, and theology reveal the complexity of this construct. We

---

[30]Ricoeur, *Oneself*, 188-89.
[31]Ricoeur, *Oneself*, 172.

have tried to operationalize alterity with some degree of parsimony by focusing on two relevant constructs: (a) intercultural competence and (b) social justice commitment. Within the field of psychology, there is a growing theoretical recognition that intercultural competence and a commitment to social justice are important but distinct professional qualities. Yet there has been limited research investigating both constructs together. We have not found relevant research that has used literature on alterity as part of a conceptual framework.

Intercultural competence (IC) involves the developmental capacity to relate sensitively and effectively across cultural differences. IC involves capacities for awareness of cultural differences in combination with intercultural knowledge and relational skills. While some might consider intercultural competence separate from spiritual formation, our research has found the opposite. We have measured intercultural competence using the Intercultural Development Inventory (IDI), a sophisticated assessment tool that uses computer-generated algorithms for scoring. Among seminary students, IDI scores were positively associated with spiritual well-being, gratitude, meditative prayer, humility, and spiritual seeking.[32] Intercultural competence is also negatively associated with two indices of spiritual pathology—spiritual grandiosity and spiritual instability. The interculturally competent practice of frame-shifting, or reflecting on the perspective of someone who is culturally different from oneself, is conducive to effective ministry in diverse settings and is associated with healthy Christian formation and interpersonal well-being. Given the correlations among the IDI and various facets of spiritual formation, we consider the IDI one of the best available indices of Christian spiritual maturity.

Intercultural minimization is probably the most common orientation toward cultural diversity in educational, training, and ministry contexts and involves an ethnocentric focus on similarities across cultural groups

---

[32]Jankowski and Sandage, "Meditative Prayer"; Sandage and Harden, "Relational Spirituality"; Sandage and Jankowski, "Spirituality."

to limit alterity anxiety. Emphasizing similarities can be effective in some situations, such as developing initial unity and generating concern for equality. But it is problematic when used perpetually. Minimization ignores the richness of differences impacting intercultural interactions. An intercultural stance that "we are all really alike" does not lead to differentiated understanding of meaningful cultural differences. It can also deny dynamics of social privilege and oppression. In some religious contexts, theological principles or perspectives may be used to support intercultural minimization. This typically involves undervaluing contextualization in theology, missions, and ministry. One could believe a theological proposition is universally true (e.g., God is sovereign), but effective ministry demands effective application of truth in context. Those who operate from intercultural minimization tend to struggle with such contextualization.

Some in conservative Christian contexts have suggested intercultural minimization is necessary for avoiding moral relativism, yet minimization was not associated with even mid-level conventional moral development in a study of undergraduates. Higher levels of intercultural competence were positively associated with moral development.[33] These findings suggest intercultural competence is more conducive to morality than minimization.

Defensiveness and reversal are two forms of intercultural polarization that can also inhibit intercultural competence. Those operating from intercultural defensiveness assume their culture is superior to others. Those engaging in reversal feel their own culture is inferior while other cultures are idealized. Both polarized orientations generate considerable levels of negative emotion in intercultural encounters—anger and paranoia for intercultural defensiveness and shame or guilt for intercultural reversal. These polarized templates impede mature alterity by making it difficult to accurately understand other cultures or one's own

---

[33]Leilani Endicott, Tonia Bock, and Darcia Narvaez, "Moral Reasoning, Intercultural Development, and Multicultural Experiences: Relations and Cognitive Underpinnings," *International Journal of Intercultural Relations* 27 (2003): 403-19.

cultural influences. Intercultural experiences become more negative than reinforcing.

Social justice commitment is the second dimension in our view of mature alterity and can be defined as "active concerns and commitments related to social justice advocacy."[34] The empirical literature on social justice commitment related to psychology and other helping professions has grown substantially in the past decade.[35] A commitment to social justice is emphasized in some Christian traditions, including our own primary religious backgrounds (SJS, Wesleyan; DRP, Catholic; JM, Quaker). However, social justice has long generated debates, particularly within conservative Christian contexts. Some have warned that "social justice" efforts can compromise the essence of the gospel.[36] We have published four studies of social justice commitment (SJC) with Christian seminary students and, like IC, have found it to be positively associated with a variety of salutary spiritual formation factors, including hope, forgiveness, DoS, humility, and positive religious coping.[37] Our SJC measure focuses on a concern for women, persons of color, and the impoverished. These studies, using Christian samples, suggest social justice concerns are consistent with healthy Christian spiritual formation.

The positive correlation between hope and SJC has been replicated, supporting the claims of social justice theorists and theologians including Martin Luther King Jr., Cornel West, Paulo Freire, A. Elaine Brown Crawford, Michelle Clifton-Soderstrom, James Cone, and

---

[34]S. J. Sandage and J. Morgan, "Hope and Positive Religious Coping as Predictors of Social Justice Commitment," *Mental Health, Religion, & Culture* 17 (2014): 557-67, 558.

[35]Sandage and Morgan, "Hope," 557.

[36]Sandage and Morgan, "Hope," 565.

[37]P. J. Jankowski, S. J. Sandage, and P. C. Hill, "Differentiation-Based Models of Forgiveness, Mental Health and Social Justice Commitment: Mediators Effects for Differentiation of Self and Humility," *Journal of Positive Psychology* 8 (2013): 412-24. S. J. Sandage and J. Morgan, "Hope and Positive Religious Coping as Predictors of Social Justice Commitment," *Mental Health, Religion, & Culture* 17 (2014): 557-67. S. J. Sandage and P. J. Jankowski, "Spirituality, Social Justice, and Intercultural Competence: Mediator Effects of Differentiation of Self," *International Journal of Intercultural Relations* 37 (2013): 366-74. S. J. Sandage, S. Crabtree, and M. Schweer, "Differentiation of Self and Social Justice Commitment Mediated by Hope," *Journal of Counseling and Development* 92 (2014): 67-74.

Jürgen Moltmann.[38] The fact that SJC is positively associated with hope (but not gratitude) and IC with gratitude (but not hope) in our studies further suggests these are differing aspects of alterity, which empirically map onto somewhat different virtues. Yet both SJC and IC have been positively associated with DoS and humility. DoS mediated in the relationship between spiritual well-being and SJC in one study,[39] and both DoS and humility mediated the relationship between forgiveness and SJC in another.[40] This supports both our theory that DoS is a central underlying dynamic in healthy relational spirituality and mature alterity and also our growing attention to humility in our empirical and conceptual work. DoS and humility form a useful set of core constructs for integrative work on spiritual formation and alterity since DoS is a term that emerged in social science and humility has a long history in theology, spirituality, and virtue ethics.

PRACTICAL IMPLICATIONS

We will briefly describe some practical spiritual formation and training implications of the theory and research reviewed above on relational spirituality and alterity.

First, IC and SJC were only modestly positively correlated overall in our research, suggesting there is a need to emphasize both in spiritual formation programming and training. The correlation between these two dimensions of alterity gets much stronger at high levels of IC, which points to mature alterity as an integration of IC and SJC. Some individuals exhibit a high level of SJC without corresponding competence across cultural differences. This could lead to sincere efforts at social justice activism that are ineffective when these individuals encounter actual cultural differences. We have seen this many times from well-intentioned ministers,

---

[38]See Sandage and Morgan (2014), 558-61, and Sandage, Crabtree, and Schweer (2014), 69.
[39]S. J. Sandage and P. J. Jankowski, "Spirituality, Social Justice, and Intercultural Competence: Mediator Effects of Differentiation of Self," *International Journal of Intercultural Relations* 37 (2013): 366-74.
[40]Jankowski, Sandage, and Hill, "Differentiation-Based Models."

counselors, missionaries, or activists who desire to make a positive difference in contexts of oppression but end up offending others with differing cultural frameworks.

Second, our research shows both IC and SJC are related to spiritual formation and relational maturity in Christian samples. While detractors may see training efforts encouraging mature alterity as a left-wing political agenda, our research indicates that healthy Christian spiritual formation and relational development are the real issues at stake. Also, it is important to consider that trainees who are struggling in spiritual formation or relational development (e.g., high grandiosity, insecure attachment) might have difficulty progressing toward IC and SJC. We do not know the causal directions in how these factors are related, but our practical experience suggests diversity training and social justice work both necessitate attention to relational growth and healthy practices of self-regulation (i.e., DoS). Growth in mature alterity involves an integration of psychological and spiritual development.

Third, we recommend use of the IDI as an assessment tool in efforts to promote Christian spiritual formation and ministry, missionary, and therapeutic effectiveness. Many people receive diversity training without any assessment or individualized feedback. This contributes to situations where people overestimate their IC or remain unclear about what they might work on for growth in IC. Moreover, diversity training efforts that do not use individual assessments risk a minimization-based or "one size fits all" approach to training, which fails to tease out differing intercultural strengths and needed growth areas. This tends to disadvantage those at higher levels of IC who can also benefit from tailored training.

Fourth, as we have suggested throughout this chapter, healthy relational dynamics are important for containing crucible-like processes of transformation and growth. Since experiential learning is (a) key to growth in IC and SJC and (b) often anxiety-provoking and stressful, it is important to provide trainees with relationships that provide a balance of challenge and support, allowing processing of new experiences. Given the importance of relational factors for growth in mature alterity, we suggest forming relationships (e.g., small group, classroom, mentoring) that can provide sustained holding environments for processing diversity and justice conversations. Too many diversity training efforts are brief and do not make use of sustained relationships as a source of gain. This is probably problematic for dominant group members who find it easy to maintain the homeostasis of social segregation in their lives.

Fifth, Christian and other religious communities (e.g., congregations, schools) are often characterized by high levels of sociocultural homogeneity. This can require extra effort for some to depart from the familiarity of sociocultural and religious enclaves and gain diversity experience for learning. We emphasize the phrase "for learning." Diversity encounters where the sole focus is "doing ministry" or "serving others" can become poorly differentiated "rescue projects." Learning and authentic relating promote the humility necessary to be effective.

Finally, leaders in various systems often have disproportionate influence on the alterity ethos of that system. Leaders can set an example of differentiation and humility by seeking out mentors and peers who can foster their growth in mature alterity. They can help their systems consider the role of IC and SJC in their visions and missions and be accountable in those areas. They can pursue necessary resources, helping people in their system to grow. Conversely, leaders can commit to defense, reversal, or minimization, consciously or unconsciously blocking IC and SJC initiatives in their systems.

Given the array of research supporting a positive relationship between mature alterity and healthy relational spirituality, these practices may not only create healthier community and work settings, they may also foster spiritual growth. Seminaries, clinical training programs, and other contexts of higher education can be useful sites for more sophisticated research designs that could validate such causal inferences, and we hope researchers and practitioners will find ways to collaborate in developing and testing interventions to promote mature alterity.

CULTIVATING THE FRUIT
OF THE SPIRIT

CONTRIBUTIONS OF POSITIVE PSYCHOLOGY
TO SPIRITUAL FORMATION

EVERETT L. WORTHINGTON JR., BRANDON J. GRIFFIN,
AND CAROLINE R. LAVELOCK

In the beginning was the Word, and the Word was with God, and the Word was God. . . . And the Word became flesh and dwelt among us, and we have seen his glory, glory as of the only Son from the Father, full of grace and truth.

JOHN 1:1, 14

For centuries, prudent and sincere thinkers have sought to describe the formation of the human spirit. These pioneers in philosophy, religion, and science wrestle with a timeless question, "What is the good life?" Yet it seems as if every religion, every generation, every person offers a different answer to that same question. Each one's perspective is a unique understanding of human flourishing, and one must first envision what it means to flourish before one's life can be formed to be good. This is the charge of positive psychology, to describe human flourishing through virtue, which can in turn be employed to shape the formation of the human mind, spirit, and body.

Christian intellectuals throughout history have amassed an extensive body of literature on the topic of spiritual formation. Theological heavyweights such as the early church fathers, the Reformers, and contemporary theologians from a myriad of Christian traditions contribute countless pages of invaluable text on spiritual formation for the edification of the church and its members.[1] In this present chapter and in the interest of brevity, we only mention a few modern definitions to compare theologically and psychologically oriented approaches to defining spiritual formation.

In his book *Renovation of the Heart*, Dallas Willard defines spiritual formation as the "the Spirit-driven process of forming the inner world of the human self in such a way that it becomes like the inner being of Christ himself."[2] Willard's definition is reminiscent of Paul's admonition to the Roman church (Rom 12:2), which highlights the personal transformation of one's own thinking to align with the mind of Christ. Yet, for some, Willard's perspective overlooks the critical role of the Christian community in the spiritual formation of its members. Wilhoit suggests that spiritual formation is the "intentional communal process of growing in our relationship with God and becoming conformed to Christ through the power of the Holy Spirit."[3] Likewise, Greenman and Kalantzis offer a perspective on spiritual formation that acknowledges the sanctification of both individuals and communities. They suggest that spiritual formation is the believer's "continuing response to the reality of God's grace shaping us into the likeness of Jesus Christ, through the work of the Holy Spirit, the community of faith, for the sake of the world."[4] Greenman and Kalantzis's definition resonates with the approach of our chapter,

---

[1] For a review, see G. L. Sittser, *Water from a Deep Well: Christian Spirituality from Early Martyrs to Modern Missionaries* (Downers Grove, IL: InterVarsity Press, 2007).

[2] D. Willard, *Renovation of the Heart: Putting on the Character of Christ* (Colorado Springs: Nav-Press, 2002), 22.

[3] J. C. Wilhoit, *Spiritual Formation as If the Church Mattered: Growing in Christ Through Community* (Grand Rapids: Baker Academic, 2008), 23.

[4] J. P. Greenman, "Spiritual Formation in Theological Perspective," in *Life in the Spirit: Spiritual Formation in Theological Perspective*, ed. Jeffrey P. Greenman and George Kalantzis (Downers Grove, IL: InterVarsity Press, 2010), 24.

especially because it emphasizes the role of the Trinity that re-forms a community of fallen yet redeemed believers for the benefit of all creation (Jn 1:1-12; Acts 2:44; 2 Cor 5:11-21).

In concert with Willard, we propose that spiritual formation is a divine activity in which people participate alongside the Holy Spirit in their sanctification (Phil 1:6). In conjunction with Wilhoit and with Greenman and Kalantzis, we maintain that the process and outcome of spiritual formation requires relationship both to God and to others. People are fashioned in the relational *imago Dei* (Gen 1:26-27), and Christian virtue can therefore not be expressed apart from living in communion with the triune God, the church, and the world at large. In these ways, our definition of spiritual formation is similar to the definitions offered by some modern theologians. Nevertheless, while theologians deliberate the reasons why the formation of Christian virtue is important (i.e., to be conformed to the character of Christ), our approach is to apply the scientific method to investigate how Christian virtue is developed over the life span to foster the well-being of both individuals and communities.

POSITIVE PSYCHOLOGY

Positive psychology is a relatively new subfield of psychology.[5] Two views predominate. In one, positive psychology is the science of happiness or well-being (usually thought of as subjective well-being). In the other, which we prefer, positive psychology is the psychological science of eudaimonic character strength or virtue.[6] In the first, positive psychology examines character strength and virtue as a vehicle by which people sometimes experience subjective well-being, achieve a

[5]M. E. P. Seligman and M. Csikszentmihalyi, "Positive Psychology: An Introduction," *American Psychologist* 55, no. 1 (2000): 5-14.

[6]E. L. Worthington Jr., "A Christian Psychologist Looks at Virtue," *Bibliotheca Sacra* 170, no. 1 (2013): 3-15; E. L. Worthington Jr., "Four Christian Virtues," *Bibliotheca Sacra* 170, no. 2 (2013): 123-36; E. L. Worthington Jr. et al., "Virtue in Positive Psychology," in *Virtues and Their Vices*, ed. K. Timpe and C. Boyd (New York: Oxford University Press, 2014), 433-57; E. L. Worthington Jr. et al., "The Contributions of Christian Perspectives and Practices to Positive Psychology," in *Positive Psychology of Religion*, ed. Chu Kim-Prieto (New York: Springer, 2014), 47-70.

sense of meaning, and enjoy transient and enduring happiness. In the second, positive psychology is focused on character strength and virtue, not on happiness, though happiness is derivative of (but not necessarily contingent on) acting relatively consistently with virtue. In our preferred definition of positive psychology, virtue and character strength are *eudaimonic*—that is, they are thought to be good for oneself and for others.

Virtue, spiritual formation, and one's concept of God are closely related. The word *eudaimonia*, which positive psychologists borrow from the ancient Greeks to describe a sense of well-being that extends beyond momentary happiness, initially embedded the idea of virtue within a theistic context. Eudaimonia was necessarily spiritual for the Greeks; it referred to living one's life in such a way as to merit the gods' favor.[7] The ancient Greeks tended to believe that the courageous, prudent, just, and temperate leader would help others as he or she manifested individual virtue. Thus in antiquity, focus on the good of others was more derivative than direct.

From the perspective of (a Christian-accommodated) positive psychology, we assert that spiritual formation is the work of the Holy Spirit to cultivate Christian virtue among individuals and communities whose character is being transformed to the character of God as it is revealed in the person of Jesus Christ. Spiritual formation is a process that can happen at any time and under any life circumstance, but it consistently results in being shaped by the expression of grace within the context of relationships with God, with others inside and outside of the church, and within ourselves.

Importantly, positive psychology is a psychological science. It includes basic scientific understanding and applied or clinical science, just as the subfields of psychology (e.g., cognitive psychology, social psychology) and psychology as a whole do. Thus we are unapologetically empirical in our approach. By this we mean that we believe that

---

[7]R. L. Woolfolk and R. H. Wasserman, "Count No One Happy: Eudaimonia in Positive Psychology," *Journal of Theoretical and Philosophical Psychology* 25 (2005): 81-90.

people apprehend the world primarily through observation—and that includes generating theories and scientific explanations to account for those observations. We attempt to create coherent narratives to explain life, which are embodied in theologies—including systematic, biblical, and practical theologies—and in scientific theories. Theories, used scientifically, are comprehensive explanations that rely on many interlocking and generally consistent theoretical explanations supported by data (i.e., observations that are meaningful in the context of a theory). Therefore, we draw on Christian theologies and scientific theories to provide an analysis of spiritual formation, especially the development of Christian virtue.

THEORY OF VIRTUE

Character strengths are aspects of a personality that are deeply ingrained. Virtues are those character strengths that are integral to eudaimonia, that are inherently good and worthy of development. Virtues, then, can be considered character strengths, but character strengths are not necessarily virtues. One might be resilient to the strain of stress and hardship, have a keen sense of pursuing a healthy lifestyle, or be likable and agreeable. Those are character strengths, but they are not necessarily moral virtues. Morality requires a community to decide what is virtuous.[8]

In the present chapter, we highlight a few of the virtues that we see as crucial to Christian life. Although many other Christian virtues exist than those we address, we limit ourselves to a few that positive psychology has empirically studied. Furthermore, we take the psychological point of view that a virtue is something that is perceived to be morally good. As Christians, we hold that there are true and absolute virtues, which are aspects of the *imago Dei*. Yet, we also believe that less than 100 percent agreement exists across different theologies, religious communities, and religious traditions regarding the exact nature of Christian virtue. Thus psychologically, we treat a virtue as something

---

[8]J. Graham and J. Haidt, "Beyond Beliefs: Religions Bind Individuals into Moral Communities," *Personality and Social Psychology Review* 14, no. 1 (2010): 140-50.

that a person perceives to be morally good (i.e., aligned with the character of Christ), and that perception is typically informed by the religious communities to which one belongs, the sacred texts that one reads, and the religious rituals or spiritual exercises that one practices. In spite of degree of agreement or disagreement of what the virtues are and what character strengths are virtues, each person will likely prioritize virtues differently.

We suggest a virtue theory in which every person creates a hierarchy of virtues, which is a framework that informs human behavior according to the virtues that are more cognitively salient and accessible.[9] Also, virtue hierarchies might shift over the lifespan in reaction to God's plans for the person. An example of an experience that might cause a dramatic shift in a person's hierarchy of virtues is conversion to the Christian faith, which is then continually refined by a nearly infinite number of experiences thereafter. More generally, Worthington and Sandage (2015) observe that times of spiritual transformation might move spiritual believers from places of stable dwelling to seeking and perhaps back to dwelling. During each phase of spiritual transformation, virtue hierarchies can shift dramatically.

Nevertheless, some virtues are routinely found in the hierarchies held by most Christians. We believe that various Christian theologies, communities, and traditions are in substantial agreement regarding the virtues such as love, forgiveness, humility, gratitude, patience, and mercy. Our claim is that positive psychology has things to say about each of these virtues (and about many other Christian virtues) that we hope will help Christians understand the virtue and actively participate in the development of Christian virtue with the direction of the Holy Spirit. Namely, we assert that positive psychology, as a scientific study of eudaimonic virtue can inform the Christian community—the church—of ways to promote Christian virtue. Whereas different

---

[9]E. L. Worthington Jr., "Virtue Orientations" in *Approaching the Gospels Psychologically*, ed. Fraser N. Watts (Philadelphia: Templeton Foundation Press, 2007), 155-73; Worthington et al., "Virtue in Positive Psychology."

theologies, communities, and traditions will be drawn to different virtues that we discuss—because they tend to value them differently— we believe we can put forth a way of understanding virtue as part of spiritual formation.

RELATIONAL APPROACH TO THE FORMATION OF CHRISTIAN VIRTUE

People live in a relational world, having relationships with other people, with supernatural agents, and with the created order. Relationships are primary.[10] They precede human culture, church, writing, arts, humanities, science, and technology. Spirituality too is fundamentally relational.

We use the term *relational* broadly to include both human relationships— within, between, and among agentic beings—and relational contexts that agents have with non-agentic things.[11] Humans are formed spiritually— and indeed in all respects (i.e., biologically, emotionally, motivationally, cognitively, behaviorally, socially, and experientially)—through their relationships and their response to those relationships. People develop virtue because they are formed via of all of those relationships.

Christian spiritual formation is more relational than merely cognitive or based in individual private moral or spiritual experience. Thus Christian spiritual development is as much about developing families, communities, friendships, and work environments—that is, relation- ships in different life settings—as it is about becoming more emotionally attuned to God. Of course, we acknowledge that God is forging internal spiritual changes in each individual. But we want to attune all our rela- tionships to God. Christian spiritual formation is as much about pro- moting virtue in others (or perhaps even more) as about promoting virtue in oneself. Virtues share something in common: they all involve

---

[10]F. L. Shults and S. J. Sandage, *Transforming Spirituality: Integrating Theology and Psychology* (Grand Rapids: Baker Academic, 2006).

[11]D. E. Davis, J. N. Hook, and E. L. Worthington Jr., "Relational Spirituality and Forgiveness: The Roles of Attachment to God, Religious Coping, and Viewing the Transgression as a Desecration," *Journal of Psychology and Christianity* 27 (2008): 293-301; E. L. Worthington Jr. and S. J. Sandage, *Forgiveness and Relational Spirituality* (Washington, DC: American Psychological Association, 2015).

self-denial.[12] Courage forgets the self and acts bravely. Prudence (i.e., practical wisdom) takes non-self-serving means to good ends. Justice is about insuring that all people have equal opportunities. Forgiveness sets aside one's right to justice. Humility places the good of others over the good of oneself. We could go on (see Comte-Sponville's treatments of major virtues).[13] This is the understanding we have adopted of eudaimonia. It is not just doing good for oneself, but it is virtue for self and for others. This is where positive psychology and Christian spiritual formation meet.

WHAT DOES EUDAIMONIC VIRTUE REQUIRE OF US?

Forming eudaimonic virtue requires a variety of things of us, which we formulate as a set of hypotheses for Christian spiritual formation. These hypotheses can be treated as a "model" of formation of virtue that could be investigated as a systematic research program. The hypotheses, if supported, could then form the basis of a project to promote higher levels of Christian spiritual formation in the church and society.

These hypotheses are not comprehensive, but we have intentionally listed actions that could be taken at different levels of generality. Some hypotheses concern what individuals can do to build virtue; others involve what social structures can do, including families, churches, scientists and clinical scientists, workplaces, and political and secular societies.

Hypothesis 1: Eudaimonic virtue requires relationships. Fundamentally, the development and practice of eudaimonic virtues requires relationships—with God, others, self, memories, things, and other virtues. In those relationships, one has the challenge and opportunity to act virtuously. If virtue is to be for self and other, there must be an "other" in some form. Humans do not exist in a vacuum, nor do growth and development occur in vacuums.

---

[12]A. Comte-Sponville, *A Small Treatise on the Great Virtues: The Uses of Philosophy in Everyday Life*, trans. Metropolitan Books (New York: Holt Paperbacks, 2002).
[13]Comte-Sponville, *Small Treatise.*

Hypothesis 2: Relationships to others—eudaimonic virtue requires em-pathic or cognitive perspective-taking. If virtue is relational and must be good for oneself and the other person (or other people), then we must be able to know what others would perceive to be good and helpful for their spiritual formation. We must be able to look at people and see their needs, thus requiring empathic or cognitive perspective-taking. Individuals use empathy, but so must institutions—like the church and a civil society—by encouraging empathy through advocating it and its development.[14]

It is possible to understand a person's needs even if one cannot make oneself identify empathically with a person's cognitive perspective. For example, we might cognitively understand a violent criminal's needs but be unable to see things from his emotional perspective. Thus eudaimonic virtue requires at best both cognitive perspective-taking and empathic concern. But we can progress with either if we must. Empathy is nec-essary to strongly pursue virtue for the sake of self and other. Of course, it is possible to be motivated to virtue for one's own self-esteem or for one's relationship with God. Ideally, all of these relationships direct one toward other-oriented virtues.

Hypothesis 3: Relationships to others—eudaimonic virtue requires accountability to various audiences. People usually make fast and in-tuitive decisions, but when there is time, slow and reasoned decisions (usually supporting the intuitive initial impressions) will occur about whether an audience will perceive one as being responsible.[15] Slower rea-soning is usually carried out for reasons not of making a decision but of justifying an intuition. The reasons we are generating are for persuasion (of ourselves or others in an immediate, general, or spiritual audience), almost never to inform a priori rational decision-making. The ordering of the priority of audiences is individually determined. For the very

---

[14]M. H. Davis, "Measuring Individual Differences in Empathy: Evidence for a Multidimensional Approach," *Journal of Personality and Social Psychology* 44 (1983): 113-26.

[15]J. S. Lerner and P. E. Tetlock, "Bridging Individual, Interpersonal, and Institutional Approaches to Judgment and Decision Making: The Impact of Accountability on Cognitive Bias," in *Emerg-ing Perspectives on Judgment and Decision Research*, ed. S. L. Schneider and J. Shanteau (New York: Cambridge University Press, 2003), 431-57.

religious person, one's belief about how God sees one might be number one; for the sociopath, the person right in front of one; for the narcissist, oneself; and for the social chameleon, observers.

Accountability, then, is an individual virtue and yet it exists in social context that motivates virtue and spiritual formation. The audiences must care about virtue and value it; thus the church and general society must seek to foster justice, responsibility, and accountability. Without societal approval and public valuing of accountability, virtues like truth, honesty, responsibility, accountability, and conscientiousness will not develop well individually nor be widely disseminated. Even virtues like compassion, love, and forgiveness require accountability.

Hypothesis 4: Relationship to self and others—eudaimonic virtue requires that one's internally experienced virtues fit with one's sociometer. Leary described sociometer theory.[16] His idea was that people continually monitored the social impression they were making (hence sociometer), using cues in their social environments to do so. If the sociometer reading declines, then one is motivated to repair the damage and do something within the social environment that will change the other person's perception of one.

A person who spends a lot of time with others who do not value the same virtues is likely to take actions others disapprove of. The cognitive and potentially empathic understanding of this discrepancy affects one's internal sociometer. People sense that they are suffering a decline in reputation or social status and are motivated either to change their be- havior to act more often in ways that result in social approval, or they are motivated to escape. If one cannot escape (i.e., one is locked into a par- ticular relationship), then one is likely to either conform or suffer lowered self-esteem.

Hypothesis 5: Relationships to past experiences—eudaimonic virtue requires a history of reward for acting virtuously. People's view of human nature typically includes how they view virtue. For some, people

---

[16]M. Leary, "Sociometer Theory and the Pursuit of Relational Value: Getting to the Root of Self-Esteem," *European Review of Social Psychology* 16 (2005): 75-111.

seem inherently good. Virtue might be seen as lurking beneath the surface, and if one could get rid of the cares of the world, or societal strictures, then virtue might naturally burst forth. For others, humans seem inherently flawed, and perhaps the flaw might often be tied to selfishness. However, research has also shown that there are many times when people act not in light of their own self-interest but to further the interests of their group.[17]

We see people as having by nature tendencies toward all three: other-centeredness, self-centeredness, and in-group centeredness. We might expect to see each of these emerge at various points in a person's life. Each motive might lead to virtuous actions and to the building of a virtuous character, though the motives for which people act virtuously will be rewarded alongside the action. Those motives can make a lot of difference in how much virtues generalize to other situations. Their rewards—in terms of social acceptance and approval, usually from their close friends, family, or primary groups—will affect what people do in the future and how they construe their motives and virtues in the future.

Hypothesis 6: Relationships to other virtues—virtue is organized as hierarchy of virtues. Depending on these rewards (and punishments, of course), people develop the aforementioned hierarchy of virtues that reflects the virtues they attempt to manifest most often. One's social relationships tend to strongly influence which of the aspects of human nature come to characterize each person most strongly.

We believe that each of the many virtues is enacted by most people at some time. But one's personality and character tend to be defined more in terms of the virtues they enact most frequently or in particularly salient acts for which they gain a reputation. For instance, some people become known as honest because their communities can count on seeing that virtue enacted whenever it seems to be under strain.

Related virtues tend to be rewarded more often in some communities than in others. Thus it may be that related virtues clump together in

---

[17]S. G. Post et al., *Altruism and Altruistic Love* (Oxford: Oxford University Press, 2002).

people's virtue hierarchies.[18] Some communities emphasize the conscientiousness-based virtues. These might include responsibility, accountability, conscientiousness, self-control, justice, fairness, protection of others from harm, freedom from coercion, patience, prudence, respect, etc. These virtues tend to inhibit self-interested or even group-interested behavior that would provide centrifugal forces that tear communities apart. Other communities tend to emphasize the warmth-based virtues. These might include empathy, sympathy, care, compassion, loyalty, humility, and love. These virtues draw us to other people. They draw people together in a sense of kinship and pursuit of common values, visions, missions, goals, and objectives. Other virtues draw us toward knowledge, wisdom, discernment, continuity, and tradition. These are epistemic virtues. They seek to hold communities together because the communities share common sources of knowledge and values. Still other virtues are sacred virtues. They draw us toward spirituality (closeness of intimacy with what we hold to be sacred) and responses to the sacred of elevation and awe, reverence, sacrifice, submission, purity, and transcendence. They hold communities together because they provide a sense of unity under the sacred. They subdue self-interest not by inhibiting it but by attracting selves to something felt to be far beyond the individual or even the community—the sacred.

Some of these categories have empirical support. Worthington, Berry, and Parrott factor analyzed people's ratings of the degree to which they valued each of eighteen classic virtues.[19] The identified virtues were limited in that they did not include those that we posited above as epistemic or sacred virtues. Thus, a priori, the empirical findings were limited in this early work on types of virtues. Worthington, Berry, and Parrott found that there was an overall factor of virtue; some people just valued virtue in general more than did others. Those people tended to

---

[18]Worthington, "Virtue Orientations," 156-57.
[19]E. L. Worthington Jr., J. W. Berry, and L. Parrott III, "Unforgiveness, Forgiveness, Religion, and Health," in *Faith and Health: Psychological Perspectives*, ed. T. G. Plante and A. Sherman (New York: Guilford, 2001), 107-38.

evaluate their behaviors more in terms of ones that were good or ones that were bad. A second order factor analysis of the residuals found that there were two sets of virtues, which Worthington, Berry, and Parrott termed warmth-based and conscientiousness-based virtues as described above.

Worthington, Berry, and Parrott hypothesized that the warmth-based virtues were those that tended to draw people toward others. They were labeled warmth-based virtues and were hypothesized to activate areas in the brain related to Gray's behavioral activating system.[20] The other virtues were labeled as conscientiousness-based values, and they were hypothesized to be virtues that requires the exercise of willpower to inhibit indulgence. These were also hypothesized to activate areas in the brain corresponding to Gray's behavioral inhibition system. Additional variance was still unexplained and was accounted for by each of the eighteen classic virtues. There has been some evidence supporting this categorization of types of virtues.[21]

By extending the Worthington, Berry, and Parrott findings, we might also anticipate that warmth-based virtues should be expected to be intercorrelated highly but less correlated with conscientiousness-based virtues and vice versa. However, in a study of virtue promotion by Lavelock, Worthington, Greer, Lin, and Griffin (under review), researchers found that interventions to promote warmth-based virtues also generalized to gains in conscientiousness-based virtues and vice versa.[22] Thus the relationships among virtues merit further research. Additionally, humility might be key to experiencing a number of virtues because it gets one's focus away from self-interest and onto the interest of others, and (as we observed earlier in concordance with Comte-Sponville) self-denial seems to be at the root of most virtues.[23]

---

[20]J. A. Gray, *The Neuropsychology of Anxiety: An Enquiry into the Functions of the Septo-Hippocampus System* (New York: Oxford University Press, 1982).

[21]J. W. Berry et al., "Forgiveness, Moral Identity, and Perceived Justice in Crime Victims and Their Supporters," *Humboldt Journal of Social Relations* 29, no. 2 (2005): 136-62.

[22]Lavelock et al., "A Qualitative Review and Integrative Model of Gratitude and Physical Health," *Journal of Psychology and Theology* 44, no. 1 (2018): 55-86.

[23]Comte-Sponville, *Small Treatise.*

Hypothesis 7: Relationships to the environment—eudaimonic virtue requires situations that stimulate virtues temporarily to the top of the hierarchy. Social psychology has always championed the power of the situation.[24] We suggest that the virtues that rise to the top of their hierarchy of virtues at any particular time are strongly dependent on the situational context. The situational demands elevate specific virtues temporarily higher up, more accessible to consciousness, in the hierarchy of virtues, depending on which virtue seems to be called for. People respond to situational cues and to the internal feelings that are triggered by various cues. When asked to justify their behavior later, a person might draw upon a behavior-consistent virtue. Those virtues that are close to the surface (due to either the situational triggers or the person's own practiced virtues) will be the most likely candidates to be adduced post hoc or even used silently to oneself during the moment of action to justify behavior in a particular situation. This self-justification is especially needed when two or more virtues come into conflict with each other.

Take, for example, Milgram's classic obedience experiments.[25] The "experimenter" provides an authoritative explanation to a subject, the "teacher," who is to deliver electric shocks to a helpless "learner" (who it in reality a confederate of the experimenter) to help the "learner" learn a list of words. The "experimenter" provides a minimal justification for the "teacher" to continue to deliver shocks (i.e., "The experiment requires that you continue") that appeals to authority (i.e., the "experimenter" or the scientific "experiment"). Furthermore, the "experimenter" attempts to defuse alternative explanations by saying things like, "You can keep the money [$5]," which eliminates the idea that one was delivering shocks to get remuneration, or "Although the shocks might be painful, they are not harmful," which tries to minimize the idea of actually

---

[24]S. Milgram, *Obedience to Authority: An Experimental View* (New York: Harper & Row, 1974); P. Zimbardo, *The Lucifer Effect: Understanding How Good People Turn Evil* (New York: Random House 2007).

[25]Milgram, *Obedience.*

harming the "learner," or "I'll take responsibility," to alleviate the sense of accountability.

About two-thirds of the "teachers" delivered shocks at what they thought were very high levels ("Danger, XXX," printed beneath "450 volts"). When asked later "Why did you keep delivering what you thought might be harmful shocks even though the person in the other room was screaming for mercy?," "teachers" did not appeal to the pressures of the situation, which we have hypothesized that people are largely unaware of as causal influencers. They appealed to virtues. They did not appeal to inherent fallenness of humans, or flawed human nature, or their love of inflicting pain. They gave reasons like, "It was for the good of science," "I didn't want to mess up the study," or "The results might help others in the future." Each of those were strong stimuli in an experimental situation, which triggered the highly salient virtues of cooperating with science or helping others.

It is important to note that not all people gave what they thought to be the full 450 volts of shock to the "learner." In one condition, in which the experimenter stood near the "teacher" and the "learner" could be heard yelling through the wall, 62 percent of the "teachers" gave the full complement of shocks. This might seem morally appalling. But 38 percent of the participants did not deliver the maximum. That means that in those 38 percent, although they faced the same situational pressures as the 62 percent, acted on other virtues, which permitted them to refuse to continue to deliver shocks.

Individual differences clearly exist in people's hierarchies of values, and the ones who resisted the social pressure of the physically near "experimenter" must have had more salient values of empathy, sympathy, compassion, mercy, or love. Alternatively, values of strength to resist authority, autonomy, or freedom from coercion might have dominated and could have also led to refusing to deliver additional shocks. As for the 62 percent who did continue, their values of obedience, knowledge, and perhaps even humility that the experimenter knew best may have risen to the top of their hierarchy along with not wishing to mess up an experiment or wanting to help future beneficiaries of the research. Those valued virtues that led to either compliance or resistance to the scientific authority's demands were made salient through their histories, their reward structures, their communities, their more robust association with other virtues, and their more frequent practice of salient virtues.

Let us note, however, that most people do not make decisions based on conscious reference to their value hierarchies. Most do not logically consult their virtue hierarchies and think, "What should I do in this situation?" Rather, they respond to the relationships that are made most salient—those triggered by cues like environmental ones or other thoughts or emotions triggered in situations. Later, people construct virtue-relevant explanations for explaining why they did what they did.

Hypothesis 8: Relationships to others and to the environment— eudaimonic virtue requires participation in a community that values others. Another strong situational context is community, where virtues are often displayed. For example, if a person is alone and is approached by a homeless person who asks directly for money, the person might frequently refuse to give the money. If the person, though, is in the company of four friends from his or her church, and if the church highly values compassion, then the person is almost certain to give money to the homeless person. If the person works for a company that encourages small-business entrepreneurship and is with work colleagues, then the person is not likely to give money. Whatever virtues are endorsed by the community are close to the surface and likely to be triggered and then acted on. Accountability, as previously mentioned, is highly relevant.

But importantly, people belong to many different communities. Often the values on various virtues are starkly different from community to community. When with fellow tennis players, competition and "no mercy" might be valued. When with other runners at a charity run-a-thon to earn money for homeless people, cooperation and mercy are prized. We might suspect that people tend to be drawn to one community more than the other. If one's personal hierarchy of virtues corresponds with community-emphasized virtues of charities, for example, the happy coincidence occurs. For some, though, there is a discrepancy between one's virtue hierarchy and the virtues valued by the community; that is, one who takes a kind and merciful approach may have difficulty understanding the cutthroat mentality at a tennis match. Thus people will tend to seek a person-environment fit when it comes to community and individual virtues, with the result, though, that many mismatches in community and virtue hierarchies are inevitable.

Hypothesis 9: Eudaimonic virtue requires practice and testing. Classical virtue theory might summarize virtue as occurring in a stepwise sequence.[26] According to classical virtue theory, promoting virtue begins when one gets a glimpse of the goal for which one is striving. Another way of thinking about this is that one makes a goal by elevating one or more virtues higher up in one's existing virtue hierarchy. This implies that both accelerative behaviors and decelerative behaviors might be needed to successfully change the virtue hierarchy. An accelerative behavior is one that one hopes to increase. Once the goal is glimpsed, according to this theory, virtue is promoted by practicing the virtue in real-life experiences and upholding these virtues in real-life tests.

Suppose one wishes to increase one's Christian love. One must seek to act lovingly more often than before and imagine what the end result would look like. But suppose one has used all 24-7 of their time prior to this self-improvement program. So some behaviors must be decelerated in order to allow time and resources to practice agape love. One can enter into the self-improvement program of increasing agape without considering the ramifications on the remainder of his or her time, or one can plan ahead and seek, for example, to reduce the time one spends watching television, reading, or even running or working out. If one plans decelerative behaviors intentionally, it is more likely that practicing this virtue will require reducing unwanted behaviors (i.e., watching fatuous

---

[26]Ellen T. Charry, *God and the Art of Happiness* (Grand Rapids: Eerdmans, 2010); Worthington et al., "Contribution of Christian Perspectives"; Tom Wright, *Virtue Reborn* (London: SPCK, 2010).

television shows); whereas, if one does not plan intentionally, one is likely to find that really one virtue is being traded for another. Still, if one can practice enough love, it is possible that this new loving habit of the heart will withstand real life challenges, and agape love can be thought of as having moved higher in one's virtue hierarchy.

In the first case, love might increase relative to other virtues, but the absolute time on each of those virtues did not change. Agape love floats up the hierarchy and overall the person becomes more virtuous. In the second case, agape love moves up the hierarchy at the expense of self-control (in our case). Overall, the person merely maintains virtue ground, trading virtues around in a zero-sum game. We will discuss classical virtue theory more thoroughly in our section outlining recommendations.

Hypothesis 10: Relationship to the spiritual—promotion of eudaimonic virtue for spiritual formation requires (1) strong internal values of virtues and (2) communities that support those virtues. This culminates in our consideration of Christian spiritual formation. The conclusion is not new. People must be formed in internal Christian character. But we have sought to differ with some previous approaches to Christian formation by placing less emphasis on both logical intentions and raw willpower and more emphasis on external triggers of situations, the communities people choose to spend time in, and the activities they engage in.

First, people are formed in communities, most strongly in relational groups like families, churches, work environments, civic societies, and churches. People choose those communities (to greater or lesser degree), and those choices can strongly affect their later Christian formation. Second, another thing different about our approach is our use of cognitive science and moral intuitionist theory to insist that typically much of spiritual formation is not through individual moral decisions but through arranging one's relationships with people, organizations, and things to maximize the number of times particular values reach momentary ascendancy in one's virtue hierarchy. Thus our final hypothesis is that each previous hypothesis propels the individual and all of his or her relationships to spiritual formation.

SUMMARY OF REQUIREMENTS FOR FORMATION
OF EUDAIMONIC VIRTUE

A rationalistic account of what Christian spiritual formation requires is an acknowledgment in the sufficiency of God to build within people the mind of Christ, to conform people to the *imago Dei* through the Holy Spirit. But it also is reasoned awareness that God often works through the human person and human institutions to bring about that transformation. Thus, as people who choose to honor what God has done in us, we seek to do what we can to make it more likely that our wants, needs, thoughts, emotions, motives, and actions are aimed at becoming more a reflection of Christ. That is followed by effort to act virtuously whenever opportunities arise. When no opportunities are available, one who is interested in being more virtuous might simply initiate those opportunities.

The psychology of virtue, however, suggests that, after acknowledging the necessity of divine intervention in our character formation, much of behaving virtuously is not about reasons, effort, and self-control. Much of what is needed for eudaimonic virtue development occurs outside of our immediate awareness. It has to do with our brain structures and how they are triggered, situations we find ourselves in, associations we make, the communities we join and spend our time with, the behaviors in our repertoire, other behaviors that compete with virtue, gut feelings that we ought to be moral and virtuous, available associations, reasons we use as justifications, and reward (and punishment) history that make it likely that we will act virtuously, whether we consciously think we should or not.

Much of spiritual formation is intuitive and occurs outside of explicit consciousness. So, if we take this view of spiritual formation, then how can we maximize being conformed to Christ?

SOLUTIONS TO PROMOTE EUDAIMONIC VIRTUE

We have developed ten hypotheses to understand how eudaimonic virtue works and to seek to promote an acceptance that building virtue and curtailing vice are not just matters of imposing rational solutions on rationally conceived problems. Rather, these hypotheses suggest that our approach to maximizing Christian spiritual formation should be primarily (but not wholly) nonrational. It needs to be exercises in agency but not mere rational agency. Based on this analysis, we offer several suggestions regarding how to promote Christian spiritual formation.

We might observe at the outset that traditional ways of promoting Christian formation—preaching, teaching, training in morals, using spiritual disciplines—use human effort to do so. Take preaching. The preacher prepares carefully, studies theology, reads source materials, accumulates examples, studies rhetoric, and delivers an organized sermon. The preacher uses many human actions to make way for the working of the Holy Spirit through preaching. We are recommending similar human actions through which the Holy Spirit can work. Thus we see our recommendations not as a secular contamination of spiritual disciplines or an intrusion of some secular psychology becoming imperialistic in the spiritual formation area. Rather, we see our recommendations as merely different human actions that can be sanctified by the working of the Holy Spirit just as the use of many disciplines by contemplatives have been over the ages.

Recommendation 1: Stimulate modifications in belief through rational self-persuasion and persuasion of others regarding the value of virtues. People have the capacity for rational control over behavior. We now acknowledge that a rationalistic view—in which rational thought can and should always dominate intuition, feelings, and other experiences, much like the rationalistic tradition of Socrates, Plato, and others through Kant have advocated—is untenable as a model on which to base individual, spiritual, or communal life. However, rational logic is useful; if for no other reason, it is useful to provide articulated reasons that bolster intuitive urges to be virtuous. We believe that people contain a deep-seated urge toward virtue as part of the *imago Dei*, but it has been reinforced by evolution and societally rooted practices, norms, and values. People lean toward virtue as one natural tendency—but some people more than others. Reasons are needed to bolster that tendency, and those reasons come through individual statements that value, teach, or make salient virtues directed toward helping others.

Recommendation 2: Stimulate modifications in belief through changes in practices of communities. Still, reason is only a small asset to spiritual formation; people rarely succumb to logical persuasive communications that modify their pre-existing view on issues. The persistent story of social psychology's study of persuasion, of the communication fields' studies of advertising, and political science's study of voting behavior is that it is many factors outside of normal awareness and logical arguments that are responsible for persuasion. Thus, if we want to persuade people to act more virtuously as Christians, we need to modify the external factors that influence them to act virtuously. This can mean structuring communities to more intentionally promote virtue development.

Books like Robert Cialdini's 2009 *Influence Science and Practice* or Charles Duhigg's 2012 *The Power of Habit* sing the same song regarding how to change people or what makes habits resistant to change.[27] The power is not in intentional rational persuasion but is in the environmental cues that trigger our behavior, and even in the rewards we get for changing (or staying unchanged) or the punishments we receive or anticipate for changing (or staying unchanged). Furthermore, most of these are outside of our conscious awareness. Advertisers, politicians, and influence agents arrange the environment to be consistent with the direction of influence they hope to promote. Some are more successful than others, but all work generally the same way—influence the environment.

To promote spiritual formation, we need to heed these lessons. We need to identify the triggers for the development of spirituality and for conditions that impede its development. Then, we need to modify the environment of as many people as possible to promote spiritual formation. We posit that the cues that trigger spiritual development are the ones that trigger a desire to please God and enjoy God forever. In addition, they include a desire to be part of a vibrant church, which includes developing empathic concern for individuals and societies, and

---

[27]R. Cialdini, *Influence Science and Practice*, 5th ed. (Boston: Pearson, 2009); C. Duhigg, *The Power of Habit: Why We Do What We Do in Life and Business* (New York: Random House, 2012).

to cultivate the self to its God-given potential for enabling self and others toward virtue and spiritual formation.

Recommendation 3: Engage intensely with social institutions that value spiritual development. Some social institutions already value spiritual development and need little additional convincing. These could include churches, of course, but also might be concerned with religious day care, homeschool groups, colleges and universities, and workplaces. The more time we choose to "practice" our virtue goals in social institutions—perhaps through spending time in traditional or extracurricular activities with the institution, giving money, or getting newsletters, email, or social media updates—the more opportunities we have to elevate that focal virtue to high status.

However, secluding oneself in nominal Christian organizations is not the only consideration for promoting Christian spiritual development. Belonging to Christian organizations is neither necessary nor sufficient to yield a spiritually mature adult. People are involved in a variety of organizations. One does not necessarily have to completely immerse oneself unanimously in Christian organizations and social structures to develop spiritually. If one wishes to grow spiritually within a Christian context, one needs to have the strongest organizations reflect Christian values on the virtues, such as the family, and (for many) the church. To the extent that the developing child and adolescent stays engaged with the family and church, it is possible that family and church might remain the dominant social structures, even if the person attends a secular school, university, or workplace. Additionally, while one need not belong exclusively to Christian organizations, it is not enough merely to associate with or belong to Christian organizations to develop spiritually. One must actively engage with important social structures that promote Christian spiritual development. The attention has to keep being called back to Christ. In addition, the agency of the Holy Spirit is necessary.

Thus over time, the more virtue and spiritual development in general become the (or one of the top) defining virtue(s) in our own virtue hierarchies, the more it becomes salient more often, the more we invest our time, energy, and resources in the virtue, the more being a mature Christian will be an important part of our self-definition.

Recommendation 4: Make intentional changes in environmental structures. Given that we might already belong to social groups or societal institutions that value virtues that we seek to invest in, we might also use our position as a participant or leader in those institutions to direct the institution toward promoting spiritual development. As members, we can act agentically to promote changes that lead people within the organization to develop spiritually.

Recommendation 5: Make intentional changes in reward structures. Most of the rewards in terms of social approval or favorable readings on our sociometer we receive for virtuous behavior will be social in nature. They will come through friends, loved ones, colleagues, and companions who value what we are doing. They might tell us that they admire us. But more likely they will show us that they approve of our choices. We have some choices of whom we choose to spend time with. Of course, we do not always choose the people we surround ourselves with on the basis of their stance toward our striving for virtue. But when we do have a choice, we might consider choosing those who reward us for behaving in ways we want to behave and not in ways that tempt us away from those virtues. Other rewards involve feelings of self-esteem for acting in accordance with our values or feelings of satisfaction from a match between our self-concept and our actions. We carry out these acts and experience self-esteem and self-satisfaction within our social contexts. Our communities, as we have argued, are crucial.

Recommendation 6: Seek and cherish spiritual experiences that transcend mere logic. Organized religious bodies will often promote spiritual experiences that not only stimulate cognition but that also promote spiritual connection that moves people to act more virtuously. These practices might include sermons, charitable works, devotional practices, as well as some of the disciplines practiced for centuries within the Roman Catholic Church.

Recommendation 7: Set up systematic practices of Christian virtues. In most of the foregoing suggestions, we have focused on stimulus control procedures—changing one's relationships, group environment, or living environment to promote more virtue. That is, we can act agentically to organize our social and physical environments to make virtuous acts more likely. We now turn, though, to one of the ways we can build internal structures that promote virtue—employing virtue theory.

We have acknowledged that one solution is to subject all processes to slow reasoning. But, as we have observed, modern cognitive science argues that this is impossible to do.[28] And when we think we are succeeding, often we are simply using slow reasoning to justify our intuitions, feelings, and urges. Because of this, the solution must be to try to train the virtues into the person so that they become the automatic intuitive behemoth.

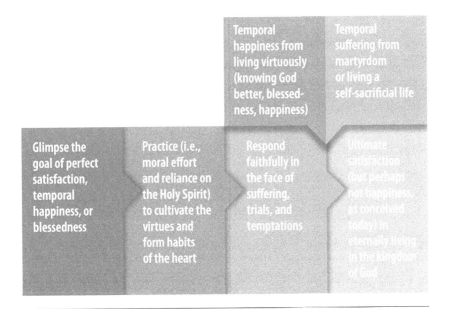

Figure 1. Schematic of virtue as a pathway to ultimate happiness (drawn from Aristotle, Augustine, Thomas, and Charry [2011] and Wright [2010])

[28]D. Kahneman, *Thinking, Fast and Slow* (New York: Farrar, Straus, & Giroux, 2011).

Learning the virtues through classical virtue theory redux. One way we can train the virtues is to employ a modernized version of the classical virtue theory described in hypothesis 9. We employ a modified version of the Christian virtue theory put forth in Tom Wright's 2010 *Virtue Reborn.*[29] Many of the themes were also explored in Ellen Charry's 2010 book on positive theology, *God and the Art of Happiness.*[30] This suggests four aspects of a virtue theory (see figure one). As a review, first, the person must glimpse the goal. Second, the person must practice the virtues until they become habits of the heart or seem second nature. Third, the virtues will be tested by life, and to further strengthen the virtues, people can elect to self-impose tests of the virtues. How they meet the tests that life places on them and the tests that they self-impose through self-control or willpower will determine whether the virtue has become real and the tests have been met with honor.[31] Fourth, people can then experience deep happiness and perhaps they might experience meaning-based temporal happiness or subjective well-being as well.[32] The sense of long-term satisfaction and deep happiness can be a result of behaving well and virtuously using this experiential theory of virtue development.

Humility is the essential first step. Humility might well turn out to be the key virtue, either before or after glimpsing the goal.[33] We need, as a precondition to being more virtuous, to be humble enough to accept that we cannot control every outcome. We do not have the perfect theology. We do not have the strength of reasoning to impose reason on every act. We have to accept that our rational, logical thinking is anemic

---

[29]Wright, *Virtue Reborn.*

[30]Charry, *God and the Art of Happiness.*

[31]R. F. Baumeister and J. Tierney, *Willpower: Rediscovering the Greatest Human Strength* (New York: Penguin, 2011).

[32]D. Keltner, *Born to Be Good: The Science of a Meaningful Life* (New York: W. W. Norton, 2009); D. Lykken, *Happiness: What Studies on Twins Show Us About Nature, Nurture and the Happiness Set Point* (New York: Golden Books, 1999); E. Diener et al., "Subjective Well-Being: Three Decades of Progress," *Psychological Bulletin* 25 (1999): 276-302; R. M. Ryan and E. L. Deci, "On Happiness and Human Potentials: A Review of Research on Hedonic and Eudaemonic Well-Being," *Annual Review of Psychology* 52 (2001): 141-66.

[33]D. E. Davis, E. L. Worthington Jr., and J. N. Hook, "Relational Humility: A Review of Definitions and Measurement Strategies," *Journal of Positive Psychology* 5, no. 4 (2010): 243-52.

compared to intuitive, fast thinking. We have to accept that our self-control will inevitably fail. We have to accept that we are not the center of the universe, but indeed we live in multiple communities, and they matter. The people we live with depend on us, just as we are mutually dependent on them. We must seek to elevate others. (This, of course is to our benefit as well, and we cannot get rid of self-benefit motives, but we can refuse to be dominated by self-benefit and instead be willing to sacrifice for others.)

Once we accept all of those, and they are inherently humble positions—they involve realistic sense of the self and an orientation to elevating others rather than ourselves—then we are ready to embrace virtue for self and others, eudaimonia.[34] The servant leader model of leadership is apropos. This model has been championed by business leaders like Robert Greenleaf, Max De Pree, and Jim Collins.[35] When we have adopted a eudaimonia-based philosophy, we can set aside self-focus and aim humbly at promoting the welfare of others. Then we are poised to try to practice such virtue until it becomes second nature.

Practice acting virtuously. When we practice virtues, we raise those virtues practiced to higher positions within our virtue hierarchy and thus make them more accessible to environmental, social, and cognitive triggers. We come to value more highly what we practice more often.

But how do we practice some virtues more often? First, we can put into practice the suggestions above about choices among friends, social organizations, and activities within those organizations. We can refer to spiritual and religious beliefs and belief structures and try to act consistently with those, seeking forgiveness from God and self-forgiveness when we fail. We can find friends who reward our behavior and do not denigrate it. We can simply, through dogged determination, try to act more in line with what we understand the mind of Christ to be more

---

[34]Davis, Worthington, and Hook, "Relational Humility."

[35]R. Greenleaf, *Servant Leadership: A Journey into the Nature of Legitimate Power and Greatness* (Mahwah, NJ: Paulist Press, 1977); M. De Pree, *Called to Serve: Creating and Nurturing the Effective Volunteer Board* (Grand Rapids: Eerdmans, 2001); and J. Collins, *Good to Great: Why Some Companies Make the Leap and Others Don't* (New York: HarperCollins, 2000).

often. We can minimize competing structures and even competing values and interests—perhaps de-affiliating with groups or friends who do not value spiritual maturity. We can seek to increase our spiritual focus, which in turn will guide many of the choices we make hour by hour. Repetitive practice is the key.

Meet life's tests and impose other self-challenging tests and try to meet them with honor. We might never steal and yet not have the virtue of honesty. We might, to the contrary, simply never have had the opportunity to steal. When tempted, we might find just how weak our honest character is. Virtues reveal themselves when they are placed under strain.

Usually, though, we do not need to concern ourselves that we will face too few tests of our virtue. Life has a way of kicking obstacles in our path, of providing temptations, or creating frequent and severe trials. If we live long enough, we will meet serious challenges to almost every virtue. Hopefully, we will successfully meet those tests when they arrive, and our virtue will be proven, consistent with classic virtue theory.

Instead of waiting on life to throw us a challenge to our Christian character, we have the capability of providing "tests" or challenges to strain our virtues and build their strength. If a person wishes to become stronger, he or she does not have to wait for a life-threatening emergency in which a person must lift an automobile. Instead, the person places himself or herself on a schedule of tests, joining a local gym and setting up a regular weight-lifting regimen. Similarly, one might design a Christian formation "lifting" program to elevate the spirit. Practicing a virtue is like doing repetitions of weights. Although weight lifting destroys a little muscle at the beginning (making the muscle sore the next day), over time the soreness becomes strengthened muscle fiber.

Experience a sense of deep happiness, not just temporal joy in the moment. When we have set a virtue before our eyes and entered into a rigorous practice schedule punctuated by tests that place the virtue under controlled strain and allow us to strengthen the virtue muscle, this will usually lead to a sense of deep satisfaction. One can be satisfied that he or she is doing something good for himself or herself or for others, and one can be satisfied that he or she is working to better the soul. Doing what is right and virtuous does not always result in hedonistic pleasure, in utilitarian outcomes (the greatest good for the greatest number), or deontological outcomes (doing what is right for the sake of right, regardless of the outcomes). But it typically does provide a sense of spiritual satisfaction.

BEING A MORE CHRISTIAN PERSON IN A MORE CHRISTIAN COMMUNITY IN A MORE CHRISTIAN SOCIETY

In this chapter, we have put forth a view of how positive psychology can contribute to Christian formation. Our theme of the chapter is that modern psychology has moved us from a Socratic, Kantian rationalism, away from a view of humanity that is ensconced in rationality and modernity. Modern psychology is more post-modern, moving us toward a sense of Christian virtue rooted in humility, forgiveness, and love that is largely experienced in various communities of which we are part. We examined positive psychology as one form of modern psychological science in which there is a body of research on the basic psychological understanding of virtues, embedded in a relational context. Also, in positive psychology, clinical scientists have developed interventions to promote those virtues.

While there is much more to Christian formation than merely developing virtues, bringing positive psychology's expertise to bear within a framework emphasizing the power of the situation and promotion of virtue can add tools to the individual Christian's or Christian community's repertoire to help people become more like Christ. We hope that our proposals might stimulate a different (supplemental) approach to the promotion of Christian formation—one that includes more attention to relationships, situations, and virtue theory and draws not only on Christian tradition but also psychological science.[36]

---

[36]E. L. Worthington Jr., *Coming to Peace with Psychology: What Christians Can Learn from Psychology* (Downers Grove, IL: InterVarsity Press, 2010).

CONCLUDING REMARKS

In this chapter, we argued that positive psychology can be a potential important partner in promoting spiritual formation.[37] First, positive psychology can help shape Christian character because positive psychology is largely about virtues, and virtues and internal aspects of being, inherent in the *imago Dei*, provide potential and motivation to act virtuously. Second, positive psychology and its relational context can help shape Christian character, as we suggest in ten hypotheses for future research programs to explore. Third, we offer recommendations by which positive psychology can be accessed by individual Christians, church bodies, and denominations to aid in Christian formation.

Positive psychology is one of many resources upon which people might draw for spiritual formation. It is a cutting-edge area of high interest in psychology, with growing empirical research that is collaborative with both religious and secular ideas and institutions. Most important, it is suited in subject matter for aiding in the understanding and promotion of spiritual formation; it is heavily concerned with virtues and their promotion, consistent with many religious traditions and the values therein. Thus it is accessible to Christians who wish to take an active, agentic part in their spiritual formation.

---

[37]Worthington, *Christian Psychologist* and *Four Christian Virtues*; Worthington et al., "Virtue in Positive Psychology"; and Worthington et al., "Contributions of Christian Perspective."

BORN TO RELATE

IN TRAUMA, IN TRANSFORMATION,
IN TRANSCENDENCE

MARIE T. HOFFMAN

"[Every human being] is formed to be a spectator of the created world and given eyes . . . [to] be led to its author by contemplating so beautiful a representation," writes John Calvin in his commentary on Romans 1.[1] Elaborating on Calvin's thoughts, theologian Belden Lane adds, "Calvin knew that human desire at its best is but a mirror of God's own desire for relationship."[2] Calvin's religious anthropology commences with humans hard-wired to desire relationship with the Creator who desires relationship with them.

Relationship is also at the heart of psychoanalysis. Though Sigmund Freud attempted to distance himself from his relational, Jewish ontology due to the virulent anti-Semitism of his day, his entire psychoanalytic method of cure was based on the interaction of persons in relationship and the ensuing insight that emerged.

Returning psychoanalysis even closer to its Judaic roots, Ronald Fairbairn, psychoanalyst, Scottish object relations theorist, and lifelong

---

[1]Quoted in Belden Lane, "Spirituality as the Performance of Desire: Calvin on the World as a Theatre of God's Glory," *Spiritus* 1 (2001): 1.
[2]Lane, "Spirituality," 9.

Christian, envisioned the infant as born with an innate inclination toward relationship. Psychoanalyst Stephen Mitchell, acknowledging Fairbairn's decisive paradigm shift to a comprehensively relational model, stated: "Fairbairn was suggesting that object-seeking, in its most radical form, is not the vehicle for satisfaction of a specific need, but the expression of our very nature, the form through which we become specifically human beings."[3]

Fairbairn's ideas have resonated in attachment research as well as in neuroscience. In a study on prenatal twin fetal activity entitled "Wired to Be Social: The Ontogeny of Human Interaction," Castiello et al. provide empirical evidence of the innate longing to relate. They write:

> By the 14th week of gestation twin fetuses . . . display movements . . . specifically aimed at the co-twin, the proportion of which increases between the 14th and 18th gestational week. Kinematic analysis revealed that movement duration was longer and deceleration time was prolonged for other-directed movements compared to movements directed towards the uterine wall. . . .
>
> [We conclude that] . . . other-directed actions are not only possible but predominant over self-directed actions . . . grounding for the first time . . . Martin Buber's I/Thou . . . on quantitative empirical results.[4]

The emphasis on relationship as central to our humanity emerged early in the twentieth century in the field of philosophy. An interdisciplinary group of scholars began meeting at Oxford in 1924, their express purpose being the examination of the "relationship of faith and science."[5] This group included philosophers Seth Pringle-Pattison, who was mentor to psychoanalyst Ronald Fairbairn, Martin Buber, and John Macmurray, mentor to psychoanalyst Harold Guntrip. Macmurray and Buber focused on the meaning of personhood. Costello summarizes their joint interest: "[Their] project had two dimensions to it: first, the recovery of a recognition of the fully personal from the reductionism

---

[3]Stephen Mitchell, *Relationality: From Attachment to Intersubjectivity* (Hillsdale, NJ: The Analytic Press, 2000), 106.

[4]U. Castiello et al., "Wired to Be Social: The Ontogeny of Human Interaction," PLoS ONE 5, no. 10 (2010): e13199, doi.org/10.1371/journal.pone.0013199.

[5]J. E. Costello, *John Macmurray: A Biography* (Edinburgh: Floris Books, 2002), 137.

imposed by mechanical and organic categories of thinking on human persons and social institutions. . . . Second, to achieve a coherent and consistent articulation of the unique logic of personal existence."[6] Macmurray and Buber passionately emphasized the necessity of understanding personhood as existing within the matrix of relationship. Emerging from this matrix and formed by it are human motivations which lead to human actions. Macmurray averred, "Any personal activity must have a motive, and all motives are, in the large sense, emotional. Indeed, an attitude of mind is simply an emotional state."[7] In this conceptualization, Macmurray linked relational influences such as parental and cultural models with personal behavior, offering a philosophical counterpart for Fairbairn's psychological premises. Relevant to our discussion of psychology and spiritual formation, Macmurray concludes:

> Religion must be concerned with the original and basic formal problem of human existence, and this is the relation of persons. Since religion is certainly a reflective activity, this must mean, if it is true, that religion has its ground and origin in the problematic of the relation of persons, and reflects that problem. In that case religion is about the community of persons.[8]

From my vantage point as a psychoanalyst, "spiritual" formation is best conceived and practiced from the foundation of an understanding of humans as formed through relationship, marred by relationship, and transformed through relationship. Thus development in human relationships transcends categories of "the spiritual," "the physical," and "the emotional," and recognizes personal formation as a holistic, non-reductive, non-dualistic matrix of maturation.[9]

To the detriment of many, mechanistic and dehumanizing approaches to human transformation plague the theory and practice of psychology.

---

[6]Costello, *John Macmurray*, 14-15.
[7]J. Macmurray, *Persons in Relation* (Atlantic Highlands, NJ: Humanities Press, 1961), 31.
[8]Macmurray, *Persons*, 157.
[9]W. Brown and B. Strawn, *The Physical Nature of Christian Life: Neuroscience, Psychology and the Church* (New York: Cambridge University Press, 2012).

The proliferation of routinized techniques and packaged "tool kits" for the alleviation of human suffering is countered by Nancy McWilliams under the title of "Preserving Our Humanity as Therapists":

> Most of my colleagues have become alarmed at the erosion of what have for decades been the more fundamental aspects of our mission as psychotherapists: to understand; to help; to speak the truth; to make a meaningful connection with our clients that fosters their sense of agency, their capacity for enjoyment and mastery, and their ability to tolerate grief and limitation, whether or not their behavior is unconventional and inconvenient according to ordinary cultural norms.[10]

The reductionistic, nonrelational focus on symptom reduction that permeates psychological treatment protocols has spurred the development of "positive psychology" as an "add-on" to balance the pathological focus of symptom-focused therapies. Such bifurcation of treatment for pathology—and treatment toward positive virtues and traits—is not necessary in psychoanalysis, for the therapist relates to the patient with a binocular lens of life that encompasses weaknesses and strengths. Contemporary psychoanalysis through a holistic, relational approach seeks to aid the patient in maturation toward a life that encompasses human dignity, health, happiness, and virtue in contrast to mere cessation of symptoms. Psychoanalytic treatment parallels a journey of sanctification and discipleship when practiced by a clinician and patient committed to Christian faith.

In this chapter I will present a psychoanalytic approach to human suffering that is holistic, relational, and resonant with Christian theology. I will first posit that since relationship-seeking is central to our human personhood, then relationship-ruptures must be implicated in human trauma and the genesis of psychopathology. Developing an epistemology from theology, neuroscience, and psychology, I will then suggest that loving, human relationship is essential to human transformation. Last, I will posit that personal healing is not merely an individual

---

[10]N. McWilliams, "Preserving Our Humanity as Therapists," *Psychotherapy: Theory, Research, Practice, Training* 42, no. 2 (2005): 140.

phenomenon experienced solely for personal relief of suffering, but it embodies transcendence as it becomes a relational enactment of redemption in God's kingdom.

BORN TO RELATE: IN TRAUMA

Cathy was exhilarated when she married Peter. He was a worship leader whose father and grandfather had pastored his country church. She had now "moved beyond" her less-than-stellar beginning—though truth be known, she was also intimidated by the Christian pedigree of Peter and his family. Cathy was born in a small Pennsylvania town to parents whose family history held many secrets. Suicides and untimely deaths dotted the genogram, but Cathy knew few specifics. Nonetheless, she was a bright woman, rising within the ranks of her church community and bringing many to faith in Christ through her youth work.

Life moved along well for Cathy until the day her eighteen-year-old nephew committed suicide. The chaos of her childhood, the mixture of sadness and rage at her nephew's father—her brother—and the feelings of unbearable inferiority to her husband's family all came crashing in upon her bucolic life. When she came to see me, her moods were cycling from despair to rage, and she feared her own destructiveness. Once, when angry at her husband, she had taken a pair of scissors and cut to pieces several pairs of his pants. On another occasion, in an explosive rage, she rammed her car into the parked car he occupied. In sessions, she would vacillate from rageful woman to panic-stricken child.

Understanding such behavior from Calvin's perspective, one comprehends that though the created order was initially marked by internal and external harmony, a cataclysmic relational event reorganized a world now separated from God and others. This world became marked by "absence of the sympathy or affinity that formerly aided understanding, and the loss of harmony within ourselves in the plurality of conflicting motives and emotions."[11] Jonathan Edwards recapitulates Calvin's linkage of separation from God to alienation with others:

> [Each person] shrank, as it were, into a little space, circumscribed and closely shut up within itself, to the exclusion of all things else. Sin, like some powerful astringent, contracted his soul to the very small dimensions of selfishness; and God was forsaken, and fellow-creatures forsaken, and man retired within himself.[12]

The Biblical narrative further describes how sin becomes repetitive, reflecting a "bondage of the will." This tenacious pull toward such behavior leads Paul to cry in Romans 7:24, "Wretched man that I am! Who shall deliver me from this body of death?"

"Bondage of the will" was a familiar theme in the Scottish Free Church sermons of Ronald Fairbairn's youth, an often-sung hymn proclaiming, "Thy pow'r alone, O Son of God, Can this sore bondage break."[13] Extrapolating from his Reformed heritage and his philosophical studies, Fairbairn proffered a relational perspective on the "bondage of the will." To Fairbairn, the repetition of sinful behavior did not implicate a lack of will, though he did acknowledge its enslavement. Rather, he understood the compulsion to repeat sinful behaviors as derivative of a relational longing. Children, needing to remain attached to parents who have failed them, internalize parental behaviors and repeat them, ensuring a relational connection through identification. This identification is a perspective for understanding "the iniquity of the fathers" being visited "on the children" (Ex 20:5). When one attaches to the significant caretaker through this unconscious identification, he or she often will relate to others in the present out of that identification. Enslavement to sin is more than an individual pathology; it is a relationally transmitted pathology.[14]

---

[11]J. G. Shortt, "Toward a Reformed Epistemology and Its Educational Significance" (unpublished doctoral dissertation, University of London, 1991), 7.

[12]J. Edwards, *Charity and Its Fruits* (Edinburgh: Banner of Truth Trust, 1852), 158.

[13]Bonar, "Not What My Hands Have Done," *Trinity Hymnal*, 403.

[14]M. Hoffman, *Toward Mutual Recognition: Relational Psychoanalysis and the Christian Narrative* (New York: Routledge, 2011).

Some of the literature in spiritual formation emphasizes how the bondage of the will may be overcome through spiritual disciplines. Such perspectives can lack a recognition that personal bondage to sin is a compulsive repetition and recreation of transgenerationally transmitted identifications that emanate from and pervert the God-designed longing for relationship. When persons trying to practice the disciplines fail to be changed, they are sometimes perceived as "double-minded." One speaker at a spiritual formation conference even suggested that although many people seek transformation there were few who truly want to change. I have rarely encountered such a person in my practice and have found patients to be deeply appreciative of a relationship that assists them to break free of relational ties that enslaved them to destructive behaviors.

Let us return to Cathy and examine how her behaviors might be motivated by such relational strivings. I came to understand that Cathy had felt marginally close to her father and very distant from her mother and brother. Largely neglected by her parents, she was never alone, for her brother would be there to rage at her, torment her, then dismiss her. Mother was perpetually ill and seeking care from Cathy, who feared that she was responsible for mother's sicknesses.

Cathy eventually came to understand that her shifts from rageful person to needy child derived from her longing to be close to mother, father, and brother. She needed to feel attached and had unconsciously become them. She behaved like the terrifying or sick mother, the neglectful father, and the rageful brother toward herself and others.

As Cathy grasped her identifications with family members and burial of any negative feelings toward them, she understood that she had been "occupied": they were actually controlling her life from within. I utilized Christian language to explain that what felt comfortable and familiar was the "natural man," and suggested that simultaneously, she was a "new creation"—the person who so lovingly reared her children, did not neglect them or terrify them. Cathy had fulfilled her need to relate through pathological identifications with her family, binding her into shameful and guilt-producing behaviors.

BORN TO RELATE: IN TRANSFORMATION

Our Savior's love moved him from being merely a hope, a wished-for Messiah spoken of by Old Testament prophets, to becoming incarnated as the Living Word to dwell among us. Why was Old Testament revelation not enough? Why was learning the truth of the law insufficient? Why is simple delivery of cognitive principles and behavioral exercises many times inadequate for interrupting the transmission of parental sins to the children? Incarnation—a relational initiative—and not just instruction was required to break the bonds that shackled humankind. Similarly, in psychotherapy validated by neuroscience, incarnation in the form of "re-enactment" of relational patterns between persons is often necessary for the breaking of old patterns and the experiencing of new.

In Cathy's case, feelings that were painful were dissociated into storage in the right hemisphere of the brain. Right hemisphere functions include the storage of highly charged memories, while the left hemisphere is more focused on verbal comprehension. Cathy was motivated by those buried feelings without recognition of their source. This points to the necessity of a psychotherapeutic approach that addresses the affective loading of dissociated mentation stored in the right hemisphere of the brain.

A psychodynamic approach targets these dissociated memories and affects, allowing them to re-occur between patient and therapist, have meaning, and eventually be comprehended by the left-brain. Efrat Ginot, in an interdisciplinary study, explains the implicit, affectively charged nature of psychoanalytic enactments:

> Neuroscientific research has demonstrated that what enactments communicate in such gripping and indirect ways are implicit, neurally encoded affective and relational patterns. Patterns formed before verbal memory was fully developed and those defensively dissociated later on by an emotionally overwhelmed sense of self. . . . What gets to be empathically known through enactments, then, are relational patterns and self-representations that cannot become recognized through verbal interchanges alone.[15]

---

[15]E. Ginot, "The Empathic Power of Enactments: The Link Between Neuropsychological Processes and an Expanded Definition of Empathy," *Psychoanalytic Psychology* 26 (2009): 292-93.

There is mounting evidence of the long-term efficacy of relational, psychodynamic approaches. In the United States, the massive NIMH funded Sequenced Treatment Alternatives to Relieve Depression (STAR*D) Study completed in 2006 found that the benefits of CBT treatments for depression erode, with relapse rates of 55 percent to 71 percent, the average time to relapse occurring in less than four months.[16] By contrast, research in the United States and Great Britain has demonstrated remarkable outcomes for psychodynamic treatment, with evidence mounting that the benefits increase over time.

The independent Cochrane Library Meta-Analysis of twenty-three randomized controlled trials with 1,431 patients receiving short-term psychodynamic psychotherapy had end-of-study effect sizes of .97 for general symptoms, .81 for somatic symptoms, .59 for depression symptoms, and 1.08 for anxiety symptoms. Nine months later outcomes improved even further with 1.51 for general symptoms, 2.21 for somatic symptoms, .98 for depression symptoms, and 1.35 for anxiety symptoms.[17]

In stunning research by Bateman and Fonagy, after eighteen months of psychodynamic treatment called "Mentalization-Based Treatment," 57 percent of patients with a Borderline Personality Disorder diagnosis no longer met the criteria for BPD. The benefits of the treatment increased over time with 87 percent of participants no longer meeting criteria at an eight-year follow-up.[18] Though cognitive-behavioral methods offer rapid alleviation of symptoms, evidence is accumulating that the effects dissipate and that the rate of recidivism is dismally high. From a theological and relational viewpoint, this comes as no surprise.

---

[16]A. J. Rush et al., "Acute and Longer-Term Outcomes in Depressed Outpatients Requiring One or Several Treatment Steps: A STAR*D Report," *American Journal of Psychiatry* 163 (2006): 1905-17.

[17]A. A. Abbass et al., "Short-Term Psychodynamic Psychotherapies for Common Mental Disorders," *Cochrane Database of Systematic Reviews* 4 (2006): CD004687, 10.1002/14651858.CD004687 .pub3.

[18]A. Bateman and P. Fonagy, "Randomized Controlled Trial of Outpatient Mentalization-Based Treatment Versus Structured Clinical Management for Borderline Personality Disorder," *American Journal of Psychiatry* 165 (2009): 556-59.

Jonathan Shedler, in his article titled "The Efficacy of Psychodynamic Therapy," summarizes research findings. He writes:

> Empirical evidence supports the efficacy of psychodynamic therapy. Effect sizes for psychodynamic therapy are as large as those reported for other therapies that have been actively promoted as "empirically supported" and "evidence based." In addition, patients who receive psychodynamic therapy maintain therapeutic gains and appear to continue to improve after treatment ends. Finally, non-psychodynamic therapies may be effective in part because the more skilled practitioners utilize techniques that have long been central to psychodynamic theory and practice. The perception that psychodynamic approaches lack empirical support does not accord with available scientific evidence and may reflect selective dissemination of research findings.[19]

The inadequacy of primarily nonrelational methods also implicates the recent clinical application of mindfulness. Originally practiced in Buddhism, mindfulness aids a patient in developing a moment-by-moment accepting awareness of one's thoughts, feelings, and experience. Jeffrey Rubin, psychoanalyst and meditation teacher, in his book *Meditative Psychotherapy: The Marriage of East and West*, while advocating the benefits of mindfulness, points out its insufficiency when used alone. He relates this story:

> One patient . . . practiced a Tibetan technique called "Touch and Go." She sat still and opened to whatever arose—often sorrow and loneliness—identified with these feelings momentarily, and then let them go. . . . "I learned," she told me very confidently, "that through meditation, I could lay my feelings about my life to rest."

> Effective as it might be, her meditation also cut her off from feedback about her emotions. She didn't yet realize that addressing their meaning was vital to figuring out what haunted her. The loss and abuse that she thought were put to rest, returned in the form of her symptoms and suffering. She had spent eighteen years anesthetizing herself with meditation, instead of dealing with the experiences of her childhood which caused her such sadness.

---

[19]J. Shedler, "The Efficacy of Psychodynamic Therapy," *American Psychologist* 65, no. 2 (2010): 98.

My patient called our therapy, "Touch and stay" because we contacted and stayed with her feelings of sadness and loss in the past and the neglect . . . in the present. She was able to grieve and mourn.[20]

While initial improvement often is experienced through mindfulness, mindfulness does not foster the witnessing of suffering through a comforting attachment to a caring human, the deepest need our patients bring. As with this patient, success is often short-lived or new symptoms emerge, necessitating a redoubling of meditation attempts.

The power of incarnation, with its emphasis on relationship, makes possible the enacting of and repair of a previous relational trauma and is supported theologically in Scripture as well as empirically in neuroscience. But does incarnation lead us directly to resurrection? Both theology and psychoanalysis would say no. There can be no resurrection without death. Simply relating kindly and with positivity will not stop the cycle of attachment to bad behaviors and identifications.

Written shortly before his death, "The Use of an Object" (1969) was British psychoanalyst Donald Winnicott's unwitting translation of his early Wesleyan theology into theory.[21] Winnicott believed that unless the therapist received and survived the patient's attacks, which come as a result of childhood distortions, the patient will never see others and themselves apart from those formative distortions. Patients come to us peering through the misty lenses of past relationships and identifications. And we in turn look back at them through our own and unwittingly become sin for our patients. We endure the punishment and rebuke that both we and significant others before us deserved, and we also suffer unjustly for sins committed by others and transferred on to us. It is only then, Winnicott theorized, that the mist clears, and the newness of resurrection is possible. When we survive "crucifixion," our patients can see that we and others are not the wounding parents they thought we were.

---

[20]J. Rubin, *Meditative Psychotherapy: The Marriage of East and West* (New York: Abiding Change Press, 2013), locations 243 and 259 of 4053, Kindle.

[21]D. Winnicott, "The Use of an Object," *International Journal of Psychological Analysis* 50 (1969): 711-16.

The therapist may aptly say, "I am crucified with Christ, nevertheless, I live." Such focus on the relationship between patient and therapist moves the locus of redemption from mere verbal discourse to the messy environs of hand-to-hand combat with evil.

Let us return to Cathy's story. Cathy began to see a reduction in outbursts, and when she did experience them, she self-regulated more quickly. But the sense that she was bad and sick and dangerous—a consequence of her relationship to her mother—continued to surface. It is at this point that my dog Rudy becomes a character in Cathy's story.

Rudy came to us when just a few months old, following the death of another beloved Pomeranian. He was cute as a button, but his brain cells were just not fully developed. Cathy always brought treats for my dogs, whom she deeply loved. On an ordinary day, she came in and gave Rudy his treat. We went on with our session until she commented to me that Rudy had not moved in a while. I looked down and to my horror, Rudy was not breathing. I don't know how long he had been in this state, but it was long enough that he involuntarily defecated. I screamed, "My dog is dead, my dog is dead," as I ran to him, held him upside down and performed the Heimlich to no avail. His lifeless body did not respond. Finally, I laid him on the floor and did CPR—compressions, breaths—as my terror-stricken patient watched. I cleared his airway by hand, and found a treat lodged sideways. But still, no respiration. I tried a second course of CPR. Still nothing. I was giving up hope, but Cathy, who had begun studies in medicine years before, pleaded, "Try one more time." I did, and Rudy began to cough. He was very disoriented, but so were we. He curled up on my lap and slept as Cathy and I talked of what had just happened. How do you go on in a session after something like this?

My mind went quickly to what must have been stirring in Cathy. I asked her what she felt, and we discovered that this incident led to the heart of her fears: her love and her hate were destructive. Her treat had nearly killed my dog. We explored her feelings of responsibility for her mother's well-being, which could oscillate to virulent hatred at her mother's total self-absorption. We discussed her feelings of envy for her brother, who had been favored, and her guilt over her wishing him ill. Through our shared horror for Rudy's apparent demise, I had not only witnessed Cathy's terror, but I had vicariously experienced the terror that Cathy felt. Until Cathy's dissociated fear spontaneously emerged, it had been unavailable for her to recollect or acknowledge, and we had been unable to access what had perpetually held her in bondage. When Cathy experienced my humanness, my panic, she was also able to relinquish her idealization of me and be reassured that her own intense feelings were normative. Cathy's desire to feel normal and good became more often realized, and she was further freed from the repetitive cycles of anger that kept her in bondage to her past.

BORN TO RELATE: IN TRANSCENDENCE

Ronald Fairbairn understood the analyst's task as finding an entrée into the closed internal world of the patient to offer a redemptive relationship with a real "other." Fairbairn variously characterized the analyst's function as: "messiah," "saviour," "exorcist," and "evangelist."[22] The patient comes to experience the analyst as a new, good relationship, hopes for the possibility of something better, and in Fairbairn's words "may be induced" to relinquish the bad and attach to the good.

More than a century before Fairbairn's contributions, the founder of the Free Church of Scotland, Thomas Chalmers, presaged Fairbairn's formulations in a legendary sermon titled "The Expulsive Power of a New Affection." I will replace Chalmer's use of the word *world* with the term "bad relationship."

> The love of the world [bad relationship] cannot be expunged by a mere demonstration of the world's [bad relationship's] worthlessness. But may it not be supplanted by the love of that which is more worthy than itself? The heart cannot be prevailed upon to part with the world [bad relationship], by

---

[22]M. Hoffman, *When the Roll Is Called: Trauma and the Soul of American Evangelicalism* (Eugene, OR: Cascade Books, 2016).

a simple act of resignation. But may not the heart be prevailed upon to admit into its preference another, who shall subordinate the world [bad relationship] and bring it down from its wonted ascendancy? . . . It is not by exposing the worthlessness of the former, but by addressing to the mental eye the worth and excellence of the latter, that all old things are to be done away and all things are to become new. . . . In fullest accordance with the mechanism of the heart, a great moral revolution may be made to take place upon it.[23]

What Fairbairn deduced from this famous sermon was translated into his work with patients. Fairbairn realized that the therapist stood in the role of Christ to the patient, and through forging a deep, loving relationship could release the enslaved patient from bondage, enabling them to respond to and give love in external reality.

The renewed capacity to see others in reality—without a projection of past identifications on to present relationships—becomes the means for transcending old patterns of relating and converting that knowledge into an empathy for suffering others. The ashes of our own pain become the very substance with which we transcend our past through feeling others' pain and bringing comfort to them in alignment with God's redemptive design. We are not simply released from bondage to feel better but to fulfill the Father's heart, "Thy kingdom come."

In psychoanalysis, providing relief from pathology has never been the final destination of treatment. Shedler concurs:

The goals of psychodynamic therapy include, but extend beyond, alleviation of acute symptoms. Psychological health is not merely the absence of symptoms; it is the positive presence of inner capacities and resources that allow people to live life with a greater sense of freedom and possibility.[24]

This broader view of the psychoanalytic vocation is reflected in the Shedler-Westen Assessment Procedure (SWAP) that assesses inner

[23]T. Chalmers, *The Expulsive Power of a New Affection* (1855; Minneapolis, MN: Curiosmith, 2012).
[24]J. Shedler, "The Efficacy of Psychodynamic Psychotherapy," *American Psychologist* 65, no. 2 (2010): 98-109.

capacities and resources to be developed in psychotherapy.[25] The list of mental health characteristics was consensually validated by clinicians across the spectrum of orientations, though psychodynamic psycho-therapy is unique in its intentional attempt to facilitate their development as part of the treatment process. Mentally healthy persons are those who

- are able to use their talents, abilities, and energy effectively and productively

- enjoy challenges; take pleasure in accomplishing things

- are capable of sustaining a meaningful love relationship characterized by genuine intimacy and caring

- find meaning in belonging and contributing to a larger community (e.g., organization, church, neighborhood)

- are able to find meaning and fulfillment in guiding, mentoring, or nurturing others

- are empathic; are sensitive and responsive to other people's needs and feelings

- are able to assert themselves effectively and appropriately when necessary

- appreciate and respond to humor

- are capable of hearing information that is emotionally threatening (i.e., that challenges cherished beliefs, perceptions, and self-perceptions) and can use and benefit from it

- appear to have come to terms with painful experiences from the past; have found meaning in and grown from such experiences

---

[25]D. Westen and J. Shedler, "Revising and Assessing Axis II, Part 1: Developing a Clinically and Empirically Valid Assessment Method," *American Journal of Psychiatry* 156 (1999): 258-72; D. Westen and J. Shedler, "Revising and Assessing Axis II, Part 2: Toward an Empirically Based and Clinically Useful Classification of Personality Disorders," *American Journal of Psychiatry* 156 (1999): 273-85; D. Westen and J. Shedler, "Personality Diagnosis with the Shedler-Westen Assessment Procedure (SWAP): Integrating Clinical and Statistical Measurement and Prediction," *Journal of Abnormal Psychology* 116 (2007): 810-22.

- are articulate; can express themselves well in words
- have an active and satisfying sex life
- appear comfortable and at ease in social situations
- generally find contentment and happiness in life's activities
- tend to express affect appropriate in quality and intensity to the situation at hand
- have the capacity to recognize alternative viewpoints, even in matters that stir up strong feelings
- have moral and ethical standards and strive to live up to them
- are creative; are able to see things or approach problems in novel ways
- tend to be conscientious and responsible
- tend to be energetic and outgoing
- are psychologically insightful; are able to understand self and others in subtle and sophisticated ways
- are able to find meaning and satisfaction in the pursuit of long-term goals and ambitions
- are able to form close and lasting friendships characterized by mutual support and sharing of experiences[26]

In her personal notes titled "What Are We Helping Patients Toward? Reflections on Overall Psychological Health," psychoanalyst Nancy McWilliams offers sixteen similar "positive" qualities that "constitute health, good character, and the good life," and which psychoanalysts seek to nurture in their patients. She enumerates these as:

1. Love

2. Work

3. Play

[26]Shedler, "Efficacy of Psychodynamic Psychotherapy," 106.

4. Movement toward a secure attachment pattern

5. Sense of agency or autonomy

6. Self and object constancy or identity integration

7. Ego strength and resilience

8. Realistic and reliable self-esteem

9. Sense of abiding values, ethics, integrity

10. Affect tolerance and regulation

11. Insight, reality testing

12. The capacity to mentalize

13. Flexibility of defenses

14. Balance between self-definition and self-in-relationship

15. Sense of vitality, enthusiasm, passion

16. Acceptance, capacity to mourn, surrender, meaning-making[27]

In the course of her treatment, Cathy began to experience the development of many of these qualities. A particularly striking development occurred when she returned to school to complete her medical training. Although in mid-life, the constraints of parents who did not encourage her academically were now diminished. Cathy excelled in her studies. Concurrently, she worked in a medical setting in which she experienced deep compassion for suffering people. She had longed to heal her mother and could not. She had longed to be comforted and was not. Now, as an adult, she could offer to herself and others what had been denied her in childhood.

A more surprising development emerged not in her career but in her marriage. A previously undisclosed revelation by Peter of a long-buried falsehood enraged Cathy. She had been the defective wife while Peter had been the saint, and it had all been a lie. Her rage returned with a vengeance, and some of Cathy's maturational gains were eclipsed. For months Cathy

[27]N. McWilliams, "What Is Mental Health? An Exploration of Wellness That Goes Beyond Symptom Relief," video, February 12, 2012, www.youtube.com/watch?v=AacLpZajJa4.

remained regressed, distant from Peter, for whom she felt unbaiting rage, until a space opened in which she could mourn. Only after Cathy's illusions of Peter's perfection and her supposed defectiveness were laid bare could she see her role in maintaining Peter's defenses against knowing his own suffering and recognizing both his own neediness and his own evil. She needed him to be her savior. Cathy began to see that Peter's family, who had appeared spotless, was riddled with falsehood and unacknowledged pain. After a significant period of her reactive disdain of Peter and his family, Cathy gingerly moved toward empathy for her husband, whom she eventually understood as someone who suffered from his own unacknowledged wounds, just like she had. After this reparative period in her marriage, old feelings of defectiveness projected on to her by her parents and brother only rarely threatened her, and she could experience empathy and forgiveness toward Peter who could now acknowledge his own shortcomings. Peter is in his own psychotherapy, and together they have come to see themselves as broken and wondrous, enjoying their marriage more than they ever had thought possible.

CONCLUSION

Religion scholar Martin Marty describes the radical relationality of our God as exemplified in His grace, and I find it fitting as a way of introducing my final thoughts in this chapter. He writes:

> God had the freedom to remain unrelated; instead God was moved to create a universe, to situate humans in it, and to move towards them. . . . God is love. . . . This reality suggests that God is moved by nothing other than that love to visit humans, bring them back to God, and restore them. This love, unmotivated and spontaneous—which means that it does not need to find redeeming qualities in its object—finds expression in grace. Grace . . . exemplifies the revelation of the divine character in action and the relation of the divine to human beings. Consequently, grace is conceived as personal, a movement from the being of God to the drama of human existence.[28]

---

[28]M. Marty, "Grace," in *A New Handbook of Christian Theologians*, ed. D. Musser and J. Price (Nashville, TN: Abingdon Press, 1992), 209-11.

My work as a psychodynamic clinician is an extension of God's grace in this world. It is radically relational, radically hopeful, and radically committed to full restoration of the image of God in each patient with whom I meet. In over twenty-five years of full-time practice as a clinical psychologist, I have found no more powerful means of transforming the lives of patients than working in this fashion. I am privileged to not only see the alleviation of symptoms but to partner in the development of potentials and virtues.

The preference for left hemisphere, verbal understanding, or the reliance on mechanistic approaches to our patients has promised much but yielded little lasting change. Consequently, many who feel hopeless have received treatments that targeted a part of the brain that did not carry the weight of their tragedies; these treatments often exclude relational elements not fully reducible to the laboratory, such as comfort, love, and hope.

I close with a note that Cathy gave me, sharing her feelings of disbelief and wonder at the growth that has occurred in her life. She writes:

> Projectors are artists. They make an art of drawing portraits of themselves on your soul. Their blackness, their shame, their emptiness, their evil. When you've been trained as a child to allow them to paint their portrait over yours, you become confused. In your heart, you know the ugly picture they've painted doesn't look like you. But you begin to doubt yourself. It hurts, deeply. Sometimes you know the portrait they've painted looks familiar, but you're not sure why, because you're focused on the hurt you feel and the urgent desire to defend yourself. If only you can step out of yourself, turn and look yourself in the face, you would instantly see the transparent portrait of the projector layered over your own face.

> The psychologist teaches you what has happened and it's like standing in front of a portrait at the art museum, studying it, captivated by it. And then you recognize the distortion for what it is. An obliteration of the goodness of your heart, reflected in the distorted face. When you've learned to identify the projector and the unique feeling when he paints his face over yours, you become free to peel off the offending layer. And you begin to see the real person you are. And you want to cry, because you weren't allowed to see it before. It's good, just like you knew it was.

GIVE UP CHILDISH
WAYS OR RECEIVE THE
KINGDOM LIKE A CHILD?

SPIRITUAL FORMATION FROM A
DEVELOPMENTAL PSYCHOLOGY PERSPECTIVE

JUSTIN L. BARRETT

Imagine teaching an English-speaking three-year-old Spanish using the following sort of instruction: "Remember that when you conjugate the present tense of the verb *tocar*, that the third person singular, *él* and *ella*, and the second person formal, *usted*, are the same, namely *toca*." Huh? Three-year-olds do not learn language this way, even if sixteen-year-olds may (or not). When it comes to language learning, different modes of instruction and learning are appropriate for different points in development. Perhaps a similar perspective should be brought to the study of spiritual formation and its applications.

In this chapter I make a simple suggestion: when it comes to spiritual formation, scholars and church leaders should approach the topic from a developmental perspective, at least in part. By a developmental perspective I mean that spiritual formation takes place during someone's lifelong development, and hence, spiritual formation may take on different characteristics or involve different efforts and disciplines depending upon one's place in development. More crudely, we should not assume that spiritual formation (and the spiritual exercises that might cultivate it) will look the same in a five-year-old and a seventy-five year old.

THE CHALLENGE

Interest in spiritual formation seems to be swelling in Christian seminaries, colleges, and churches, but a common operating assumption appears (to this observer, at least) to be that spiritual formation is all about adults—and possibly young adults at that—and therefore children (and older adults) are not given the same attention.[1] This initial oversight may be forgiven because most scholars in this area have traditionally been surrounded by adults or late adolescents in their care: parishioners, young monastics, college undergrads, seminarians, and so on. Or perhaps spiritual formation is regarded as something beyond the reach of children because children are not conceptually mature enough to understand and know God with any depth. To get mature faith, perhaps we need mature people. As 1 Corinthians 13:11 says, "When I was a child, I spoke like a child, I thought like a child, I reasoned like a child. When I became a man, I gave up childish ways."

What if, to the contrary, certain aspects of spiritual formation are ready for growth earlier in life than adulthood? Or what if, at least in some ways, early cultivation will tend to reap greater harvests than waiting for adulthood? Even if some aspects of spiritual formation lie beyond the reach of children, developmental sciences have made great contributions to our understanding of human thought and behavior by recognizing that sometimes insights into the adult form are obtained

---

[1]My focus will be on children and younger adolescents because my developmental expertise is with those ages, but similar considerations may apply to older adults. That is, it may be that aspects of spiritual formation look very different for older adults than for young adults, and rapid growth on some dimensions may be most suited for a mature life and mind.

most readily through the study of how the organism got there—that is, through development.

Let me be clear: the developmental approach I am suggesting to be part of the scholarly and pastoral concern with spiritual formation is not merely taking insights from adulthood concerning, say, spiritual discipline and coming up with "junior-sized" models that appear age appropriate. Imagine taking silent solitude and adapting it to six-year-olds. What would four-year-old lectio divina look like? No. Rather, I am suggesting the church seriously explore the ways that spiritual formation takes place in children, adolescents, adults, and senior adults and develop ways to cultivate spiritual formation that may, at times, be entirely different for the various points in development and not merely "dumbed down" or "amped up" versions of each other.

SPIRITUAL FORMATION

In a previous psychological research project concerning whether decisions to follow Christ bore spiritual fruit in a particular ministry context, I was repeatedly asked by ministry staff members whether such a study "left room" for the Holy Spirit. The assumption seemed to be that psychological factors are causally complete and determinative. That is, if we can discover psychological factors or mechanisms that bear on some aspect of spiritual growth, then we are tacitly saying that the Holy Spirit was not involved, that the psychological explanation is complete and eliminates the need for any other. I reject such a view as both scientifically naïve and theologically worrisome. Psychological explanations are never complete or determinative in any domain, and since when does Christian theology teach that the Holy Spirit never works through the natural mechanisms that God created? Whether one views "spiritual formation" as denoting how one's spirit is formed or as how the Spirit forms us into the likeness of Christ (or both), psychological science has a contribution to make in understanding it.

Just which kind of contribution psychology can make to our understanding of spiritual formation is partially a function of one's particular theology concerning how God brings about spiritual formation. Christians hold a continuum of perspectives. On one end, spiritual formation is the work of the Holy Spirit alone. Humans have no active role at all in the process. On the other end, the Holy Spirit grants new desires, but it is up to individuals (perhaps with the help of their local church) to implement the best tools to protect and satisfy these new godly desires. Personally, I am drawn to the parable of the sower in Matthew 13, in which it appears that people have the responsibility to prepare the soil for God's seed to take root and maximize its yield. Spiritual formation, then, is a partnership that God invites us into with him.

Regardless of which of these three views of spiritual formation you find most satisfying, psychology has something to contribute. If one assumes spiritual formation is entirely the work of the Holy Spirit and humans have no willful contribution to make, and assuming that the Holy Spirit is generally orderly in his dealing with humans, then the psychological study of spiritual formation may help us understand how the Holy Spirit typically works and, perhaps, also help identify the obstacles that get in the way of the Holy Spirit's typical work strategy. The study, then, would be analogous to studying how, for instance, adrenaline impacts human thought and behavior: it will have an impact regardless of human will, but how, what, and why are still legitimate areas of scientific inquiry. In both of the two other models of how humans may contribute to their own or others' spiritual formation, psychological study may help reveal general patterns of spiritual formation as well as obstacles to and aids in its growth.

For the sake of my discussion here, I will presume that people can play some role in spiritual formation of themselves or at least of others. I will also take spiritual formation to have something to do with coming to know God in a loving relationship and coming to evince the fruit of the Spirit. I take these two aspects of spiritual formation to be uncontroversial. Before turning to these two areas of spiritual formation, I introduce two developmental concepts.

KEY DEVELOPMENTAL CONCEPTS

Two recurrent patterns discovered by developmental psychologists may prove important for the study and practice of spiritual formation: sensitive periods and loss of flexibility with aging. A sensitive period (in extreme forms called a "critical period") is a window in development during which exposure to an idea or practice contributes much more to learning than exposure outside that window. For instance, when it comes to discriminating different sounds that make up human speech, it appears that zero- to twelve-month-old babies are more adept at distinguishing closely related consonant sounds from other languages than are adults. That is, we seem to lose the ability to distinguish sounds that our native language does not distinguish. Exposure to a language early, then, pays off more than the same exposure later in life. For this, among other reasons, humans have a sensitive period for language learning.[2] We observe what appear to be sensitive periods in many domains from binocular vision to food preferences to social attachment.[3] Sensitive periods in development, whether in infancy, childhood, or adolescence are caused typically by the human mind having a receptiveness and flexibility to learn that is different before or (more often) after the sensitive period. That is, often we see with aging a loss of flexibility in information processing not unlike losing physical flexibility.[4] If you do not stretch your body in certain ways, it gets harder to gain that flexibility later. Likewise, in many areas of thinking and acting, failing to use our minds in particular ways may make it harder to do so later.

Given that we see sensitive periods and related loss of psychological flexibility in many domains, perhaps we should explore whether spiritual

---

[2]Steven Pinker, *The Language Instinct* (New York: HarperCollins, 1994).

[3]David H. Hubel, *Eye, Brain, and Vision* (New York: Scientific American, 1988); Elizabeth Cashdan, "A Sensitive Period for Learning About Food," *Human Nature* 5, no. 3 (1994): 271-91; John Bowlby, *Attachment*, 2nd ed. (New York: Basic Books, 1982).

[4]Of course, in some ways we can gain flexibility with aging and learning, particularly in higher-order thought that draws together information from different domains. Exactly why various sensitive periods exist is an area of scholarly debate and should not be equated with a simple loss of brain or neuronal *plasticity*.

formation, or some aspects thereof, likewise have sensitive periods of development. Does failure to exercise spiritual disciplines, for instance, earlier in life make it harder to do so later in life?

ON KNOWING GOD

A couple of years ago, I was at a conference with a colleague who is an atheist living in the European country that is commonly regarded as the least religious country in the world, and yet when his daughter was three and a half, she walked up to her father and said, "God is everywhere all the time." He was stunned. As a good psychologist, he tried to discern where his daughter "caught" an idea about God but could not discover any social cause. Further, a little over a year later, not only did she still believe in a god but "God" is for her an invisible, ever-present elderly woman. It is very unlikely this god concept was the product of rigorous indoctrination behind the back of the atheist parents. Something else was going on here.

Such stories can be multiplied many times over. Anecdotally, many children show receptiveness to the idea that there are supernatural beings or gods of one sort or another, a receptiveness that appears underexplained by parental beliefs or straightforward enculturation. This apparent ease with which children form a belief in God resonates with theological reflections in various faith traditions too. I once had a Hindu Brahmin explain to me that children find thinking about God easier than adults because they have been with God more recently than adults and have not yet forgotten. According to Islamic theology, children have a *fitrah*, an instinct or disposition toward the divine. In Christianity the comparable concept is the *sensus divinitatis*, an inchoate sense of the divine that naturally draws humans to God. This concept finds its chief scriptural inspiration in the first chapter of Paul's letter to the Romans. These anecdotes and theologies suggest that children do have some access to God by virtue of just being human, but do we have any independent scientific evidence to support this idea? It appears so.

As I have summarized in my book *Born Believers*, a number of developmental psychologists and cognitive scientists of religion—both theists and non-theists—have converged on the general idea that children have natural dispositions that make them receptive to the idea of God.[5] For instance, Deborah Kelemen answered her titular question, "Are Children Intuitive Theists?" affirmatively, primarily because of her own research showing that children have a strong natural tendency to see design and purpose in the natural world and to connect that apparent purpose with someone who purposed it.[6] Similarly, Margaret Evans has found that children are more attracted to creationist (or even spontaneous emergence) accounts of the origins of animals than to evolutionary accounts, even contrary to parents' and teachers' instruction.[7] Marjorie Taylor has found that a majority of children have invisible friends, showing that intentional beings without visibly present bodies are not a conceptual problem for even preschoolers, and Bradley Wigger found that these invisible friends tend to have supernatural knowledge or perception, even though no cultural institutions or parents have taught them these ideas.[8] That is, children can spontaneously invent invisible super-friends, demonstrating that such ideas are not conceptually beyond the pale. My own collaborators and I have found that children in America, China, Ecuador, Israel, Mexico, and the United Kingdom easily attribute super knowledge, super perception, and perhaps immortality to other beings,

---

[5]I say "idea of God" because the evidence primarily concerns their conceptual receptiveness to God and not necessarily forming any devotion or relational attachment to God. The theists may see this evidence as supporting the idea of a *sensus divinitatis* or similar aspect of Common Grace planted in humanity. Atheist and agnostic writers in this area see such evidence of natural receptivity to the idea of God as a partial explanation for why belief in gods and God is so widespread absent conclusive empirical evidence. Justin L. Barrett, *Born Believers: The Science of Children's Religious Beliefs* (New York: The Free Press, 2012).

[6]Deborah Kelemen, "Are Children 'Intuitive Theists'? Reasoning About Purpose and Design in Nature," *Psychological Science* 15 (2004): 295-301.

[7]E. Margaret Evans, "Cognitive and Contextual Factors in the Emergence of Diverse Belief Systems: Creation Versus Evolution," *Cognitive Psychology* 42 (2001): 217-66.

[8]Marjorie Taylor, *Imaginary Companions and the Children Who Create Them* (New York: Oxford University Press, 1999); Bradley J. Wigger, "See-Through Knowing: Learning from Children and Their Invisible Friends," *Journal of Childhood and Religion* 2, no. 3 (2011), childhoodandreligion.com/JCR/Welcome.html.

including God.[9] Whereas some cross-faith and cross-national differences were detected, the general pattern was remarkable ease in reasoning about super properties and, in many cases, even over-attributing super properties to agents that adults would not normally treat as super knowing or perceiving. In some cases, children reason about God's divine attributes more accurately than comparable human attributes in their mothers or friends.[10] Taken together, children seem to naturally have conceptual equipment that make thinking about a super knowing, super perceiving, immortal, invisible creator not all that challenging.

Given that children find many theological concepts easier than a previous generation of developmental psychologists might have thought, perhaps there are other theological concepts that children may have a leg up on. I speculated in *Born Believers* that the doctrine of grace is one of these concepts worth a careful look. Adults seem to have considerable trouble with the idea of unmerited favor from God. *Surely God expects something in return for my salvation. Surely someone who is a worse sinner than I am should pay a higher price.* The fact that pastors have to revisit grace repeatedly suggests that this doctrine does not jibe neatly with adult psychology. But what about children? One obstacle for adults seems to be their entrenched sense of reciprocation, tit-for-tat. *God gives me something, so I have to give something.* Young children, in contrast appear to have no such hang-ups. When an adult gives them an unmerited, unexpected good gift, their response is not typically, "Oh, now I need to give

---

[9]For data from the United States, see for instance, Justin L. Barrett, Rebekah A. Richert, and Amanda Driesenga, "God's Beliefs Versus Mom's: The Development of Natural and Non-Natural Agent Concepts," *Child Development* 72, no. 1 (2001): 50-65. For data from China and Ecuador, see Tyler S. Greenway, Gregory S. Foley, Brianna C. Nystrom, and Justin L. Barrett, "Dogs, Santa Claus, and Sun Wukong: Children's Understanding of Nonhuman Minds," in *Religious Cognition in China: "Homo Religiosus" and the Dragon*, ed. R. Hornbeck, J. Barrett, and M. Kang (Springer International, 2017), 97-110. Studies were conducted in Mexico with Yukatek Maya children by Nicola Knight, and in Israel and the United Kingdom by Emily Burdett. Nicola Knight, "Yukatek Maya Children's Attributions of Belief to Natural and Non-natural Entitites," *Journal of Cognition and Culture* 8 (2008): 235-43; Emily Reed Burdett, "Cognitive Developmental Foundations of Cultural Acquisition: Children's Understanding of Other Minds" (unpublished DPhil dissertation, University of Oxford, 2012).

[10]Barrett, *Born Believers*.

you something," but gratitude. Perhaps, then, in some ways, grace is less a stumbling block for children and this is what Mark 10:15 intimates: "Truly, I say to you, whoever does not receive the kingdom of God like a child shall not enter it."[11] More research is wanted here.

My "born believers" thesis does not entail that all of Christian theology is conceptually easy for children. Many particulars of the Christian life and Christian beliefs have to be learned from trusted adults. Such learning is facilitated by a secure relational attachment to parents. A secure attachment is characterized by confidence that their parents are responsive to their needs but allow them a developmentally appropriate degree of autonomy. Children with a secure attachment style with their Christian parents tend to mature gradually in a relationship with God in the general theological tradition of their parents. Children with insecure attachments with their Christian parents are more likely to have sharp "conversion" experiences that may lead them to other faith traditions or even to reject God.[12] Likewise, it may be that whereas basic cognition encourages children to receive the idea of God, basic social interactions with caregivers may be critical for helping children develop a genuine quality relationship with God.

ON CULTIVATING SPIRITUAL FRUIT

"But the fruit of the Spirit is love, joy, peace, patience, kindness, goodness, faithfulness, gentleness, self-control; against such there is no law. And those who belong to Christ Jesus have crucified the flesh with its passions and desires" (Gal 5:22-24).

Recent evolutionary psychological considerations of where moral intuitions come from has given rise to Moral Foundations Theory.[13] Moral

---

[11]I am not suggesting that such an interpretation exhausts what Mk 10:15 may mean. Perhaps there are multiple ways in which one must receive the kingdom of God like a child.

[12]Sarah Schnitker et al., "Attachment Predicts Adolescent Conversions at Young Life Religious Summer Camps," *International Journal for the Psychology of Religion* 22 (2012): 198-215; Pehr Granqvist and Lee A. Kirkpatrick, "Religious Conversion and Perceived Childhood Attachment: A Meta-analysis," *International Journal for the Psychology of Religion* 14 (2004): 233-50.

[13]Jonathan Haidt and Craig Joseph, "The Moral Mind: How 5 Sets of Innate Moral Intuitions Guide the Development of Many Culture-Specific Virtues, and Perhaps Even Modules," in *The*

Foundations Theory proposes five emotional, intuitive engines of morality that are cross-culturally present but differentially emphasized or amplified in different communities.[14] That is, we all have emotion-laden intuitions that drive our moral thinking, but these foundations may be directed or discouraged by cultural factors. These five moral foundations are: harm/care, fairness/reciprocity, in-group/loyalty, authority/respect, and purity/sanctity. Jonathan Haidt and Craig Joseph argue that these foundations underlie most untutored, folk reflections on why something is right or wrong, even from an early age.[15] People will tend to consider whether an act is an instance of harming versus caring for another; whether an act is fair or shows appropriate reciprocity; whether someone is showing loyalty to or betraying their group, showing respect to those in authority, avoiding impure acts, substances, or people, and otherwise treating sacred things appropriately. Interestingly, Haidt and Jesse Graham provide evidence that even within a single nation (the United States), we can see differences in how these foundations are emphasized, with political liberals thinking primarily in terms of harm/care and fairness/reciprocity but conservatives more evenly employing all five foundations like most peoples all over the world.[16] That these intuitive foundations can be tamped down or amplified in different cultural and sub-cultural contexts opens the possibility that aspects of moral development may have a sensitive period for tuning.

How, then, does this observation bear upon the cultivation of spiritual fruit? Some overlap appears to exist between Haidt's moral foundations and aspects of the nine-fold fruit of the Spirit depicted in Galatians 5.

Innate Mind, ed. P. Carruthers, S. Laurence, and S. Stich (New York: Oxford University Press, 2007), 365-92.

[14]Jonathan Haidt, Silvia Helena Koller, and Maria G. Dias, "Affect, Culture, and Morality, or Is It Wrong to Eat Your Dog?," *Journal of Personality and Social Psychology* 65 (1993): 613-28, doi:10.1037/0022-3514.65.4.613; Richard A. Shweder, Manamoban Mahapatra, and Joan Miller, "Culture and Moral Development," in *The Emergence of Morality in Young Children*, ed. J. Kagan and S. Lamb (Chicago: University of Chicago Press, 1987), 1-83.

[15]Haidt and Joseph, "Moral Mind."

[16]Jonathan Haidt and Jesse Graham, "When Morality Opposes Justice: Conservatives Have Moral Intuitions That Liberals May Not Recognize," *Social Justice Research* 20 (2007): 98-116, doi: 10.1007/s11211-007-0034-z.

A full mapping is beyond the scope of this chapter and, to my knowledge, beyond existing scholarship. Here I focus on just two aspects of the fruit in relation to moral foundations: faithfulness and kindness.

Faithfulness. Faithfulness consists in the ability to be trusting of and devoted to others. To not show faithfulness toward one's family or friends, for instance, would be a violation of the in-group/loyalty foundation. Faithfulness is closely associated with loyalty. Further, when directed at God, parents, or authority figures, it constitutes appropriately submitting oneself to that person in authority and treating them with due respect, trusting their guidance, leadership, or protection. In this context, faithfulness is related to the authority/respect foundation. If Haidt and Joseph are correct, then faithfulness to God, the church, spouses, friends, and family are supported by two early-developing, cross-culturally recurrent moral foundations, authority/respect and in-group/loyalty.[17] Yet if Haidt and Graham are correct, then faithfulness springs from a foundation that is culturally vulnerable: political liberals may have less access to this foundation.[18] An uncomfortable implication, requiring further empirical evidence, would be that political liberals may be handicapped in the cultivation of faithfulness.

What is not clear is whether the loss of these two foundations (authority/respect and in-group/loyalty) are due to poor investment in early development or the result of counter-instruction and indoctrination (e.g., "don't trust those in authority"). Given that these foundations are cross-culturally recurrent, it may be that children will naturally acquire them unless cultural peculiarities tamp them down. In either case, targeted cultivation of faithfulness may be possible and most fruitful early in life by encouraging the growth of these two moral foundations. Exactly how that is accomplished I leave for future research.

Kindness. Kindness receives impetus from the harm/care moral foundation. Harm/care is a foundation springing from the fact that humans are intensely social animals having uniquely close attachments to others.

---

[17]Haidt and Joseph, "Moral Mind."
[18]Haidt and Graham, "When Morality Opposes."

Humans feel empathy and compassion for each other, which motivates acts of kindness, gentleness, and nurturance. Harming others without their consent is generally considered immoral in any cultural environment. Likewise, failing to care for a member of one's group (e.g., family, tribe) is generally considered immoral the world over. One way in which psychologists and educators have tried to cultivate kindness (and combat bullying and other antisocial behavior) in children is through intervention programs that are designed to improve a key emotion behind kindness: empathy. For instance, the Roots of Empathy program that has been used with hundreds of thousands of children in Canada (primarily), the United States, and elsewhere is meant to generate empathy by appealing to one of the harm/care contexts key to human experience and survival, mother-infant interaction. The Roots of Empathy program features monthly classroom visits by a parent and infant that serves as an object lesson and reflection point for lessons on perspective-taking, caring for others, and understanding emotions.[19] Quasi-experimental evidence suggests that such interventions are effective.[20]

Notably for my argument here, it appears that this Roots of Empathy intervention is most effective with younger children (e.g., kindergarteners) and less effective with middle-schoolers.[21] Sadly, prosocial behavior (without the intervention) has been found to decline through the school years.[22] These two pieces of developmental evidence suggest that kindness may require cultivation in childhood and the most effective interventions may prove to be in early childhood. Waiting until adolescence or adulthood may require much greater effort to achieve the same progress. As with faithfulness, however, more research is needed for these speculations to become conclusions.

---

[19]Kimberly A. Schonert-Reichl et al., "Promoting Children's Prosocial Behaviors in School: Impact of the 'Roots of Empathy' Program on the Social and Emotional Competence of School-Aged Children," *School Mental Health* 4, no. 1 (2012): 1-12.

[20]Robert G. Santos et al., "Effectiveness of School-Based Violence Prevention for Children and Youth: Cluster Randomized Field Trial of the Roots of Empathy Program with Replication and Three-Year Follow-Up," *Healthcare Quarterly* 14 (2011): 80-91; Schonert-Reichl et al., "Promoting."

[21]Santos et al., "Effectiveness."

[22]Schonert-Reichl et al., "Promoting."

My point in discussing moral foundations theory in relation to faithfulness and kindness is not to make any definitive claims about their relationships or developmental course. I only wish to raise the possibility that some aspects of the fruit of the Spirit may best be actualized through investment in early childhood. A little investment early may be more valuable than bigger investments later. That is, perhaps faithfulness and kindness have sensitive periods in development.

I am not arguing that all aspects of the fruit of the Spirit have the same sensitive periods or even sensitive periods at all. Instead, it may be that some aspects of spiritual formation require frequent revisiting throughout development or build upon earlier-developing character strengths and, hence, will only blossom later.

IMPLICATIONS AND CONCLUSION

Evidence from developmental psychology supports the idea that young children may have natural receptivity to learning about God and acquiring moral sensibilities that underwrite the fruit of the Spirit. If so, considering spiritual formation from a developmental perspective may importantly amplify current scholarship and practice surrounding spiritual formation.

Scholarship. I have hinted at a few topics that seem to me in need of scholarly attention. In addition to investigating whether moral foundation theory may contribute to understanding spiritual formation and the specific questions concerning whether faithfulness and kindness are most effectively cultivated in childhood, several big questions may guide a program of research on spiritual formation from a developmental perspective.

- What investments in spiritual formation are most effective at which points in development? For instance, it may be that empathy interventions are most effective in early childhood whereas self-control interventions aid adolescents and young adults most. Perhaps fasting, for example, promotes positive spiritual formation in adults but not in elementary school children.

- Relatedly, are there sensitive developmental periods for particular aspects of the fruit of the Spirit? For acquiring character strengths and virtues? Is investment in knowing God more profitable in preschool than later in childhood or even adulthood? Comparisons with other domains of learning (including language, music, and morality) should open us to some surprising answers in this regard.

- How do we understand immature versions of spiritual fruit? For instance, what does self-control look like for a five-year-old as compared with a seventeen-year-old and a forty-year-old? Does gentleness, for instance, take on different forms at different points of development? Does a relationship with God have different qualities depending upon one's point in cognitive and social development?

Practice. Answers to these questions for scholarship will surely impact how we think about activities of the church or of individuals in attempting to prepare the soil and water the seeds of spiritual formation. Even without answers to these questions raised above, however, existing developmental evidence prompts me to offer the following suggestions.

Children need secure attachments to their parents and caregivers. Secure attachment leads to many positive developmental outcomes and a better soil for spiritual formation appears to be one of them.[23] Warm, responsive, non-anxious, predictable parenting is a great field for growing spiritual fruit. I recommend the church assist parents with support and training that will maximize the chance for secure attachments with their children. Churches frequently require premarital counseling before marrying couples; perhaps they should require pre-parental counseling before dedicating or baptizing infants.

Children should be taught about God early and organically.[24] Parents and adult friends of children should not be shy about talking about God's activity in the world and God as an invisible but present person. Children

---

[23]Lee A. Kirkpatrick, *Attachment, Evolution, and the Psychology of Religion* (New York: Guilford Press, 2005).

[24]I offer more speculations and suggestions with more complete explanations elsewhere: Barrett, *Born Believers*, chapters 10 and 11.

can understand more about what an invisible, powerful person can see, know, and do better than we might think. Do not be afraid to talk about God's super attributes. Give children opportunities to think about God's beliefs, desires, and actions in real life and not just as abstracted lessons for Sundays at church. Do not set talk about God apart as special or even suspect by using different language such as prefacing everything with "I believe . . ." We do not say, "I believe oxygen is entering my lungs when I breathe," but simply, "Oxygen is entering my lungs when I breathe."

In summary, though children are undoubtedly immature in many ways, they too are fearfully and wonderfully made in God's image and are called to spiritual formation. That spiritual formation begins with life and can be aided or frustrated by the activities of people around them. I encourage the church to begin a serious consideration of how spiritual formation may be better understood and encouraged by taking a developmental perspective. The result will help children become the people God has created them to be and will likely also cast adult spiritual formation in a fresh light.

CONTRIBUTORS

JUSTIN L. BARRETT

Justin Barrett is the Thrive Professor of Developmental Science and is the chief project developer for the Office for Science, Theology, and Religion Initiatives (STAR) at Fuller Seminary's Graduate School of Psychology. Dr. Barrett is author of *Born Believers: The Science of Children's Religious Belief* (Atria, 2012), *Cognitive Science, Religion, and Theology: From Human Minds to Divine Minds* (Templeton, 2011), and *Why Would Anyone Believe in God?* (AltaMira, 2004). He is a founding editor of the *Journal of Cognition and Culture*.

EARL D. BLAND

Earl Bland is a professor of psychology at Rosemead School of Psychology, Biola University. Prior to coming to Biola, he was professor of psychology and dean of the School of Behavioral Sciences and Counseling at MidAmerica Nazarene University. Dr. Bland edited *Christianity and Psychoanalysis: A New Conversation* (IVP, 2014). He also serves as a board member of the Society for the Exploration of Psychoanalytic Therapies and Theology and maintains a practice as a psychoanalytic psychotherapist.

ELLEN T. CHARRY

Ellen Charry is the Margaret W. Harmon Professor of Systematic Theology Emerita at Princeton Theological Seminary. She designed and administered a program in interfaith understanding for theology students
at the National Conference of Christians and Jews under grants sponsored by the Pew Charitable Trusts (1985–1991). Dr. Charry is author of
God and the Art of Happiness (Eerdmans, 2010) and *By the Renewing of
Your Minds: The Pastoral Function of Christian Doctrine* (Oxford University Press, 1999).

JOHN H. COE

John Coe is a professor of philosophy and spiritual theology and director
of the Institute for Spiritual Formation at Talbot School of Theology,
Biola University. His research focuses on understanding the nature of
spiritual and psychological health, the history of spirituality, the work of
the Holy Spirit in personal change, and the interface among psychology,
spirituality, and philosophy. Among other publications, Dr. Coe coauthored *Psychology in the Spirit: Contours of a Transformational Psychology*
(IVP, 2010) and the "transformational psychology view" in *Psychology
and Christianity: Five Views* (IVP, 2010). He is the founding editor of the
Journal of Spiritual Formation and Soul Care.

THOMAS M. CRISP

Tom Crisp is a professor of philosophy at Biola University and scholar-in-
residence at Biola's Center for Christian Thought. His areas of interest include metaphysics, epistemology, philosophical theology, and social ethics.
He has published articles in *Noûs, Philosophy and Phenomenological Re-
search, Oxford Studies in Metaphysics, The Oxford Handbook of Metaphysics,
Analysis, Synthese,* and *The American Philosophical Quarterly* and is
coeditor of *Knowledge and Reality: Essays in Honor of Alvin Plantinga*
(Springer, 2006), *Christian Scholarship in the Twenty-First Century:
Prospects and Perils* (Eerdmans, 2014), and *Neuroscience and Soul: The
Human Person in Philosophy, Science, and Theology* (Eerdmans, 2016).

ROBERT A. EMMONS

Bob Emmons is a professor of psychology at the University of California, Davis, the founding editor-in-chief of *The Journal of Positive Psychology*, and director of the Emmons Lab, a long-term research project designed to create and disseminate a large body of novel scientific data on the nature of gratitude, its causes, and its potential consequences for human health and well-being. He is the author of the books *Thanks! How the New Science of Gratitude Can Make You Happier* (Houghton-Mifflin, 2007), *Gratitude Works! A 21-Day Program for Creating Emotional Prosperity* (Jossey-Bass, 2014), and *The Little Book of Gratitude* (Gala, 2016).

C. STEPHEN EVANS

Steve Evans is University Professor of Philosophy and Humanities at Baylor University and professorial fellow at the Institute for Religion and Critical Thought at Australian Catholic University, Melbourne. His published works have focused on Kierkegaard, philosophy of religion, and the philosophy of psychology. He has written fifteen single-authored books, including *God and Moral Obligation* (Oxford University Press, 2013). Dr. Evans's *Natural Signs and Knowledge of God* (Oxford University Press, 2010) won the C. S. Lewis Prize for best book in philosophy of religion between 2007 and 2012.

BRANDON J. GRIFFIN

Brandon Griffin completed his PhD in psychology at Virginia Commonwealth University and is currently a clinical and translational researcher at the San Francisco VA Medical Center, where he specializes in positive health psychology and develops interventions for military veterans seeking treatment for PTSD. Dr. Griffin has coauthored articles or chapters in the *Journal of Positive Psychology*, *Self and Identity*, *Wiley Handbook of Positive Clinical Psychology* (Wiley, 2016), and *Handbook of Humility: Theory, Research, and Applications* (Routledge, 2017).

BRUCE HINDMARSH

Bruce Hindmarsh is James M. Houston Professor of Spiritual Theology at Regent College (Vancouver, BC). He is the author of *John Newton and the English Evangelical Tradition* (Eerdmans, 2001), *The Evangelical Conversion Narrative* (Oxford University Press, 2008), and *The Spirit of Early Evangelicalism: True Religion in a Modern World* (Oxford University Press, 2018). Dr. Hindmarsh has been a Mayers Research Fellow at the Huntington Library, a holder of the Henry Luce III Theological Fellowship, past-president of the American Society of Church History, and a fellow of the Royal Historical Society.

MARIE T. HOFFMAN

Marie Hoffman is a clinical psychologist, psychoanalyst, and the cofounder of the Brookhaven Center for Counseling and Development in Allentown, PA. She is associate professor of psychology at New York University's postdoctoral program in psychotherapy and psychoanalysis and visiting professor at Rosemead School of Psychology, Fuller Theological Seminary, and Wheaton Graduate School. She is the author of *Toward Mutual Recognition: Relational Psychoanalysis and the Christian Narrative* (Routledge, 2010).

JAMES M. HOUSTON

Jim Houston is Board of Governors' Professor of Spiritual Theology at Regent College (Vancouver, BC). Dr. Houston helped to found Regent College and cofounded the C. S. Lewis Institute in Washington, DC, of which he remains a senior fellow. He is the author of a long list of books, including *The Transforming Friendship* (Lion, 1989), *The Mentored Life: From Individualism to Personhood* (NavPress, 2002), *Joyful Exiles: Life in Christ on the Dangerous Edge of Things* (IVP, 2006), and five volumes in the Soul's Longing Series (Cook, 2005–2007).

CAROLINE R. LAVELOCK

Caroline Lavelock completed her PhD in psychology at Virginia Commonwealth University and completed a postdoctoral fellowship at the counseling center of the University of Illinois, Chicago. Dr. Lavelock has coauthored several workbook interventions on developing humility, forgiveness, and patience that were tested for efficacy. Other coauthored articles have appeared in journals such as the *Journal of Positive Psychology*, *Journal of Psychology and Theology*, *Journal of Clinical Psychology*, and *Journal of Counseling Psychology*.

JONATHAN MORGAN

Jonathan Morgan is a PhD candidate studying the psychology of religion at Boston University. His research focuses on the relationship between religious engagement and self-regulation, with special attention to the consequences of this relationship for cooperation and mental well-being. He has coauthored multiple articles and chapters detailing this research in such places as *Religion, Brain, and Behavior*, *Neuropsychologia*, and *The New Reflectionism in Cognitive Psychology* (Routledge, 2018).

DAVID R. PAINE

David Paine received his PhD in counseling psychology at Boston University and is currently a postdoctoral fellow at the Albert and Jesse Danielsen Institute. Dr. Paine's research interests include relational spirituality, religious practice, spiritual struggles, humility, disappointment, meaning, and the integration of psychology and theology. His coauthored articles appear in journals such as *Journal of Spirituality in Mental Health*, *The Family Journal*, and *Mental Health, Religion, & Culture*.

STEVEN L. PORTER

Steve Porter is a professor of theology and philosophy at Talbot School of Theology and at Rosemead School of Psychology (Biola University). Dr. Porter has contributed articles to *Faith and Philosophy*, *Journal of Psychology and Theology*, *Themelios*, *Religious Studies*, *Journal of Analytic*

Theology, and *Journal of Psychology and Christianity*. He authored *Restoring the Foundations of Epistemic Justification* (Lexington, 2005) and coedited *Christian Scholarship in the Twenty-First Century: Prospects and Perils* (Eerdmans, 2014) and *Neuroscience and Soul: The Human Person in Philosophy, Science, and Theology* (Eerdmans, 2016). Dr. Porter serves as editor of the *Journal of Spiritual Formation and Soul Care* and scholar-in-residence at Biola University's Center for Christian Thought.

STEVEN J. SANDAGE

Steve Sandage is the Albert and Jessie Danielsen Professor of Psychology of Religion and Theology at Boston University and Director of Research at the Danielsen Institute. His books include *The Faces of Forgiveness: Searching for Wholeness and Salvation* (Baker, 2003), *Transforming Spirituality: Integrating Theology and Psychology* (Baker, 2006), and *The Skillful Soul of the Psychotherapist: The Link Between Spirituality and Clinical Excellence* (Rowman & Littlefield, 2014). Dr. Sandage has also authored numerous articles and chapters in areas such as forgiveness and related virtues, spiritual development, marriage and family therapy, relational development, intercultural competence, and suicidology.

SIANG-YANG TAN

Siang-Yang Tan is a professor of psychology at Fuller School of Psychology and senior pastor of First Evangelical Church (Glendale, CA). Some of Dr. Tan's many publications include *Lay Counseling* (Zondervan, 1991), *Counseling and Psychotherapy: A Christian Perspective* (Baker, 2011), *Full Service: Moving from Self-Serve Christianity to Total Servanthood* (Baker, 2006), and *Disciplines of the Holy Spirit* (Zondervan, 1997) with Douglas Gregg. He is associate editor of the *Journal of Psychology and Christianity*, contributing editor for the *Journal of Psychology and Theology*, consulting editor for *Edification: Journal for the Society of Christian Psychology*, and editorial consultant of the *Journal of Spiritual Formation and Soul Care*.

GREGG A. TEN ELSHOF

Gregg Ten Elshof is a professor of philosophy at Biola University and scholar-in-residence at Biola's Center for Christian Thought. His areas of interest include metaphysics, epistemology, modern philosophy, and Confucianism. Dr. Ten Elshof has published articles in such journals as *Midwest Studies in Philosophy*, *The Modern Schoolman*, *Grazer Philosophische Studien*, *The Journal of Philosophical Research*, and *International Studies in Philosophy*. His book *I Told Me So: Self-Deception and the Christian Life* (Eerdmans, 2009) won Christianity Today's 2009 Book Award for Christian Living. He is also author of *Confucius for Christians* (Eerdmans, 2015), and he coedited *Christian Scholarship in the Twenty-First Century: Prospects and Perils* (Eerdmans, 2014) and *Neuroscience and Soul: The Human Person in Philosophy, Science, and Theology* (Eerdmans, 2016).

EVERETT L. WORTHINGTON JR.

Ev Worthington recently retired after forty years as a professor of psychology at Virginia Commonwealth University. He continues to be extremely active in research, having written over 30 books and 350 scholarly articles and chapters on topics including forgiveness of others, self-forgiveness, character strength, humility, religion and psychology, and couples therapy. Two of his publications are *Forgiving and Reconciling: Bridges to Wholeness and Hope* (IVP, 2003) and *Moving Forward: Six Steps to Forgiving Yourself and Breaking Free from the Past* (WaterBrook Press, 2013). The REACH Forgiveness program and other resources are available free of charge for churches or individuals at www.evworthington-forgiveness.com/.

This volume was produced through an initiative of the Biola University Center for Christian Thought (CCT) supported by the John Templeton Foundation to explore integrative research in psychological sciences and Christian spiritual theology and formation.

Biola University's Center for Christian Thought exists to reconnect Christian scholarship with the academy and the church. Our academic research and public engagement programs seek to stimulate, refine, and express Christian scholarship through collaborative interdisciplinary research, in order to promote an understanding of spiritual, philosophical, scientific, and theological inquiry among scholars, religious leaders, and laypeople.

CCT's values and emphases focus on theological imagination, creativity, principled pluralism, and the intersection of perspectives from different cultural sectors, academic disciplines, denominations, and backgrounds. Our founding vision maintains a commitment to religious and theological inquiry that celebrates Christian ecumenism in the spirit of humility, wonder, open-mindedness, practical wisdom, and public engagement.

Visit cct.biola.edu to access The Table—CCT's platform for articles, podcasts, videos, and events.

CAPS

An Association for Christian Psychologists,
Therapists, Counselors and Academicians

CAPS is a vibrant Christian organization with a rich tradition. Founded in 1956 by a small group of Christian mental health professionals, chaplains and pastors, CAPS has grown to more than 2,100 members in the U.S., Canada and more than 25 other countries.

CAPS encourages in-depth consideration of therapeutic, research, theoretical and theological issues. The association is a forum for creative new ideas. In fact, their publications and conferences are the birthplace for many of the formative concepts in our field today.

CAPS members represent a variety of denominations, professional groups and theoretical orientations; yet all are united in their commitment to Christ and to professional excellence.

CAPS is a non-profit, member-supported organization. It is led by a fully functioning board of directors, and the membership has a voice in the direction of CAPS.

CAPS is more than a professional association. It is a fellowship, and in addition to national and international activities, the organization strongly encourages regional, local and area activities which provide networking and fellowship opportunities as well as professional enrichment.

To learn more about CAPS, visit www.caps.net.

The joint publishing venture between IVP Academic and CAPS aims to promote the understanding of the relationship between Christianity and the behavioral sciences at both the clinical/counseling and the theoretical/research levels. These books will be of particular value for students and practitioners, teachers and researchers.

For more information about CAPS Books, visit InterVarsity Press's website at www.ivpress.com/christian-association-for-psychological-studies-books-set.

Finding the Textbook You Need

The IVP Academic Textbook Selector
is an online tool for instantly finding the IVP books
suitable for over 250 courses across 24 disciplines.

ivpacademic.com